RIBA Book of British Housing

RIBA Book of British Housing

1900 to the present day

Ian Colquhoun

Second Edition

Foreword by Jack Pringle,
President of the Royal Institute of British
Architects 2005–2007

ELSEVIER

AMSTERDAM • BOSTON • HEIDELBERG • LONDON • NEW YORK • OXFORD
PARIS • SAN DIEGO • SAN FRANCISCO • SINGAPORE • SYDNEY • TOKYO
Architectural Press is an imprint of Elsevier

Architectural Press

Architectural Press is an imprint of Elsevier
Linacre House, Jordan Hill, Oxford OX2 8DP, UK
30 Corporate Drive, Suite 400, Burlington, MA 01803, USA

First edition 1999
Second edition 2008

Copyright © 2008, Ian Colquhoun. Published by Elsevier Ltd. All rights reserved

The right of Ian Colquhoun to be identified as the author of this work has been asserted in accordance with the Copyright, Designs and Patents Act 1988

No part of this publication may be reproduced, stored in a retrieval system or transmitted in any form or by any means electronic, mechanical, photocopying, recording or otherwise without the prior written permission of the publisher

Permissions may be sought directly from Elsevier's Science & Technology Rights Department in Oxford, UK: phone (+44) (0) 1865 843830; fax (+44) (0) 1865 853333; email: permissions@elsevier.com. Alternatively you can submit your request online by visiting the Elsevier web site at http://elsevier.com/locate/permissions, and selecting *Obtaining permission to use Elsevier material*

Notice
No responsibility is assumed by the publisher for any injury and/or damage to persons or property as a matter of products liability, negligence or otherwise, or from any use or operation of any methods, products, instructions or ideas contained in the material herein. Because of rapid advances in the medical sciences, in particular, independent verification of diagnoses and drug dosages should be made

British Library Cataloguing in Publication Data
Colquhoun, Ian
  RIBA book of British housing design : 1900 to the present day – 2nd ed.
  1. Dwellings – Great Britain – Design and construction
  2. Architecture, Domestic – Great Britain
  I. Title II. Colquhoun, Ian, RIBA book of 20th century British housing III. Royal Institute of British Architects
  728'.0941'0904

Library of Congress Catalog Number: 2007941697

Typeset by Charon Tec Ltd (A Macmillan Company), Chennai, India
www.charontec.com

Printed and bound in Slovenia

ISBN: 978-0-7506-8254-1

For information on all Architectural Press publications
visit our website at www.architecturalpress.com

08 09 10 11   11 10 9 8 7 6 5 4 3 2 1

Working together to grow
libraries in developing countries

www.elsevier.com | www.bookaid.org | www.sabre.org

ELSEVIER   BOOK AID International   Sabre Foundation

Contents

Foreword to the first edition — vii
Foreword to the second edition — ix
Acknowledgements — xi
Introduction — xiii

Chapter 1	**British Housing: 1900 to the Present Day**	**2**
	The early years: 1900–1918	3
	Homes fit for heroes: 1918–1939	4
	Years of hope: 1945–1951	6
	In pursuit of an ideal: 1951–1979	10
	New directions: 1979–1997	25
	From 1997 into a new century	35
Chapter 2	**London**	**48**
Chapter 3	**The English Regions**	**160**
	Eastern England	162
	The Midlands	181
	North-east England	191
	North-west England	203
	Southern England	231
	South-west England	263
	Yorkshire and Humberside	283
Chapter 4	**Wales**	**300**
Chapter 5	**Scotland**	**312**
	Introduction	314
	Inter-war years policies	315
	Years of ambition: 1945–1979	315
	Post 1979: a new culture	318
Chapter 6	**Northern Ireland**	**356**
	Introduction	357
	Projects	361

Abbreviations — 371
Bibliography — 373
Index — 379

involvement of chartered architects in their housing aspirations. If we and they can work together, quality could become the norm.

Ian Colquhoun's book charts progress from the housing legacy of the Industrial revolution, through the exodus of people from the cities to the new suburbs and the countryside beyond, to present forecasts of a need to build large amounts of new housing. Where this is to be provided, and how, are key issues at both national and local levels. The lessons to be drawn from the experience of the past century are vital to this debate. I therefore congratulate the author, and the RIBA Housing Group, on this book and I commend it to all those who will have a responsibility for, and an interest in, creating our future homes and housing environments.

Foreword to the second edition

Jack Pringle, President of the Royal Institute of British Architects, 2005–2007

Housing

What more important endeavour could there be than housing? And what greater bandwidth could the subject have from the most modest cottage to iconic works of the masters, from the socio-economic and political impact of housing billions of people when hundreds of millions of them are below the poverty line and further hundreds of millions are migrating from place to place? Add the impact on climate change of heating and cooling these dwellings. It is a big subject.

We live in the UK on a densely populated island with a historically prosperous economy based initially on land (wool) then industry and now information, banking, technology, the arts and service companies. We have moved around the island over time depending on which location was generating the wealth. First the countryside, then the industrial Midlands and North, the South-east and now spreading back to provincial successful areas such as Bristol, Leeds and Manchester. As fast as prosperous Brits emigrate to warmer climes others pour into the UK to find work and a new life. London is one of the few first-world cities, that is expanding. It is certainly a world city and argues that it is the capital of Europe.

Here in the UK we have had our successes and failure's with housing. But we should not let the failure's of the past inhibit the successes of the future. Despite a few model towns and garden suburbs, we have not been great formalists in planning our settlements. The Victorians developed with ruthless efficiency and their terraced house remains one of the most sophisticated and effective forms of mass housing. Private capital developed great tracts around cities following the expansion of railway and transport links on an informal basis. The Edwardians followed suit with their leafy semis in the suburbs.

Post-war we were less successful. Le Corbusier's vision of villages in the sky, which may have been workable in the apartment dwelling culture of the continent where concrete looks good under blue skies, did not translate well in the grey wet UK where time was of the essence in building hundreds of thousands of homes fit for heroes on slashed budgets using under researched prefabricated concrete systems. Architects of the day were blamed, not entirely fairly, and generally pushed out of housing for the next three decades.

Mrs Thatcher killed public housing in large volumes and contributed to the growing housing shortage. Private developers found that they had a seller's market and buyers generally bought on location, price and then design. So in the right place for the right price, they did not need well-designed products and need not trouble themselves with awkward architects, they could sell rubbish. And they did.

But have we a new dawn in the twenty-first century? Consumers know more about design, which is now a colour supplement (and a footballers' wives) subject. Kevin McLeod's "Grand Designs" and the RIBA's "Building of the Year" get prime time audiences of a million on the television. No one wants concrete jungles and no one wants neo-tudorbethan pastiches. Modern, light, safe, well-designed homes for our lifestyle is what we all want, whether it is a studio flat for the youngster making his or her way, or a family home for bringing up kids.

This is a great opportunity for architects to serve our community, add carbon neutral and the lack of land to the mix and it is no mean task. But I know we are up to it.

Enjoy Ian's book. He is a friend and colleague who I have high regard for.

Acknowledgements

Housing design has been at the centre of most of my architectural life. To be a member of the RIBA's Housing Group from 1977 to 1990 was both a privilege and an education, and I am most grateful to the Institute's for its continual support. David Rock, former RIBA President wrote the foreword for the first edition and President 2005–2007, Jack Pringle, the foreword for this edition.

I wish to thank the following people in connection with the first edition: RIBA Housing Group Members – Bernard Hunt (Chair), Chris Johnson, Richard Lavington, David Levitt, Stuart Mackie, Mary McKeouwn, David Moore, David Parkes, Chris Purslow, the late Martin Richardson, Chris Rudolf and the RIBA officer, Bernadette Hammerson-Wood. The Royal Incorporation of Scotland, Jim Johnson, Roan Rutherford, Derek Lyddon, Ian and Marjorie Appleton, and Dr Tom Begg's excellent books on Scottish housing all helped with the chapter on Scotland. Professor Tom Woolley of Queen's University, Belfast, Jim McClusky, of the Royal Ulster Society of Architects, the Northern Ireland Housing Executive and the Belfast office of the NHBC helped me understand the housing scene in Northern Ireland. The RIBA Awards Office and Nancy Mills supplied details of award winning schemes and various RIBA Regions gave helpful advice on schemes to visit. John Bartlett provided information on MoHLG experiments into extendible housing. Elain Harwood, Nigel Wilkins and Gaynor Roberts of English Heritage gave information on projects that have been listed. Dr Jingmin Zhou helped with research and the preparation of plans. Her husband, Lyang Sun, also helped with the drawings. Rita Johnson, who assisted with typing the first edition, has sadly passed away and is greatly missed. Thanks go to my son, Christopher, who prepared the photographs for the second edition and took those for which he is credited.

My thanks also go to the Hull School of Architecture in the University of Lincolnshire and Humberside (now the Lincoln School of Architecture in the University of Lincoln). Norman Arnold, Greg Ritchie and Richard Havenhand and a group of students put together an exhibition based on the first edition, which was displayed at the RIBA in London during the summer of 1999.

The book benefited much from the huge amount of work on housing undertaken by the Commission for Architecture and the Built Environment (CABE) and Building for Life, which it established and is a major force for raising quality in housing design. CABE's publications and website, especially that of Building for Life, were most valuable sources for research.

Design for Homes, of which I have been a Board Member since 1990 has given much support to me in producing this second edition. Other Board Members and staff are Bernard Hunt (Chair), Yolanda Barnes, David Birkbeck (Chief Executive), Jack Cassidy, Clive Jackson, Chris Johnson, Richard Lavington, David Lunts, David Levitt, David Moore, Richard Mullane (Manager), Stephen Mullins, Barry Mundy, Peter Redman and John Wier. Peter Redman very kindly gave time to discuss

ACKNOWLEDGEMENTS

the future housing scene in Britain. Amongst its many interests Design for Homes supports the management of the Building for Life awards scheme and manages the annual national Housing Design Awards.

I very much appreciate the receipt from architects and housing developers of plans and photographs of the schemes illustrated. I apologise for not including everything but space would not allow it. The book entailed endless travel throughout Britain. I was always warmly welcomed by people I specifically arranged to meet but there are simply too many to list.

Authors need good support from their publishers and I cannot thank Jodi Cusack, Lucy Potter and Lisa Jones of Elsevier/Architectural Press enough for their help, advice and support in producing the second edition, together with that of Neil Warnock-Smith and Marie Milmore for the first edition. Finally, the book would not have been possible without the endless support of my wife, Christine who, throughout the period of research and writing of both this and the first edition, helped with travel arrangements, photography, filing, proof reading, etc. plus all the normal things of life which I had little time to do.

I took all the photographs myself except where photographers or others are specially credited in the figure captions. The project architects provided plans and drawings unless otherwise stated. I particularly wish to thank CABE, Building for Life and Design for Homes for their help with photographs. Whilst every effort has been made to trace the owners of copyright material, in a few cases this has proved impossible and I apologise to any copyright holder whose rights have been unwittingly infringed.

Whilst I received information and support from many sources, the book is an independent piece of work and I am responsible for the choice of schemes and opinions expressed.

Professor Ian Colquhoun
6th October 2007

Introduction

This book is about British housing and its design from 1900 to the present day. The period of time ends as it began with a forecasted need for large numbers of new housing. In 1900, this was to replace the slums left by the industrial revolution. Today it is to build affordable housing for sale and rent for a rapidly growing number of new households, the majority of which are single people and couples with no children, often young or elderly. Many are black and ethnic minority households. There is a huge population explosion in the South-East of England and an urgent need to address acute housing problems in the towns and cities. There is a shortage of affordable housing for people living and working in rural areas. There is general agreement that additional housing should be centred on the re-use of existing buildings and the development of brownfield sites to offer new life to urban areas. Yet many people have little affinity to urban life and have an inherent distrust of new concepts due to the failures of the 1960s housing. The problem for architects is that these generalisations hide great achievements and in reality the twentieth century, and particularly the first few years of the twenty-first, have witnessed an outflow of great creativity in housing design which continues to attract worldwide attention and admiration.

For most of the twentieth century action focused on new development, mainly the reconstruction of residential areas built at the time of the Industrial Revolution. The vast majority of the new housing was built by local authorities with mixed success. Private housing was built in the suburbs but only rarely were these designed by architects. In the last two decades of the century, architects turned their attentions to the regeneration of inner-city areas and the refurbishment of 1960s estates. They established a trend for more environmentally friendly and community-based development. The first years of the new century saw the continuation of this but also a complete explosion of new ideas, which has transformed design and given society new confidence in what architects can achieve.

It was the interest in British housing from overseas that prompted the idea for this book. The RIBA frequently receives requests for information on housing, many from people wishing to visit schemes for themselves. There is also a need for a simple up-to-date primer, which can introduce the subject to visitors, students and practitioners. The book includes schemes from every decade from 1900. Many of the projects included have received national acclaim and awards for their design quality. A number of schemes over 30 years old have been included by English Heritage on the statutory list of buildings of "special architectural or historic interest" which now includes post-Second World War housing.

The first chapter of the book provides an historical overview. This enables the projects in the main body of the book to be seen against the political, social, economic and cultural background of the time when they were designed. The projects, which are described in later chapters, are highlighted in bold type in Chapter 1. Space in the book limits the number of plans and photographs but they have been selected to demonstrate the great variety of design ideas. For people who want further information there are plenty of references to journals and other publications. There is a generous inclusion of schemes from 2000 to the present day so that the remarkable change in design approach can be fully appreciated.

Anyone engaged in housing design can benefit considerably from looking at other people's work and by talking to the managers of the projects and the residents. Visits will give first-hand experience. I have been to all the schemes and taken almost all of the photographs. Where schemes are within reasonable walking distance of railway, underground or metro-stations, the nearest stop has been given. In some instances private transport is essential. No detail has been given of travel in Northern Ireland. Most projects can be viewed from the public highway but respect for people's privacy is essential. Permission should be sought before entering private grounds and it is not possible to visit sheltered housing for elderly people and other schemes providing specialist care without first seeking the agreement of the owners of the building.

I sincerely hope you find this book useful.

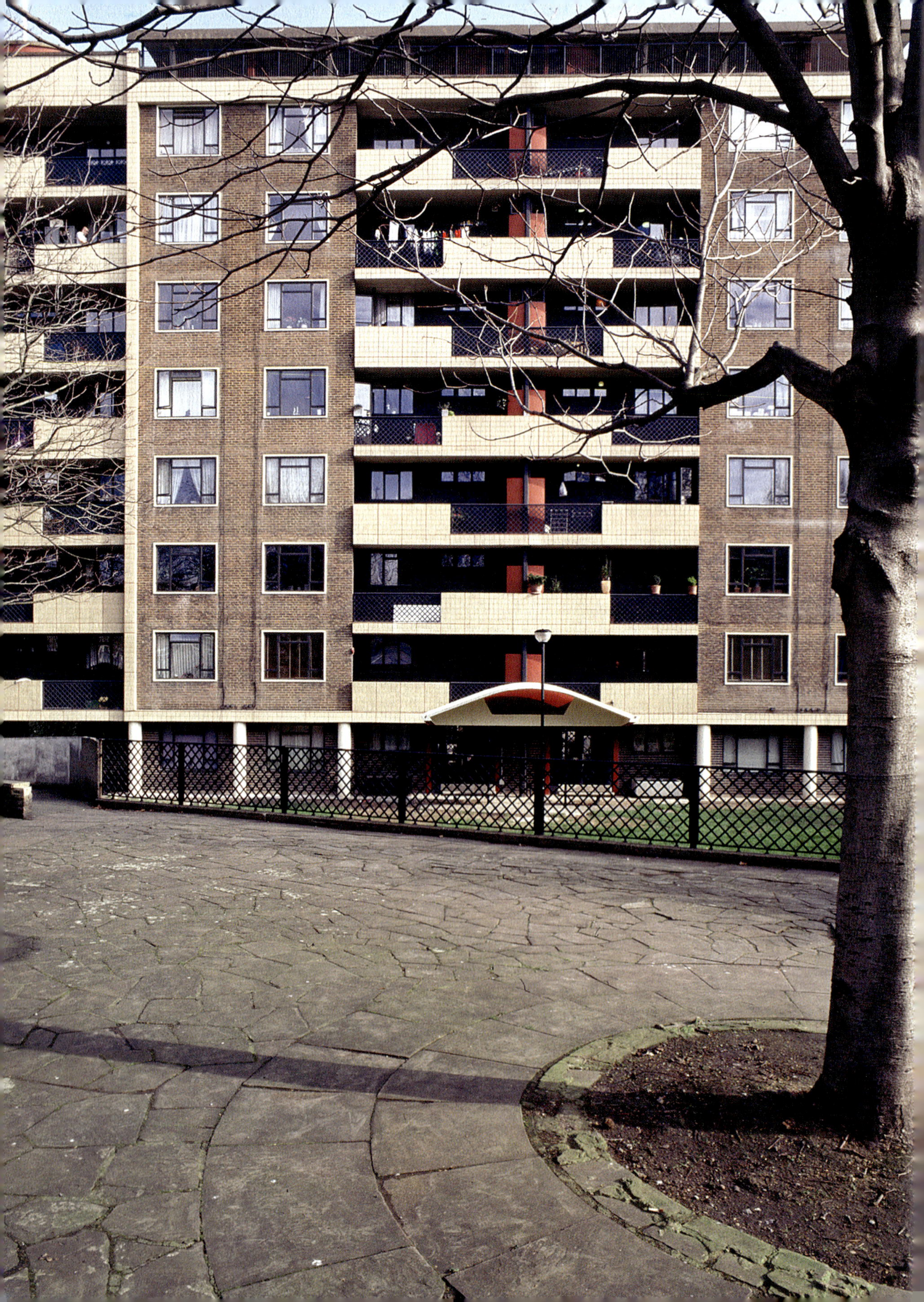

British Housing: 1900 to the Present Day

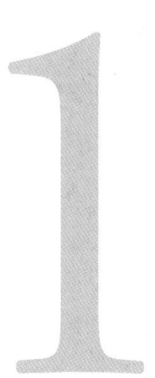

The early years: 1900–1918

It was not until the turn of the twentieth century that a real effort was made to deal with the huge legacy of poor housing handed down by the industrial revolution. In the nineteenth century a number of philanthropic individuals and organisations attempted to provide better housing for the working classes. Titus Salt's village at Saltaire, near Bradford, Peabody Trust housing in London and William Lever and George Cadbury's Garden Villages of Bourneville and Port Sunlight still remain as monuments to individual people who saw the benefits of decent housing for their workers.

Garden cities

The publication of Ebenezer Howard's *Tomorrow: A Peaceful Path to Real Reform* (retitled in 1902 *Garden Cities of Tomorrow*) [1] and the formation of the Garden City Association in 1898 led to the founding of **Letchworth Garden City** in 1902 and **Hampstead Garden Suburb** in 1906. At the same time, Joseph Rowntree started to build **New Earswick, York.**

Ebenezer Howard saw his garden cities in economic, social and political terms as well as physical. His vision was to create new self-sufficient "social cities" of 250,000 people, set with their own commerce and industry in the countryside. Each social city would consist of a central core of 58,000 people connected within a circle of six independent and widely spaced garden cities, each with populations of 32,000. His plans included an agricultural belt to be farmed on behalf of the community and to serve as a barrier to limit urban development. It remains the only new town where the land originally acquired for the development is still held in trust for the community [2]. Excess money from rent would be used to set up pension funds and community services. Any profit arising from development in the town must be used for the benefit of the community as a whole. In these ways he was unknowingly the first advocate of sustainable development.

Howard's ideas were ably translated in architectural terms by architects Raymond Unwin and Barry Parker (Fig. 1.2). Their design set out to avoid the monotony of the uniform grid plans of nineteenth century housing. They restricted density to 12 houses per acre

Figure 1.1 Lubetkin's flats at Spa Green still in excellent condition (p. 7).

Figure 1.2 Cottage housing in Letchworth.

(30 dw/ha) and planned the layout carefully to take advantage of the existing landform, trees, hedgerows and other natural features of a site. Their cottage designs reflected the popular English romantic ideals of the time [3], producing an architectural quality, which "materialised the Englishman's ideal conception of home as a unit of house and garden combined" [4]. This fundamentally remains the housing preference of most British people today.

Government intervention

Despite Howard's energy, the garden city movement merely touched the fringe of the housing problems of the time and clearly a more concerted effort was required. Under the Housing of the Working Classes Acts of 1890 and 1900 local authorities were empowered for the first time to buy and develop sites to build houses for rent. The legislation was not mandatory but a few authorities were quick to respond. The London County Council (LCC), founded only a few years previously in 1888, built both tenement blocks (**Boundary Street**) and cottage estates of two-storey housing with gardens at both front and rear (Totterdown Fields, **Old Oak Estate** and **White Hart Lane**).

Homes fit for heroes: 1918–1939

It took a world war and the fear of revolution to bring about real change. Reconstruction after the war meant a totally new outlook and spirit of concern to deal with the problems. In his speech to the electors of Wolverhampton in 1918, the Prime Minister, David Lloyd George, vowed, "to make Britain a fit country for heroes to live in" [5]. His words were embodied into legislation in the 1919, Housing and Town Planning Act, introduced into parliament by the Minister of Health, Christopher Addison. The Act instructed local authorities to survey the housing needs of their area and prepare programmes for meeting them. For the first time local authorities could seek government subsidy to support their programmes. Subsidy, in some form or other remained a feature of British housing for many years to come.

Garden city ideals

There was no doubting the preference for garden city housing. The Tudor Walters Report of 1919 [6] embraced this fully. A prominent member of the committee was Raymond Unwin. His influence ensured design criteria, which remained in place for a quarter of a century. The key features were semi-detached houses and short terraces made up of wide frontage houses with densities of 12 dwellings per acre (30 dw/ha) in towns and 8 per acre (17 dw/ha) in the countryside and a minimum planning distance of 70 ft (21 m) between adjacent rows of dwellings. In many cities and towns, the "cottage" estates, began to be laid out with great care and pride by local authorities [7].

The garden city movement rejected the city as it then existed and searched for better solutions based on the countryside and the village. Layouts were to take their form more naturally from the site and the dwelling design was to reflect a rural image [8]. At this time the debate began on how to accommodate the motorcar, which began to have an impact on the urban scene in terms of dealing with through traffic and congestion. It also gave access for more people to live in the new suburbs and the countryside beyond.

There was disagreement amongst architects on layout arising from the contrast between Parker and Unwin's theories and the *beaux-arts* style of straight roads and formal symmetrical layouts advocated by Patrick Abercrombie and Professor C.H. Reilly of Liverpool University [9].

Addison Act, 1919

This Act became the basis for all local authority housing built during the inter-war years. The Ministry of Health "Housing Manual" of 1920 illustrated typical cottage plans. The Tudor Walter's report recommended separate parlours, but the Health Ministry preferred non-parlour types because these were considerably cheaper to build. Kitchens were merely "sculleries" and the bathroom was on the ground floor with the coal store nearby. They lacked many of the facilities that are now taken for granted but, at the time, they were great improvements on previous housing.

A lowering of quality

The lowering of subsidies by the Wheatley Act in 1924 and subsequent funding cuts during the recession reduced standards and general design quality. The early images of Parker and Unwin, which had formed the basis of the Tudor Walters Report, were rationalised and simplified. The difference in quality became evident. The Garden City Association felt betrayed. Ebenezer Howard had campaigned for the construction of 50 new towns. In reality, **Welwyn Garden City** founded in 1919, was to be the only other new town built until after the Second World War.

Most had built in cookers and refrigerators as part of factory made kitchen/bathroom units (Fig. 1.3). Under the powers in the 1944 Temporary Housing Programme, local authorities built over 150,000 prefabs. They were generally intended to have a lifespan of around 20 years, but most far exceeded this expectation. As late as the early 1990s the "little palaces" were still popular with their occupants. A few, which have in recent years been modernised (**Wake Green, Birmingham**) will undoubtedly have a long life.

The neighbourhood unit

Both the Dudley Report and the 1944 Housing Manual [11] recommended planning new housing in neighbourhood units. These varied in size from 5,000 to 10,000 people and contained smaller homogeneous housing groups of between 100 and 300 dwellings. Neighbourhoods of this size could support a primary school, a range of local shops and other community facilities.

Scandinavian influence

The influence of post-1930 housing by Scandinavian architects was considerable in the early years after 1945. Their projects featured in many journals and government publications and were admired for their modest domestic scale and use of natural materials. Scandinavian layouts followed principles first used in 1930 by Walter Gropius for his Seimensstadt housing in Berlin, where blocks of flats were arranged in rows on an east–west orientation in open landscape to allow maximum sunshine penetration into living rooms. Sunshine was perceived in Britain to be important to good health. Therefore the layout principle was widely accepted and no one had any doubts about separating the housing from the streets. Amongst the first schemes laid out this way were **Churchill Gardens** and **Roehampton**.

1949 Housing Act

The Health Minister, Aneurin Bevin, was concerned to ensure that council housing would be available for a wide cross-section of society. His ideas were incorporated into the 1949 Housing Act, which removed the obligation on local authorities to provide housing only for the working classes. They were now free to create balanced communities and to meet all housing need irrespective of social class. [12] He believed that good housing was important to health and he wanted to create housing for everyone in which the doctor, the baker and the butcher all lived next door to each other. Regrettably, this opportunity was never developed as local authorities concentrated on meeting their most critical housing problems.

The 1949 Housing Manual [13] contained minimum space standards for dwellings that have not been bettered even by the 1961 Parker Morris standards. The Manual criticised the monotony of the pre-war estate: "Unity and character are best achieved in low-density areas by the use of terraces and semi-detached houses in contrast with blocks of flats, and public buildings, and in other areas by a mixture of three-storey terraces and multi-storey flats and maisonettes" [14].

Much attention was given to the need for careful design in rural areas, which was exemplified in the new village housing in **Ditchingham**, **Norfolk** (Fig. 1.4). High-density housing was seen as necessary in urban areas and examples illustrated in the manual included the **Spa Green** (Fig 1.1) and **Woodbury Down Estates in London**. The Manual contained a chapter on the use of non-traditional systems of house building. It advised of the economies in time, labour and

Figure 1.4 Tayler and Green at Ditchingham, 1948.

cost that could be effected by the prefabrication of internal parts and fittings to fit a shell of standard size, whether in brick or in other forms of construction.

Mixed development

The concept of "mixed development" was based on the social perception that people would, in accordance with their needs, freely move from one kind of dwelling to another within an estate. The first home of the typical young family would be a flat in a tower or a four-storey block. Here the first child would be born. After the arrival of the second child a house with a garden would be more suitable. With the approach of old age, the occupants could find a house too large for their reduced needs and a more manageable flat or a bungalow would now be preferable. Mixed development appeared in every town and city (**Roehampton** and **Gleadless Valley Sheffield**), but the concept was flawed because mobility between the various forms of dwellings never became a practical reality.

Mark 1 new towns

A major concern of the immediate post-war years was planning the overspill of population from the large cities. Patrick Abercrombie's Greater London Plan of 1944 recommended the establishment of new towns as planned settlements of balanced communities with a target population of between 50,000 and 100,000 people. In 1946 proposals were announced for the first new town at Stevenage, which was quickly followed by others at Harlow, Crawley, Hemel Hempstead, Welwyn (previously a garden city), Hatfield, Basildon and Bracknell. The designations also included Newton Aycliffe, Peterlee and Corby, which were new towns to provide workforces for large local industries. Sir Lewis Silkin, the minister for town and country planning, saw new towns as places where "all classes of community can meet freely together on equal terms and enjoy common cultural and recreational facilities". They were also to be "architectural fanfares for the common man, woman and booming baby" [15].

The planning of the new towns embraced the concepts of the neighbourhood unit and mixed development. The Development Corporations employed architects and consultants of the highest calibre including Berthold Lubetkin at Peterlee and Sir Frederick Gibberd at Harlow. Their role was significant in the development of the masterplans and determining the urban and housing design strategy. At Harlow Gibberd became a legend for his "design" [16] of the new town and many people in the town still commonly know his name.

Politically the new towns were unpopular with local authorities, which related the population loss to a fall in revenue. Rural authorities, where the new towns were designated, were concerned about all the new development in their back yard. Nevertheless over 30 new towns were built throughout the country including several in Scotland, Wales and Northern Ireland.

The Festival of Britain

The period culminated in 1951 with the Festival of Britain in London. Whilst enjoying the pleasures on the South Bank site, people were encouraged to visit the "live" architecture and planning show of the festival. The new **Lansbury Estate**, built in the East End of London, modelled all the new planning and design concepts complete with schools, a pedestrian shopping centre, churches and community buildings. The intention was to demonstrate the future to come. However, the reality in 1951 was more concerned with the general election and the return of Conservative government with promises of new approaches to housing development. The scene had been set for what was to be an explosion in housebuilding over the next 30 years.

In pursuit of an ideal: 1951–1979

The incoming government of 1951 introduced economies and lowered standards in order to build greater numbers. Through the medium of Harold Macmillan's "People's house" (Fig. 1.5) [17], the increased use of terraces, narrower frontages to raise density and fewer internal facilities were advocated. For the first time, plans for family flats above ground floor level were recommended. Mixed development continued to be the basis of design until the emergence at the end of the 1950s of high-density housing.

High-rise development

The 1960s and early 1970s are synonymous with high-rise housing. Politicians, planners and architects alike all welcomed the move away from the suburban housing sprawl of previous years. The influence upon architects of Le Corbusier's Unité d'Habitation in

Figure 1.5 "The people's house", 1951 (MoHLG, Houses 1952, frontispiece).

Marseilles, completed in 1952, proved highly significant in promoting the modernist image. It symbolised "the futurist view of … modernity as the saviour of the housing crisis" [18].

Le Corbusier's vision was of clean, healthy housing in a green parkland setting with houses built in a mass-produced manner like ships and aeroplanes. His views were widely supported by contemporary architectural writers. In 1953, J.M. Richards and Gordon Cullen made bitter attacks in *The Architectural Review* on what they called the "prairie planning" of post-war new towns [19]. Both demanded more urban and higher-density development: "Towns should be planned as towns which is denied by the present suburban sprawl" [20]. The Unité was the concrete embodiment of Le Corbusier's longstanding theories and programmes concerning housing. Such an event had not occurred since Ebenezer Howard's day and it started a process of questioning and reappraisal of the housing problem in Britain: "Where do we want to live? What sort of houses do we want?" [21]. This fuelled the imagination of an architectural profession eager to make its contribution to the reconstruction of Britain [22].

The first point block of flats constructed in Britain was Frederick Gibberd's eleven-storey block at **The Lawns**, **Harlow**

CHAPTER ONE • BRITISH HOUSING: 1900 TO THE PRESENT DAY

Figure 1.6 Alton West, Roehampton.

"rows" so that neighbours were kept together. Community development officers helped the people settle in and set up social activities. As it was experimental, Park Hill received extra government funding and this enabled the general standard to be higher than in later schemes built by other local authorities. Most noticeable elsewhere was the reduced width

Figure 1.8 Park Hill, Sheffield.

of the decks that became little more than access galleries.

Cluster housing

The concept of cluster housing related to the Smithson's vision of "community" and "feeling of identity", which had its origins in the "unadulterated vitality of life in the East End street" [29]. The cluster block as developed by Denys Lasdun at **Usk Street** (1952) and **Claredale Street** (1960), both in Bethnal Green, reflected these principles but neither proved popular with their occupants.

Space standards

Internally, the dwellings of the 1960s were designed to good space standards for the time. The Parker Morris report, *Homes for Today and Tomorrow*, published in 1961 [30] set out a new range of overall dwelling sizes based on thorough investigations into how people lived (Fig. 1.9). It concluded that space standards should not be concerned with room sizes but with the number of occupants. *Design Bulletin 6: Space in the Home* [31], first published by the MoHLG in 1963, developed the principle through defining spaces between the furniture in each room. From 1969 to 1981, the Parker Morris standards were mandatory for all public sector housing, but were never accepted by the private sector to which the report was also directed.

Housing Cost Yardstick

Funding levels and subsidy for new development had to be determined in relationship to Parker Morris standards. This was achieved through the Housing Cost Yardstick System introduced by the Housing Subsidies Act 1967 and set out in the accompanying manual [32]. All too quickly the yardstick became geared to density and high-rise development and minimum standards became maximum.

Contractor designed housing

There was a shortage of architects both in private and public sector practice that meant that local authorities relied heavily upon the contractors who offered a combined planning, design and construction service. In the mid-1960s authorities were inundated with representatives selling their company's systems of construction. Far too many systems were untried and tested before use. Supervision on

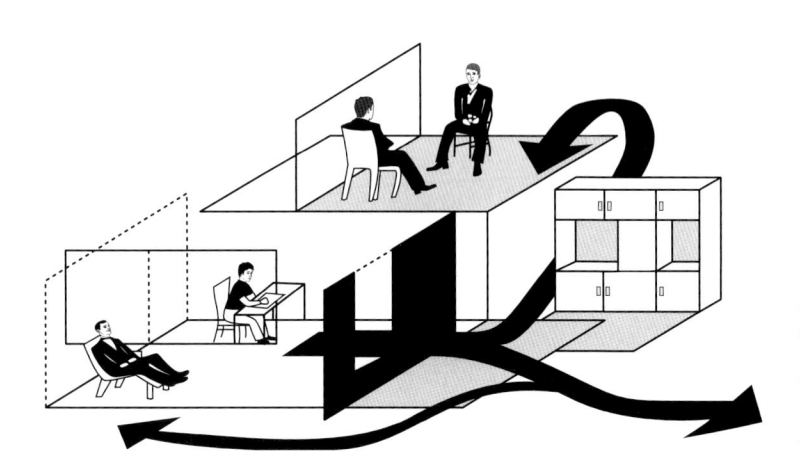

Figure 1.9 How people live: an illustration by Gordon Cullen from the Parker Morris Report, Homes for Today and Tomorrow, 1961, pp. 1 and 49 (Crown copyright).

site was often poor. Prefabricated panels were damaged at the edges and in the corners during construction, which produced leaky joints. Designs failed to consider cold bridging which caused dampness and mould growth that was to become worse where tenants could not afford to run the central heating systems. Poor construction was followed by bewildered management and poor maintenance in local authorities whose staff lacked the skills and experience to cope with the legacy handed to them.

Radburn layout

One of the key references in the Parker Morris report was to the use of layouts which segregated pedestrians and vehicles along the lines developed during the 1930s in Radburn, New Jersey, USA. The Radburn concept responded to a genuine fear of increasing danger from the growth in car ownership but there were inherent problems related to building houses in terraces whereas at Radburn the houses were detached or semi-detached with access to the front door from both sides of the house. There were also serious problems due to a lack of security in the rear parking courts and the separation of housing from the street was not liked.

Research and Development

The MoHLG's Research and Development Group under Cleeve Barr and Oliver Cox experimented with new housing forms in an attempt to set standards and collaborated with local authorities to build and test their ideas. The Research and Development Group developed its own 5 m system, which was built as a pilot project in 1961 at Gloucester Road in Sheffield. From the outset Oliver Cox expressed his concern over the way in which the development of industrialised housing was proceeding. He preferred to see a more humanistic participatory approach to housing development.

The Research Group and later the Housing Development Directorate (HDD) of the Department of the Environment, under Pat Tindale, researched key design issues and produced a whole series of bulletins, occasional papers and other publications that offered guidance and feed-back on design and development, much of which is still relevant today. Of particular merit were the design bulletins and occasional papers on topics such as mobility and wheelchair housing and research on space in the home and residential roads and footpaths conducted by John Noble [33].

Standardisation of plans

Inherent in the research into the industrialisation of housebuilding was the recognition that certain elements such as staircases and bathroom fittings could be standard even though dwellings might differ in size. This theme was developed in a series of generic plans produced in 1965 by the National Building Agency (NBA). The NBA's standard range of house shells was intended to prevent abortive time being spent on house planning and to streamline production.

Flexibility and adaptability

Concepts of flexibility and adaptability were considered through the development of pilot houses by the MoHLG at the Ideal Home Exhibition in 1962 (Fig. 1.10). The arguments were further implemented after 1967 through the development of **PSSHAK (Primary System Support Housing and Assembly Kits)**. This concept had visions of using industrialisation to offer choice. The system provided movable partitions, which enabled the tenants to decide on the relative sizes of rooms for themselves, and when one family

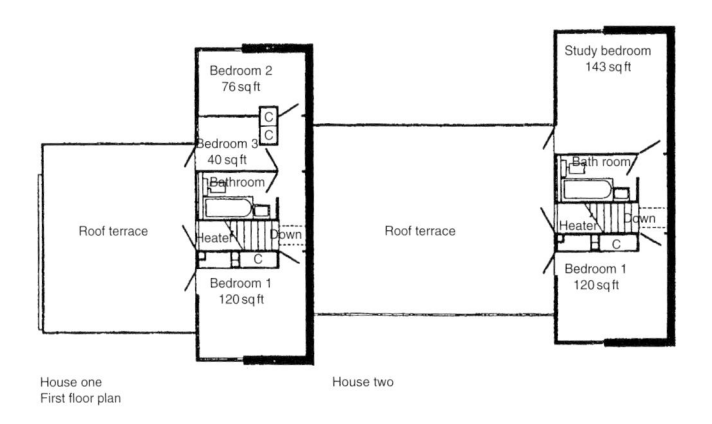

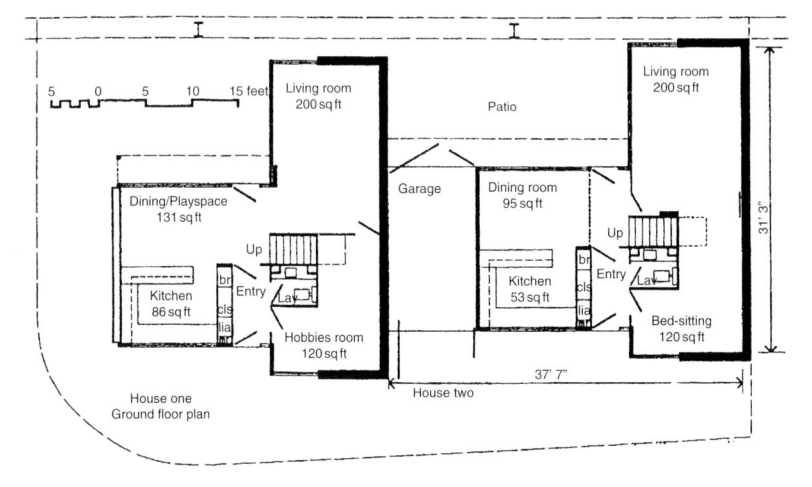

Figure 1.10
Expandable/adaptable houses designed by the MoHLG's Research and Development Group and erected at the Ideal Home Exhibition in 1962.

moved, or the children grew up, the sizes of the rooms or the size of the flat could change. A pilot scheme was built in **1977** at Adelaide Road/Eton Road, Camden.

The decline of high rise

Initially high-rise was accepted as people enjoyed modern facilities within the home for the first time. However, few people warmed to the modernist images. The rejection was heightened by the shear size and scale of many of the schemes. There were also serious problems with noise transmission between dwellings. People felt isolated and flats above ground level were clearly unsuitable for families with children. The problems were aggravated by a spiral of social and economic decline as communities were hit badly by unemployment following the collapse of traditional heavy industry from the **1970s** onwards. The gas explosion at Ronan Point in **May 1968** hastened an end to high rise and by the mid-1970s industrialised housebuilding had virtually ceased.

High density/low rise

The unpopularity of high-rise development at the end of the 1960s led to a change in direction. Housing forms were sought that accommodated families at ground level in dwellings with gardens with other dwellings above. Some solutions were ingenious,

Figure 1.11 High-density/low-rise housing, Maiden Lane, Camden.

but the over-complex forms required more sophisticated maintenance techniques which local authorities had difficulty in providing.

A conviction for modernist housing still remained an important vision for many architects in the 1970s. It was inherent in providing better housing for people.

Prominent amongst these was the Camden Borough Architect's Department, headed by Sydney Cook. Under his direction, Neave Brown, Gordon Benson, Alan Forsyth and others designed a number of highly ambitious schemes between 1968 and 1971 at **Highgate New Town**, **Maiden Lane** (Fig. 1.11), **Alexandra Road** and **Branch Hill**. Most of the Camden schemes were built on the consistent pursuit of a single idea – the linear stepped-section block based on Le Corbusier's designs as personified in Atelier 5's 1962 Seidlung Halen in Berne.

A very different approach was adopted by Darbourne and Darke for their scheme at **Lillington Street**, Pimlico, built between 1961 and 1971. Here the buildings are clad externally in brick and tile and the modelling of the blocks is designed to express individual dwelling units [34]. The approach produced a landmark project that was much admired and copied during the 1970s.

Theoretical design models

Most influential at this time were the mathematical studies of built form in the studies at Cambridge University in the 1960s by Leslie Martin and Lionel March. These proved that low-rise housing could be created at the same density as high-rise development. Two of their studies, published in *Urban Spaces and Structures* (1972) [35], related to "courtyard" housing and "perimeter" housing (Fig. 1.12).

Using hypothetical models, **courtyard housing** was shown to provide five times more accommodation than tower block development on an equivalent site. It could also achieve over half as much accommodation again as a terraced layout. The concept took physical form in Neylan and Unglass' schemes at **Bishopfield**, Harlow and at **Setchell Road**, Southwark. Phippen Randall and Parks also used a patio form in the hugely successful co-ownership scheme at **The Ryde**, Hatfield.

The principles of **perimeter housing** lie in the geometry of the "Fresnel Square". When translated into architectural terms the concept is that the traditional tower block isolated within a square of green could be developed as low-rise housing in a ring around the edge of the green without the loss of dwellings. The principle was developed into built form at **Watermeads, London Borough of Merton** and at Duffryn Lighthouse Road, Newport, South Wales (1978 MaCormac & Jamieson) [36].

Mark 2 new towns and planned overspill

Even with high-rise housing, it was impossible for local authorities to rehouse in new development within their boundaries all the people and facilities displaced from the slum clearance areas. New towns and planned overspill developments were therefore an important part of the governments overall new housebuilding programme. This policy of population dispersal was supported by town planners who considered that the social, economic and planning problems of the inner cities could not be tackled without some people being moved out. The GLC was particularly active through its "Expanded Towns

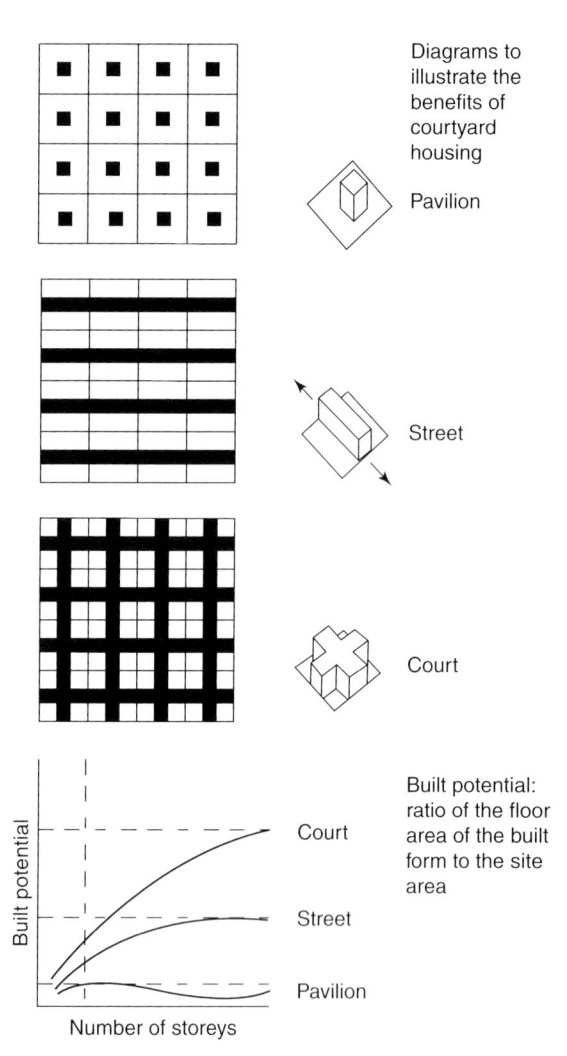

Figure 1.12 The Fresnel Square and Court housing: diagrams illustrate alternatives to high-rise housing (Redrawn with approval from Martin, L., and March, L., *Urban Space and Structures*, Cambridge University Press, 1972, pp. 36–37 and *AR*, 4/80, p. 207).

Policy" and planned overspill under the 1952 Town Development Act, which included major expansions of Basingstoke, Bletchley (later Milton Keynes), Swindon, and a number of East Anglian towns including Haverhill, Kings Lynn and Thetford.

After 1960 a further group of new towns were designated (Fig. 1.13) amongst which were Skelmersdale, Runcorn (later Runcorn and Warrington) and Central Lancashire in the North-west, Washington in Tyneside, Redditch and Telford in the West Midlands, Peterborough, Northampton and Milton Keynes in the South-East. Others were designated in Scotland and Northern Ireland. In total, from 1946, 32 new towns were built in Britain with a total population of 2.5 million. Politically the new towns were not always popular with local authorities that related the population loss to a fall in revenue. Rural authorities, where the new towns were designated, were concerned at all the new development in their back yards.

The master plans for these new towns provided an opportunity for their planners to explore a number of different models. The road grid plan at **Washington** and later at **Milton Keynes** (planned on a kilometre grid) was based on achieving a high level of personal mobility. **Runcorn's** figure-of-eight bus-only route gave an alternative emphasis to public transport. Most of the new towns experimented with new ideas in housing design. Runcorn (later Runcorn and Warrington), Washington and Telford successfully pioneered new ways of integrating the car into housing layouts. Runcorn developed the access-way (**Halton Brow**) whilst shared pedestrian/vehicular courts first appeared in Washington in the late 1960s. Milton Keynes developed complete cycle networks. High standards were set for the design of external spaces and planting. These innovations contributed much to the DOE's planning and design bulletins and occasional research papers and had a significant influence over local authorities, the planning system and the general level of quality of development.

Housing Associations – the beginnings

The Housing Association movement began in the 1830s with the Society for Improving the

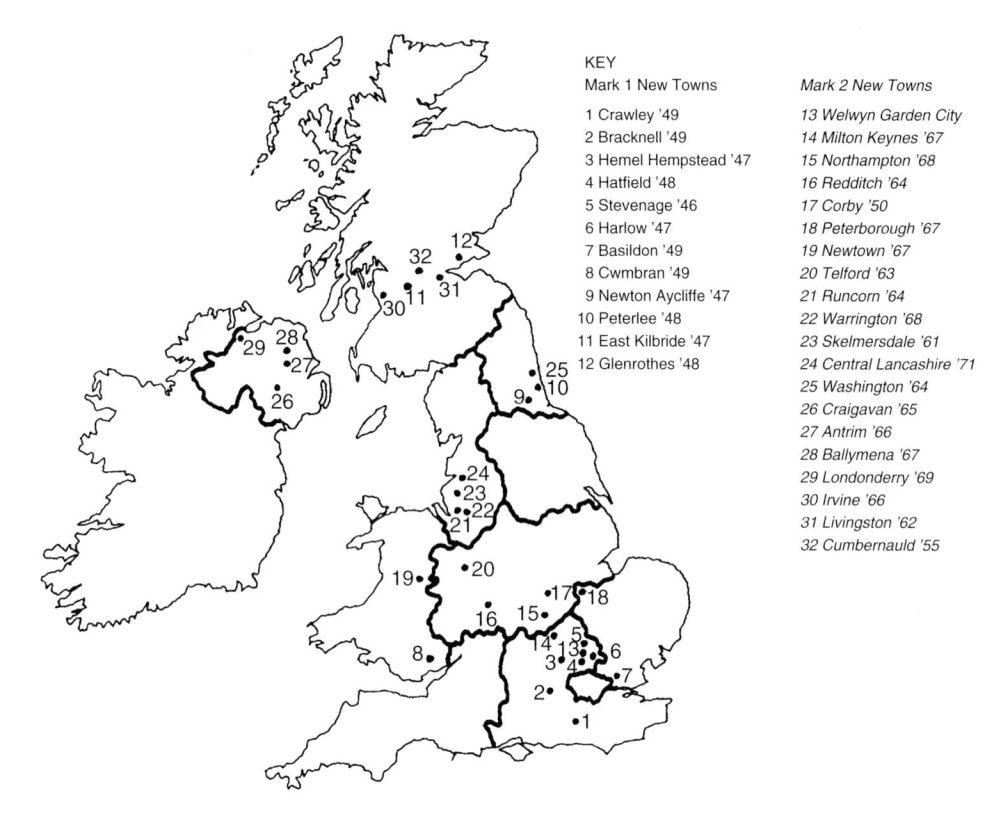

Figure 1.13 Location of the New Towns.

KEY

Mark 1 New Towns
1 Crawley '49
2 Bracknell '49
3 Hemel Hempstead '47
4 Hatfield '48
5 Stevenage '46
6 Harlow '47
7 Basildon '49
8 Cwmbran '49
9 Newton Aycliffe '47
10 Peterlee '48
11 East Kilbride '47
12 Glenrothes '48

Mark 2 New Towns
13 Welwyn Garden City
14 Milton Keynes '67
15 Northampton '68
16 Redditch '64
17 Corby '50
18 Peterborough '67
19 Newtown '67
20 Telford '63
21 Runcorn '64
22 Warrington '68
23 Skelmersdale '61
24 Central Lancashire '71
25 Washington '64
26 Craigavan '65
27 Antrim '66
28 Ballymena '67
29 Londonderry '69
30 Irvine '66
31 Livingston '62
32 Cumbernauld '55

Conditions of the Labouring Classes. However, Housing Associations were of little significance until in the 1950s when they became involved in building special needs housing, particularly sheltered housing for elderly people. They received their major boost in the 1964 Housing Act in which the government established the Housing Corporation as a promotional body and the channel of finance. Most new schemes were small with an emphasis on meeting special need and developing urban infill sites where the architects took care to make the schemes fit the sites and the localities. Prominent in this area of work was the York University Design Unit led by David Crease, which designed some highly influential housing in Heslington, York for the growing University and newly established housing associations for which he helped secure funding from the Housing Corporation (**Bretgate/Walmgate, York**) [37].

Encouraged by the 1967 Civic Amenities Act, Housing Associations became skilled in conservation and the conversion of old buildings into housing. This experience introduced associations to the larger and more difficult task of rehabilitating pre-1919 housing in inner urban areas. Working closely with local authorities, they established local offices and proved themselves particularly adept at working with communities, many of which included black and ethnic minorities. Frequently the residents were elderly owner–occupiers whose homes were in serious disrepair. The task often went far beyond this into areas of environmental improvement, helping local groups promote community activities and generating employment opportunities [38].

Improvement of pre-1919 housing

The 1969 Housing Act created a new emphasis. At this time the worst of the Victorian slums had been cleared and most of the pre-1919 housing that remained, if adequately repaired and modernised, was capable of having a longer life. Prominent amongst the early schemes in the 1970s was **Black Road, Macclesfield** where architect, Rod Hackney, worked with local residents to preserve and improve two small groups of housing which, at the time, were included in the local authority's slum clearance programme.

The 1969 Act effectively brought an end to slum clearance and gave powers to local authorities to look at older housing areas as a whole. Funding was available to designate general improvement areas (GIAs) and later housing action areas (HAAs) in which the local authority established a working relationship with houseowners, landlords and their tenants to encourage them to secure improvement grants for internal works, whilst the local authority itself organised the environmental improvements.

The rehabilitation of pre-1919 terraced housing took on its most effective form in the **enveloping** schemes devised most progressively **by Birmingham City Council** in the 1970s. Enveloping was envisaged as a form of neighbourhood improvement, which financed renovations to the external fabric of unimproved housing without a cost burden being placed on the owners. The works included new roofs, windows, chimneystacks damp proof courses, cleaning of brickwork, etc., and a measure of environmental works. The internal improvements were subsequently organised through housing improvement grants. The Housing Acts of 1984 and 1985 directed financial resources to areas of greatest need and introduced means testing for improvement grants and local authorities could no longer support enveloping from their housing investment allocations [39].

Private housing

Home ownership grew rapidly from 1950 but most speculative housing followed the pattern established before the war with layouts of detached and semi-detached houses built to average densities of around 10 dwellings per acre (25/ha). A number of specialist developers produced good schemes, for example, A. Cragie in **Jesmond, Newcastle**. Neil Wates, after visiting Seidlung Halen in Berne, commissioned Swiss architects, Atelier V to design a small group of hillside houses in Croydon (Fig. 1.14) (*Park Hill Road, Croydon, 1968 – AR, 9/70, p. 181. R. East Croydon*).

However, the most exceptional private housing of the period were the **Span housing** schemes at **Blackheath, Ham Common** (Fig. 1.15), **Highsett** in Cambridge and at other locations in the south of England. Span Developments Ltd was established in the mid-1950s by G.P. Townsend, an Architect who was formerly a partner of Eric Lyons but resigned from the partnership (and the RIBA) to become a "developer" [40]. Span's architect, Eric Lyons, thereafter produced designs with unmistakable flat and monopitched roofs, which set styles that became fashionable all over Britain. Lyons and Townsend (with their partners landscape architect Ivor Cunningham and builder/developer Leslie Bilby) shared a vision of how people might live – if shown the possibilities. It was a vision, which captured the imagination of Richard Crossman who, as Minister of Housing, gave planning consent, despite official advice, for **New Ash Green**.

Eric Lyons's greatest design achievement was to demonstrate that it was possible to

CHAPTER ONE • BRITISH HOUSING: 1900 TO THE PRESENT DAY

Figure 1.14 Atelier V's hillside housing at East Croydon.

Figure 1.15 Span housing at Blackheath.

move away from the standard housebuilder's pattern of site layout and the highway engineer's rigid requirements for the design of roads. At **Blackheath** the roads around the sites were private (and still are). This enabled him to soften their visual impact and use materials such as stone setts for curbs and a variety of materials for paving [41].

He believed that the key to successful design was the firm control by a single architect of every detail from briefing to site supervision and having total command between plants, paving and building. Supported by Ivor Cunningham's landscape design, he was able to realise these high standards. His achievement brought public acclaim and he was RIBA President between 1975 and 1977.

A distinct advantage to the design was the management company set up by Span to maintain the buildings with their roads and planting. The residents bought long leases costing £2,500–3,000 (a substantial amount for the late 1950s) – knowing that thereafter their house

23

Workshops and other buildings, intended to stimulate employment opportunities amongst communities, were incorporated wherever possible. In some instances, it proved to be more economically and/or socially viable to demolish the estate progressively and decant the tenants into new low-rise development.

There was a huge problem with the high-rise and high-density estates. Many suffered serious physical difficulties but much worse were the growth in unemployment, crime, vandalism and anti-social behaviour. Many tower blocks were demolished but others were given a new lease of life with a new outer skin in a variety of forms (**Nightingale Heights**, Greenwich; **Winterton Tower**, Tower Hamlets). With the installation of modern door entry systems, a block could offer a high degree of safety, security and privacy. Some blocks were successfully converted into sheltered housing for elderly people, complete with resident warden, concierge, community rooms and a launderette.

In addition to improving the physical fabric of estates, the process in itself was an important means of stimulating the economic and social objectives for stabilising the community and raising its self-esteem (**Kings Cross Estate Action, Cromer Street**). This multi-faceted approach to regeneration was seen as essential to the long-term sustainability of the estates.

In 1996 Estate Action was merged with the Single Regeneration Budget (SRB) to form a single pot of money for estate and urban regeneration. It became harder to secure funding and local authorities looked elsewhere. Some linked with housing developers and to established Local Housing Companies and Joint Venture Companies as a means of attracting government and private sector funding into regeneration. Hull City Council was particularly successful in this way at Victoria Dock and Gipsyville.

Community architecture

Architects made a real contribution to the regeneration of council estates through community architecture. Ralph Erskine encouraged resident participation at **Byker** in the 1970s and Hunt Thompson's pioneering scheme at **Lea View, Hackney** in the early 1980s established the model for estate regeneration. Rod Hackney was also active at **Black Road, Macclesfield**. The community architecture movement received royal assent in 1984 from Prince Charles who in his speech to the RIBA at Hampton Court said:

"To be concerned about the way people live, about the environment they inhabit and the kind of community that is created by that environment, should surely be one of the prime requirements of a really good architect ... what I believe about community architecture is that it has shown 'ordinary people' that their views are worth having".

The RIBA actively promoted community architecture. In 1988 the Housing Group published *Tenant Participation* [47] jointly with the Chartered Institute of Housing, which brought together examples of the best practice of the time [48].

Utopia on Trial

Alice Coleman's book *Utopia on Trial: Vision and Reality in Planned Housing*, published in 1985 [49], made a huge impact at the time. Her views were vigorously supported by the Prime Minister, Margaret Thatcher. The book made sweeping condemnations of local authority housing, both in its design and management. Assisted by a team of five researchers, Alice Coleman studied more than 100,000 houses mainly in Southwark and Tower Hamlets. She concluded that people were clearly happier in housing which related to streets and where the space around had a measure of defensibility and surveillance. The use of through roads rather than culs-de-sac would reduce crime [50]. The Department of the Environment commissioned her to put these views into practice in a number of estates in Southwark, Tower Hamlets (Fig. 1.17) and Westminster (Fig. 1.18). Many of her findings from this reflected those of Oscar Newman who had previously studied similar estates in the USA [51]. The final outcome was ultimately considered to be inconclusive but the concept of "permeable" street layouts is now widely accepted.

Housing Action Trusts

Housing Action Trusts (HATs) were seen by the government as the next step on from RTB: the prospect of having their home and estate improved would persuade tenants to accept transfer to an alternative landlord. After experience on the Tenants' Choice Programme in 1987, government officials made direct approaches to a number of estates to form HATs, but residents were suspicious of the intentions and refused to co-operate. The first HAT was, after much negotiation, eventually established in 1991at the **North Hull Estate**. This was followed by others at Waltham Forest (1991), Liverpool (1993), **Castle Vale**, **Birmingham** (1993), and in London – **Tower Hamlets** (1993) (Fig. 1.19) and **Stonebridge in Brent** (1994). They proved to be well-funded successful experiments in reviving estates affected by severe levels of deprivation. The process enabled the HATs to acquire the housing stock from the local authorities by direct transfer after a favourable ballot of the tenants. During refurbishment or building new housing, the tenants could vote to either return the ownership of their dwelling to the local authority or be transferred to an alternative landlord such as a local housing association. Ownership could also be taken over by the residents themselves through forming a Community Based Housing Association. HATs were to have limited lives so an important task was to prepare an "exit strategy" which generally led to the establishment of some form of Community Trust, run by residents, to protect the long-term sustainability of the physical and socio-economic regeneration measures.

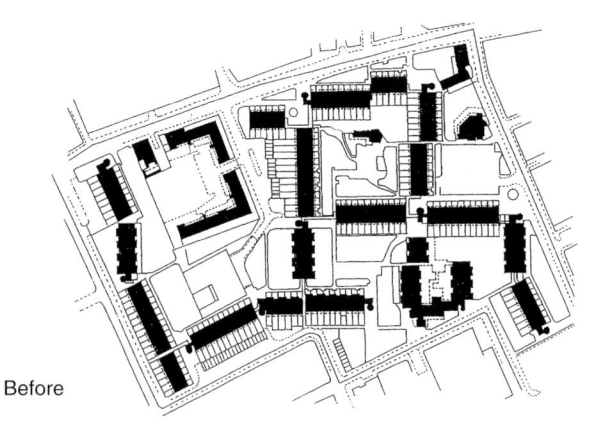

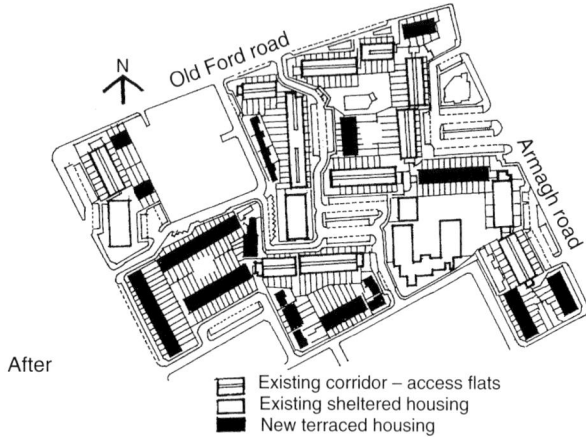

Figure 1.17 Ranwell Road Estate, Tower Hamlets, before and after the DICE intervention (redrawn with approval from B, 11/97, p. 48).

Home ownership

The government placed its emphasis on building new housing for home ownership. By 1995, home ownership had reached 67 per cent of the total housing stock but

Figure 1.20 London Docklands: Blackwall Basin, near Canary Wharf: a unique place in which to live.

new social housing. Many were involved in regenerating large 1960s housing estates working in partnership with local authorities and the private sector. Some concentrated on providing housing for elderly people and offering care facilities (**Liberty of Earley, Reading**) (Fig. 1.21). A number of associations successfully promoted new forms of housing for young people (**Swansea Foyer**) and developed low-energy housing (**BedZED; Honddu Place, Swansea**).

Partnering

In his report *Constructing the Team* [55], published in 1994, Sir Michael Latham gave added strength to people in the building industry who advocated closer working between client and builder by recommending the partnering method of procurement which he believed could cheapen costs. This has now become the accepted way for the larger housing associations (and groups of associations that have linked together for development purposes) to operate with contractors and house builders on major housing regeneration projects.

Housing co-operatives

The early 1980s witnessed the emergence of the Housing Co-operative movement. Most significant in the last quarter of the century was the growth of the par-value co-op. In normal co-operative housing, members have personal equity for their own property but in par-value co-ops they are nominal shareholders and own the development collectively [56]. From 1957 local authorities could

Figure 1.21 Liberty of Earley sheltered housing for frail elderly people; view of the garden court.

provide them with mortgages, but more importantly from 1974 they could receive the same grants as housing associations through the Housing Corporation. The greatest concentration of co-ops was in **Liverpool** and **Glasgow**. In London **the Coin Street Community Builders** created some highly imaginative housing.

Self-build

A number of housing co-operatives ventured into the area of self-build, notably the **Diggers** in Brighton. Self-build is the ultimate form of resident participation in the housing design and procurement process and its supporters argue, the most sustainable. Self-build in Britain is small in comparison with other countries. A study carried out by Sussex University in 1992 [57] showed that the self-help sector comprised just 6 per cent of the housing market in comparison to USA where it is 20 per cent. The statistics have not since greatly changed. In Sweden, Stockholm City Council has had a self-build department since the 1920s, which has been responsible for 30 per cent of all single-family dwellings in the city. The benefits of self-build for both rent and home ownership can be considerable provided residents accept the commitment and the time it takes, particularly acquiring the land and the finance. It can reduce construction costs by as much as 40 per cent which can produce cheaper homes; or the saving can be put into improving the quality of the housing such as measures to reduce energy. The unseen benefits are greater satisfaction, a sense of ownership leading to better standards of maintenance and a new vitality in housing [58].

Lifetime homes

Developed by the Joseph Rowntree Foundation, lifetime homes is about creating housing that is accessible and adaptable so that it can meet the changing circumstances of the occupants. Dwelling plans are designed to be suitable for both able-bodied people and adaptable for frail or physically disabled people.

The 16 design features for lifetime homes are indicated in Fig. 1.22 and Table 1.1. The cost at the initial construction stage of these features is small in comparison with the later cost of making adaptations and many housing associations have now adopted the standards for all their new developments.

Private housing development

Private ownership increased steadily to 67 per cent of the total stock by 1997. For most people this meant buying a new house in a speculative suburban development. The use of brown land in the inner cities grew

Lifetime Homes standards

14 Bathroom planned to give side access to WC and bath

13 Easy route for a hoist from bedroom to bathroom

First floor

11 Walls able to take adaptations

15 Low window sills

16 Sockets, controls, etc. at a convenient height

12 Identified space for future house lift to bedroom

Ground floor

7 Turning circles for wheelchair in ground-floor living rooms

10 Accessible entrance level WC plus opportunity for shower later

6 Width of doors and hall allow wheelchair access

8 Living room (or family room) at entrance level

4 Accessible threshold – covered and lit

9 Identified space for a temporary entrance level bed

12 Provision for a future stair lift

3 Level or gently sloping approach to the Lifetime Home

1 Parking space capable of widening to 3300 mm

2 Distance from the car parking space kept to a minimum

Edwin Trotter Associates

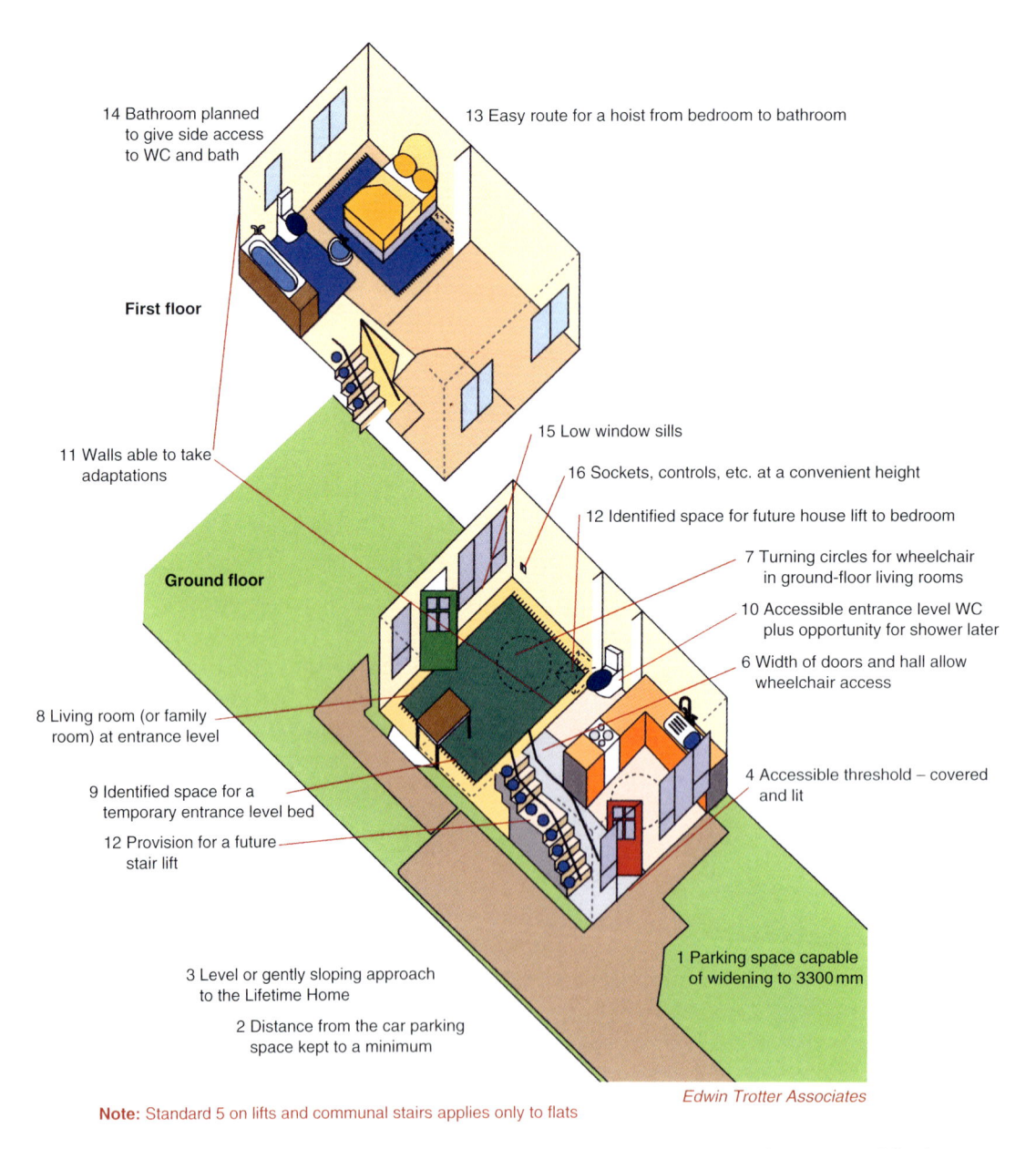

Note: Standard 5 on lifts and communal stairs applies only to flats

Figure 1.22 Lifetime Homes: design features of a three-bedroom house (from page 12 of *Meeting Part M and Designing Lifetime Homes*, edited by Caitriona Carroll, Julie Cowans and David Durton, published in 1999 by the Joseph Rowntree Foundation. Reproduced by permission of the Joseph Rowntree Foundation. Drawing copyright: Edwin Trotter Associates).

Table 1.1 Lifetime Homes Standards

1. **Car parking:** Where adjacent to the home, should be capable of enlargement to 3.3 m width.
2. **Access from car parking:** The distance from the car parking space to the home should be kept to a minimum and should be level or gently sloping.
3. **Approach:** The approach to all entrances should be level or gently sloping.
4. **External entrances:** All entrances should be illuminated, have level access over the threshold and have a covered main entrance.
5. **Communal stairs:** Communal stairs should provide easy access and, where homes are reached by a lift, it should be fully accessible.
6. **Doorways and Hallways:** The width of internal doorways and hallways should conform to Part M of the building regulations, except that when the approach is not head on and the hallway width is 900 mm, the clear opening width should be 900 mm rather than 800 mm. There should be 300 m nib or wall space to the side of the leading edge of the doors on entrance level.
7. **Wheelchair accessibility:** There should be space for turning a wheelchair in dining areas and living rooms and adequate space for wheelchairs elsewhere.
8. **Living room:** The living room should be at entrance level.
9. **Two or more storey requirements:** In houses of two or more storeys, there should be space on the entrance level that could be used as a convenient bed space.
10. **WC:** In houses with three or more bedrooms, or one level, there should be a wheelchair accessible toilet at entrance level with drainage provision enabling a shower to be fitted in the future. In houses with two bedrooms the downstairs toilet should conform at least to Part M.
11. **Bathroom and WC walls:** Walls in the bathroom and WC should be capable of taking adaptations such as handrails.
12. **Lift capability:** The design should incorporate provision for a future stair lift and a suitable identified space for a through the floor lift from the ground floor to the first floor, for example to a bedroom next to a bathroom.
13. **Main bedroom:** The design and specification should provide a reasonable route for a potential hoist from a main bedroom to the bathroom.
14. **Bathroom layout:** The bathroom should be designed for ease of access to the bath, WC and washbasin.
15. **Window specification:** Living room window glazing should begin no higher than 800 mm from the floor level and windows should be easy to open/operate.
16. **Fixtures and fittings:** Switches, sockets, ventilation and service controls should be at a height usable by all (i.e. between 450 and 1200 mm from the floor).

Reproduced by courtesy of the Habinteg Housing Association (www.lifetimehomes.org)

and many of the large house building companies established urban renewal units, formed partnerships with local authorities and housing associations and participated in seeking grant aid from the government through City Grant, City Challenge and Single Regeneration programmes. This saw the beginnings of the waterfront developments in most of the major cities and towns (**Swansea, Plymouth**) (Fig. 1.23).

Living over the shop

Some success came out of this initiative developed in the early 1990s by Ann Petherick and Ross Fraser [59] with the support of the Joseph Rowntree Foundation. Unfortunately, whilst there have been some excellent schemes, for example those run by Coventry Churches Housing Association in Granby Street, Leicester, and the Soho Housing Association at 9 Berwick Street in London,

Figure 1.23 Plymouth: successful waterfront regeneration offers new lifestyle opportunities.

the government programme was not fully taken up. Nevertheless, the concept is not forgotten as the Northern Ireland Housing Executive has recently launched a substantial living over the shop (LOTS) programme.

Housing for young people

The 1980s and 1990s witnessed the growth of young homeless people in Britain, particularly amongst the 16–26 age group. In 1995 the CHAR Inquiry into Youth Homelessness Report [60] estimated that there were between 200,000 and 300,000 homeless young people in Britain. This coincided with a huge rise in unemployment. With no work, young people were unable to find anywhere to live and with no home they could not get work.

Foyers: The most significant response to this came from the rise of the foyer movement. The idea originated in France in the 1940s. The UK network was spearheaded from 1992 by Shelter and Grand Metropolitan plc. Foyers provide accommodation, training and a job network for young people between the ages of 18 and 25. Most have been located in cities and large towns close to public transport and work opportunities (**The Swansea Foyer**). By mid-1997 there were 51 operational foyers in Britain with a total of 2,500 bedspaces nationwide. Sizes of foyers varied between 8 and over 150 bedspaces. The average length of stay was 12 months. Rents were low but Foyers could raise additional income from statutory grants, revenue from catering in their cafe/restaurants and training facilities.

Youth build: Another initiative that grew in the 1990s was self-build by young people promoted by the Young Builders' Trust and undertaken by a whole host of small organisations such as Grimsby Doorstep [61] which enables young people to improve pre-1919 terraced housing or build new housing whilst gaining training in the building industry for future employment. Regrettably, whilst these initiatives are good they have merely touched the problem of unemployment and disillusionment amongst young people.

Concern for quality/sustainability

By the mid-1990s concerns about quality in the built environment and the future impact of urban growth were being expressed in high places. Prince Charles's books *A Vision of Britain* (1989) [62] and *Urban Villages* (1992) [63] brought the issues to the public's attention. In 1994, John Gummer, Secretary of State for the Environment, outlined his concern in a remarkable publication for the government of the time, *Quality in Town and Country* [64]. This emphasised the importance of architecture in creating quality and urban design, which can reinforce a sense of community and create local pride. Above all it commented that "Quality is sustainable". John Gummer defined sustainability as "taking the longer term perspective and not cheating future generations out of the quality of life we enjoy" [65]. A whole host of guidance followed amongst the best of which was research sponsored by the Joseph Rowntree Foundation [66]. There was particular hope from the Urban Villages movement.

Urban Villages as a concept originated in the plans of the unsuccessful attempts in the early 1980s by Consortia of housebuilders to develop "Country Towns" within the greenbelt around London [67]. It was stimulated by the Urban Villages Forum established by Prince Charles who saw Urban Villages as mixed-use developments covering 100 acres (30 ha) for 5,000 residents. Housing was to be built at an average density of 20–25 dwelling/acre (50–60 dw/ha). There would be a focus on public transport and reducing car travel by building workspace as part of the development. Central to the concept were unified control of the whole site by the landowner and/or promoter of the development. Their responsibilities would be set out in the constitution of an "Urban Village Trust". Local people would be represented on this through a "Community Trust" [68]. **Poundbury** was identified by the Forum as its first demonstration project followed by **Crown Street**, Glasgow, **West Silvertown** in London Docklands, **Hulme** and the **Millennium Village**, Greenwich (Fig. 1.24).

From 1997 into a new century

Towards an Urban Renaissance

The new century was heralded in 1999 by the Urban Task Forces report *Towards an Urban Renaissance* [69]. Chaired by Lord Richard Rogers, its mission was to "recommend practical solutions to bring people back into our cities, towns and urban neighbourhoods ... to establish a new vision for urban regeneration founded on the principles of design excellence, social well-being and environmental responsibility within a viable economic and legislative framework". The publication was hugely influential.

CABE

CABE was set up in 1999 and is a statutory body funded by Communities and Local Government and the Department of Culture, Media and Sport. It is the government's advisor on architecture, urban design and public space. From the outset CABE placed design quality firmly on the modern housing agenda. Its audits of housing design in England between 2004 and 2007 "amount to a damning

Sir John Egan's report *Rethinking Construction* [81]. It has the support of the government, which is concerned that traditional trade-based technologies cannot deliver the numbers of new homes now required. The Peabody Trust has experimented with prefabricated housing at **Murray Grove**, **Raines Court**, **Beaufort Court** and **Barons Place**. These and other initiatives featured in the 2005 New London Architecture exhibition "Prefabulous London", which promoted the idea that "the prefab is now an inspirational dwelling which is becoming increasingly desirable" [82]. Sir John Egan suggested making a start on social housing which is now embodied in the Housing Corporation's scheme development criteria. Many housing associations grouped together to maximise the cost benefit from larger-scale development programmes and, with this, the potential for modern methods of construction. The private sector has been slow to respond but there have been notable exceptions (**Urban Splash Castlefields**), and some developers, particularly in the South-East of England have used timber-framed systems because of the shortage of skilled labour (**St Mary's Island**, **Chatham Maritime** – Fig. 3.109).

Transfer of local authority housing/ decent homes standard

A key government policy in recent years has been the transfer of council housing to alternative landlords, leaving the local authorities responsible only for housing strategy. The transfer options were:

- Arms Length Management Organisations (ALMOs), which are companies with tenants on the Board, set up by local authorities to manage their housing stock and carry out improvements. The housing remains council owned.

- Voluntary Stock Transfer (LSVT) where the housing stock is transferred to a RSL, either one already existing or one specially established. As the organisation is independent of the local authority it is easier to secure private sector investment.

The government also introduced measures to make all councils and housing associations bring their housing up to a "decent" standard by 2010. A decent home was defined as being warm, weatherproof and having reasonably modern facilities. Many housing organisations entered into partnering arrangements with building contractors to carry out this work more efficiently.

Housing Market Renewal

The unprecedented low demand and abandonment of housing in the north of England and the Midlands, particularly amongst the pre-1919 terraced housing, brought about the establishment in 2003 of nine Housing Market Renewal Pathfinders to tackle the issues as part of the government's Sustainable Communities Action Plan. These were at:

- Manchester and Salford (north and east/central Salford)
- Merseyside: New Heartlands (inner Liverpool, South Sefton and parts of Wirral)
- East Lancashire: Elevate (Blackburn, Hyndburn, Burnley, Pendle)
- Oldham and Rochdale
- South Yorkshire: Transform (North Sheffield, North Rotherham, South Barnsley, West Doncaster)
- Humberside: Gateway (Hull and adjacent areas of East Riding)
- Building Newcastle and Gateshead
- North Staffordshire: Renew (Stoke-on-Trent, Newcastle-under-Lyme)
- Renew Birmingham and Sandwell (North-West Birmingham and East Sandwell)

The concept of Housing Market Renewal (HMR) is different to the mass slum clearance programmes and redevelopment of the 1950/1970s, which were social housing programmes. In contrast HMR is driven by the need to enable people to enter into the housing market, and for people who cannot do this to be mixed with people who can. Consequently schemes are assessed from this point of view and not merely on cost. It also caters for a progression route from one to the other [83]. However, HMR has proved controversial. The mass housing clearances proposed was severely criticised by local communities and conservation organisations, particularly in Liverpool. They claimed that there was a bias towards clearance and that wholesale clearance of large areas of Victorian and Edwardian housing would do irreparable damage to the historic environment and destroy their local distinctiveness [84].

The HMR Pathfinders have been keen to ensure high design standards and a high level of resident participation throughout the planning and design process, the benefit of which is very obvious in the first new developments (**Selwyn Street, Oldham**).

Expansion in the south-east

In 2003, the Government responded to the seriousness of the housing shortage in the South-East of England by launching its Sustainable Communities Plan to develop new residential development in four growth areas in the south-east of England:

- Milton Keynes/South Midlands
- M11 Corridor: London/Stanstead/Cambridge/Peterborough.
- The Thames Gateway to the east of London
- Ashford in Kent.

Milton Keynes's population is planned to expand by a further 110,000 people by 2030, and an additional 28,000 new dwellings are proposed for the former new town of Corby. The first phase of major development at Northampton is at **Upton**. The Thames Gateway runs along both banks of the River Thames from London Docklands to Southend in Essex and Sheerness in Kent. It has been described as the largest regeneration project in Europe [85]. It covers 3,000 hectares of brownfield land and will accommodate up to 200,000 new dwellings by 2016 (**St Mary's Island**; **Ingress Park**).

Urban regeneration

The development of inner urban areas has expanded dramatically in recent years, including high rise/high density in the larger cities. Waterfront development is particularly popular and commercially successful. Setting the example for urban regeneration was **Urban Splash**, which started in 1993 with two men in a shed talking about the benefits of modern design, city centre living and urban regeneration. From small beginnings in Liverpool (**Old Haymarket**) and Manchester (**Britannia Wharf**, **Castlefields**), they have taken on a range of very exciting projects including the regeneration of Sheffield's **Park Hill Estate**, the conversion of Bristol's Imperial Tobacco building into housing and offices, the Lister Mills in Bradford and Royal William Yard, Plymouth into apartments, Birmingham's iconic Rotunda into housing, and the **New Islington** project in Manchester [86].

Rural housing

Housing shortage in rural areas is an acute problem. Over the past 20 years, the countryside's population has increased by more than 1 million people due to the greater mobility of the affluent commuter. This and the demand for second homes have squeezed the existing rural population out of the housing market.

Furthermore the supply of affordable housing is now extremely limited – only 5 per cent of houses in villages are social compared to the national average of 23 per cent. Consequently 45 per cent of newly forming households cannot afford to set up home where they currently live.

In July 2005 the Affordable Rural Housing Commission (ARHC) was set up by the Department of Environment, Food and Rural Affairs with Elinor Goodman as Chair. This was given the task of identifying ways of improving access to affordable housing in rural areas. It published its findings in 2006, concluding that a minimum of 11,000 affordable houses was needed each year in market towns and villages (settlements of less than 10,000 people). AHRCs estimate would be equivalent to six new houses in each settlement, which according to Elinor Goodman could be accommodated without unacceptable damage to the landscape – "Villages should be allowed to evolve, as they did in the past, but in scale and in character with their surroundings". She advises that this should be achieved through cross-subsidy from allowing some private development. This calls for sensitively designed housing on small infill sites in a way that reflects local architectural tradition (**Broadwindsor, Dorset**) (Fig. 1.28), but this quality can be difficult to achieve in social housing design because of funding limitations for housing association development [87].

Communities England

In January 2007, the government announced the establishment of a new agency, Communities England, to deliver housing and regeneration in England. It will bring together the previous functions of English Partnerships and the Housing Corporation and be responsible at national level for HMR, housing growth and urban regeneration and the

Figure 1.28 Broadwindsor, Dorset: new rural housing adds to the structure and character of the existing village.

decent homes programme. It will have a £4 billion annual budget.

Lessons for the future

The question is whether the lessons of the past have really been learnt or will the mistakes be repeated? Lessons from the past are obvious such as the lack of public investment in housing over the last 25 years and there is a clear message on climate change and sustainability. What has not changed since 1900 is that a good home in a pleasant environment within a community is key to the well-being of society. In her Review of Housing Supply in 2004, Kate Barker from the Treasury called for 45,000 social houses per year – more than double the present number. Prime Minister, Gordon Brown, has recognised this need with a projection of 3 million new homes by 2020 including permitting local authorities to build affordable houses for rent. But is it just about numbers? Surely quality is vital to sustainability and evidence from history clearly shows that the better designed and better built housing continues to serve its purpose long beyond expectancy, requires less maintenance and lasts longer. This means investing on the basis of sustainable costs rather than standard cost limits and taking account of management and maintenance at design stage.

There have been some remarkable achievements in estate regeneration in recent years and there is much to learn from this experience. The most successful were those where residents were involved right through the process from inception to management and maintenance. The Community Co-operatives and the HATs were good examples of this. The problem is that, despite the achievements there are still huge areas of poor housing in cities and towns waiting for something to happen. And when it does, we must not build large estates. Instead development should be small in scale with lots of design variety and be as socially mixed as possible. We must adopt industrialised housing with caution. It is the logical answer to building large numbers but to succeed where it failed previously it must be adaptable to human perceptions of home and environment.

Climate change is the big challenge but it needs careful planning. Projects such as Hockerton and BedZED are ground breaking but the housing development industry is struggling to master a new language. What is needed is a culture change running through housing development from the client's brief to the architects design, to the building site itself and to later management and maintenance. It is also important to learn how best to educate people to use their housing properly.

Much more attention (and research) needs to be given to the kind of housing that should be built. The majority of people in Britain aspire to a house with a garden whilst much current development is in the form of small flats, which offer little potential to young families to build a long-term home. What is really needed are much more spacious energy efficient options that will respond to the total needs of society from single young people and families to a growing and ageing population. In particular, modern homes should offer lower fuel bills and lots of natural sunlight, as well as providing green leafy places with a real sense of identity.

There is real hope amongst many people that the new awareness of design quality stimulated by CABE on one hand and TV on another will have an affect on the decision makers. Many of the schemes in the following chapters show just what can be achieved if design replaces dogma in the provision of housing. The RIBA's recent paper entitled "No more shoddy, Noddy boxes" called for higher minimum space standards and better design. Jack Pringle, commented, "For too long, many architects have been disenfranchised from the housebuilding industry" [88]. Good design needs good architects and these exist in both the large national and small local practices as evidenced in this book.

References

[1] Howard, E., *Garden Cities of Tomorrow*, Attic Books, 1997, (reprint).
[2] Reiss, R.L., *The Significance of Welwyn Garden City*, AR, 1–6, 1927, pp. 175–182; Girardet, H., *The Gaia Atlas of Cities*, Gaia Books Ltd., London, 1992, pp. 54–55.
[3] Taylor, N., *The Village in the City*, Temple Smith, London, 1973, p. 73.
[4] Hawkes, D., The architectural partnership of Barry Parker and Raymond Unwin, AR, 6/78, pp. 327–332.
[5] Swenerton, M., *Homes fit for Heroes*, Heinemann Educational Books, Oxford, 1981, p. 79.

[6] Tudor Walter's Report, *Report of the Committee to consider questions of building construction with the provision of dwellings for the working classes*, 1918.
[7] Housing and Town Planning after the War: a valuable report, AR, 9/18, pp. 19–22.
[8] Unwin, R., Town Planning: Formal or Irregular AR, 11/11, pp. 293–294.
[9] Swenerton, M., *Homes Fit for Heroes*, Heinemann Educational Books, Oxford, 1981, pp. 64–66.
[10] Yorke, F.R.S., *The Modern Flat*, The Architectural Press, London, 1937.
[11] Ministry of Health/Ministry of Works, *Housing Manual*, HMSO, London, 1944.
[12] Smith, M., *Guide to Housing*, (Third Edition 1989), The Housing Centre Trust, London, 1989, p. 13
[13] Ministry of Health, *Housing Manual*, 1949 HMSO, London, 1949.
[14] Ibid., p. 14.
[15] Glancy, J., Brave new world, *The Guardian*, 6/11/06, pp. 10–13.
[16] Lock, D., Harlow: The City Better, *Built Environment*, 3/4/83, pp. 210–217.
[17] MoHLG, *Houses 1952: Second Supplement to the Housing Manual*, 1949, HMSO, London, 1952.
[18] Nuttgens, P., *Homefront*, BBC Books, London, 1989, p. 68.
[19] Richards, J.M., *Failure of the New Towns*, AR, 7/53 pp. 29–32; Cullen, G., *Prairie Planning in the New Towns*, AR, 7/53, pp. 33–35.
[20] Ibid, p. 33.
[21] RIBAJ, 12/62, pp. 447–469.
[22] Failure of the New Densities, editorial and letters to the editor, AR, 12/53, pp. 355–361.
[23] English Heritage, Something Worth Keeping? Post-War Architecture in Britain: Housing and Houses, London, 1996, p. 3.
[24] AR, 7/59, pp. 21–35; also Taylor, N., *The Village in the City*, Temple Smith, London, p. 16.
[25] Ravetz, A., *The Place of Home*, E & FN Spon, London, 1995, p. 51.
[26] Glendinning, M., and Muthesius, S., *Tower Block*, Yale University Press, New Haven and London, 1994, pp. 121–131.
[27] Scoffham, E.R., *The Shape of British Housing*, George Godwin, London, 1984, p. 85.
[28] AD, 9/67, pp. 393–394.
[29] Glendinning, M., and Muthesius, S., *Tower Block*, 1994, Yale University Press, New Haven and London, p. 121.
[30] MoHLG, *Homes for Today and Tomorrow*, HMSO, London, 1961.
[31] MoHLG, *Design Bulletin 6, Space in the Home*, HMSO, London, 1963 and 1968.
[32] MoHLG, *Housing Subsidies Manual*, HMSO, London, 1967.
[33] DOE/DOT. *Design Bulletin 32. Residential Roads and Footpaths*, 1977 (2nd Edition, 1992), HMSO, London, DOE/HDD; Occasional Paper, 2/74. *Mobility Housing*, 1974 (AJ, 3/7/74, pp. 43–50). DOE/HDD Occasional Paper, 2/75. *Wheelchair Housing*, 1975 (AJ, 25/6/75, pp. 1319–1348). See also: *Activities and spaces: dimensional data for housing design* (AJ, 5/12/82, pp. 1–27).
[34] Scoffham, E., *The Shape of British Housing*, George Godwin, London, 1984, p. 91.
[35] Martin, L., and Marsh, L., *Urban Space and Structures*, Cambridge University Press, Cambridge, 1972, pp. 36 and 37.
[36] Colquhoun, I., and Fauset, P.G., *Housing Design in Practice*, Longman, UK, 1991, pp. 53–56; AR, 4/80, pp. 205–219; Duffryn: AR, 1/76, p. 11; AJ, 10/8/77, pp. 247–248; AJ, 13/2/80, pp. 325–334; AR, 4/80, pp. 205–214.
[37] AJ, 10/6/75, p. 677.
[38] Smith, M., *A Guide to Housing*, (Third edition), 1989, The Housing Centre Trust, London, p. 241.
[39] Ibid, pp. 95, 301–302, 296–297, 301–306.
[40] AR, 2/59, pp. 108–120.
[41] *The Architect*, July 1971, p. 42 (See also RIBAJ, 11/06, p. 16).
[42] AJ, 14/8/74, p. 366; AJ, 22/9/76, pp. 533–552.
[43] *Planning*, 10/10/97, p. 3.
[44] Nuttgens, *The Homefront*, BBC Books, London, p. 112.
[45] Scarman, Lord. T. (Inquiry Report Chairman), *Brixton Disorders*, April 10–12, 1981, HMSO, London.
[46] Church of England, *Faith in the City: a Call for Action by the Church and the Nation*, Church House Publishing, London, 1985, p. 333.
[47] RIBA/CIOH, *Tenant Participation*, 1988.

[48] McCafferty, P., Working in Association, *Prospect*, Summer 1994, p. 25 (See also *AJ*, 8/8/84, pp. 18–19.

[49] Coleman, A., *Utopia on Trial, Vision and Reality in Planned Housing*, Hilary Shipman, London, 1985.

[50] This view is still not shared by all police crime prevention officers.

[51] Newman, O., *Defensible Space – People and the Design of the Violent City*, Architectural Press, London, 1973.

[52] Parry, N., The New Town Experience, *Town and Country Planning*, 11/96, p. 302.

[53] *London Docklands*, A Builder Group supplement, March, 1998, p. 30.

[54] Ibid.

[55] Latham, Sir M., *Constructing the Team, Final Report of the Government/Industry Review of Procurement and Contractual Arrangements in the UK Construction Industry*, HMSO, London, 1973.

[56] Ravetz, A., *The Place of Home*, E&FN Spon, London, 1995, pp. 112–113.

[57] Duncan, S., and Rowe, A., *Self-Help Housing: The World's Hidden Housing Arm*, Centre for Urban and Regional Research, The University of Sussex, Brighton, 1992.

[58] *AJ*, 7.11.96, pp. 48–50.

[59] Petherick, A., and Fraser, F., *Introduction to Living over the Shop*, The University of York, York, 1992.

[60] Evans, A., *We do not choose to be homeless*, CHAR – Campaign for Homeless and Rootless (recently renamed Natural Homeless Alliance), London, 1996.

[61] Colquhoun, I., *Design Out Crime*, Elsevier, Oxford, 2004, pp. 22–23.

[62] Charles, HRH Prince of Wales, *A Vision of Britain – A Personal View of Architecture*, Doubleday, London, 1989.

[63] Aldous, A., *Urban Villages*, Urban Villages Group, London, 1992, (Foreword by HRH The Prince of Wales).

[64] DOE, *Quality in Town and Country*, HMSO, London, 1994.

[65] DOE, London, *Construction Monitor*, Issue 9, 2/95 p. 1.

[66] URBED (David Rudlin and Dr Nicholas Falk), *21st Century Homes, Building to Last*, report for the Joseph Rowntree Foundation, URBED, London, May 1995. Girardet, H., *The Gaia Atlas of Cities, New Directions for Sustainable Urban Living*, Gaia Books Limited, London, 1992.

[67] Colquhoun, I., and Fauset, P.G., *Housing Design in Practice*, Longman UK, Harlow pp. 68–69.

[68] *Urban Villages Forum Newsletter*, London, Autumn 1997, p. 9.

[69] Urban Task Force, *Towards an Urban Renaissance*, E&FN Spon, London, 1999.

[70] *R&R*, 16/2/07, pp. 16–17.

[71] *R&R*, 9/2/07, p. 2.

[72] *B*, 2/3/07, p. 12; Colquhoun, I., *Design Out Crime*, Elsevier, Oxford, 2004. pp. 237–249.

[73] Wayne Hemingway (Chair, Building for Life), www.buildingforlife.org

[74] Bentley. et al, *Responsive Environments, a Manual for Designers*, The Architectural Press Ltd, London, 1993.

[75] DETR, *Places Streets and Movement*, HMSO, London, 1998.

[76] CLG/DFT, *Manual for Streets*, Thomas Telford, London, 2007, p. 11.

[77] *The Guardian*, 13/5/06, p. 13.

[78] *The Guardian*, supplement "Building the future", 18/4/07, pp. 1–8.

[79] *R&R*, 16/2/07, pp. 20–22; *B*, 15/12/06, p. 11; *B*, 16/2/07, pp. 74–76; *B*, 19/1/07, pp. 28–30.

[80] CLG, *Eco Towns Prospectus*, CLG Publications, 2007.

[81] Department of Transport, Local Government and the Regions (DTLR), *Rethinking Construction: The Report of the Construction Task Force (Egan Report)*, DTLR, London, 1998.

[82] *AJ*, 25/5/06 pp. 28–37; *AT*, 3/99, pp. 60–64.

[83] *AJ*, 23/6/05, pp. 18–19.

[84] *RIBAJ*, 4/05, pp. 56–58; *B*, 13/1/06, p. 20; *AJ*, 8/8/06, p. 16.

[85] *R&R*, supplement – The Thames Gateway, 18/11/05, p. 3).

[86] *RIBAJ*, 11/06, p. 30; *B*, Awards supplement, 20/10/06, p. 11.

[87] *Voice* (the magazine of CPRE), Autumn 2006, p. 17; *Planning*, 26/5/06, p. 8; *Planning*, 14/4/06, p. 22; Commission for Rural Communities, *Rural Disadvantage: Reviewing the Evidence* (2006), pp. 64–83. www.ruralcommunities.gov.uk

[88] Bayley, S., Lets start thinking outside the box, *The Observer*, 15/7/07, pp. 10–11.

Barking and Dagenham

Tanner Street redevelopment, Barking, IG11
2006. Peter Barber Architects and Jestico + Whiles. U. Barking

Barking falls within the area of the Thames Gateway and has ambitions over the next 15–20 years to build 7,500 dwellings in the town centre and a further 10,000 on the Barking Reach riverside site. A start has been made with development at Tanner Street for the East Thames Housing Group by a partnership of architects Peter Barber Associates and Jestico + Whiles (Fig. 2.3).

The scheme follows on from Peter Barber's earlier Donnybrook scheme (p. 145) and replaces 3 six-storey slab blocks that had proved prohibitively expensive to repair and were beset with social problems. The 165 new apartments and houses are laid out as a network of street housing with tightly packed terraces built hard up to the back edge of footpath. The space across the street is reduced in places to as little as 9 m (30 ft) but this does not appear oppressive because of the light reflected from the white rendered walls and the recessed terraces at first floor level. At the western edge of the scheme is a nine-storey tower designed by Jestico + Whiles which forms a landmark at a square where a number of roads meet. There is a wide range of house types in the scheme from three-storey, four-bedroom town houses to one- and two-bedroom apartments in two-storey terraces. Apartments have usable open space in the form of rear patios at ground floor level or recessed terraces at first floor overlooking the streets.

BD, 16/3/07, pp. 10–13; *Housing Design Awards 2005* Publication, pp. 72–73; *AJ*, 13/9/07, pp. 23–25.

Figure 2.3 Tanner Street, Barking.

Barnet

Hampstead Garden Suburb, NW11
Started 1906. Parker and Unwin, Lutyens, Baillie Scott, others. U. Golders Green

Founded in 1906 by Dame Henrietta Barnet, this development had a most significant influence on British housing design for half a century. Here Barry Parker and Raymond Unwin produced some of their finest planning (Fig. 2.4). Culs-de-sac were used for the first time. In his book *Town Planning in Practice* 1909, Unwin described these as being "specially desirable for those who like quiet

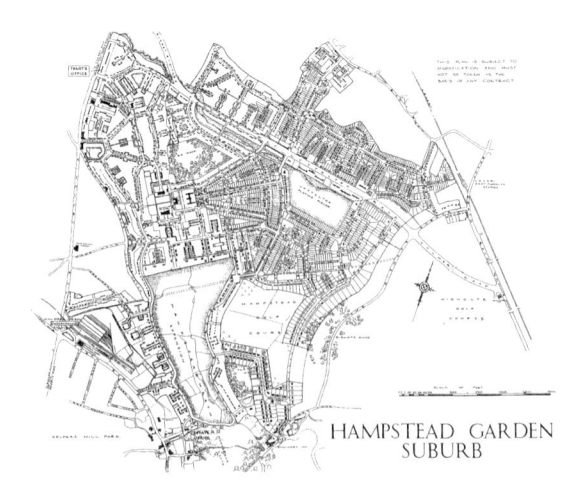

Figure 2.4 Plan of Hampstead Garden Suburb by Parker and Unwin and Sir Edward Lutyens (plan reproduced by courtesy of Hampstead Garden Suburb Trust Ltd).

for their dwellings ... particularly since the development of the motorcar" [1]. A special Act of Parliament was required to enable culs-de-sac to be built and a maximum density of eight dwellings to the acre was stipulated by Parliament because of concern regarding possible traffic problems.

The central area was planned by Sir Edwin Lutyens whose designs were more formally structured than Parker and Unwin's work elsewhere in the Suburb. The housing was designed by several architects. Amongst the finest groups are Sir Edwin Lutyens's "Wren" inspired housing (1908–1910) at Erskine Hill (on the west side of the street below the Free Church) and M.H. Baillie Scott's Waterlow Court, Heath Close (1908–1909) and 6–10 Meadway with 22 Hampstead Way (c1910). Most of the houses designed by Parker and Unwin are simple terraced cottages, but at Corringham Road (1911) Unwin successfully combined a neo-Georgian style with the intimate character of a small-scale quadrangle (Fig. 2.5). Their Temple Fortune shops and flats (1900) at the junction of Finchley Road and Hampstead Way form a powerful composition at the gateway to the Suburb. A visit should include a walk up Erskine Hill to Lutyens' Central Square with its two massive churches and Institute (1909–1910); crossing the Square to Heathgate reveals the open heathland beyond.

Henrietta Barnet's aim was to produce a socially mixed utopia in which rich and poor would live together in harmony. Each house was to have a garden and each street flowering trees. Hedges were to be cut low. There was a clubhouse in which alcohol was forbidden. After the First World War, the spirit of the founder was lost. Less interesting neo-Georgian style dwellings were built. Today, Hampstead Garden Suburb has become a middle and upper class dormitory for some 16,000 people and, as such, has lost much of its former social objectives [2].

[1] Unwin, R., *Town Planning in Practice*, 1909;
[2] *AR*, 10/57, pp. 259–262.

BRENT

Stonebridge Estate Regeneration, Hillside/Knatchbull Road/Mordaunt Road, NW10
2007. Shepheard Epstein Hunter, AFH Shaw Sprunt. Masterplanners: Terence O'Rourke Ltd.
U. Harlesden

The Stonebridge estate was, in 1995, the last of the six Housing Act Trusts (HATs) to be established. The 20 hectare (55 acre) estate of 1775 dwellings, built in the 1960s and 1970s, contained seven deck-access concrete panel slab blocks and six 21-storey towers. These were difficult to maintain, windswept, crime ridden and were thoroughly unpleasant places in which to live.

Figure 2.7 Ossulston Estate (photo by Christopher Colquhoun).

Figure 2.8 Isokon flats: first British housing in the modernist manner.

were let furnished, with services offered to the tenants such as shoe and window cleaning, bed making, dusting and refuse collection, for rents of £96 per year [1]. The project included the Isobar restaurant, which was envisaged as the social hub of the community. Commenting in 1970 on the design, Jack Pritchard said, "We had just been hit by the Bauhaus, which in fact, we went to see with Wells and Chermayeff. We were very much bowled over by that episode. We were not consciously pioneers: it just seemed the right thing to do" [2].

From 1945 the building declined and, after various ownership changes, it became almost derelict. Its significance was recognised by Grade I listing and it was recently restored and modernised internally by Avanti Architects for Notting Hill Home Ownership. An important part of the renovation was the social programme, whereby, through a mixed-tenure, cross-subsidy arrangement, 25 of the 36 dwellings were made available as affordable housing for key workers.

[1] *AR*, 11/79, p. 290; [2] *AJ*, 11/3/70, p. 595; *AR*, 3/07, pp. 84–85; *Detail*, January/February 2007, pp. 34–37.

Kent House, Ferdinand Street, NW1
1935. Connell Ward and Lucas.
U. Chalk Farm

Built for the St Pancras Housing Association, this was Connell Ward and Lucas's only social housing commission. It is one of the few examples in Britain of inter-war modern movement architecture applied to housing for low-income people. The development is in two-, five- and six-storey blocks with a small amount of open space containing children's

Figure 2.9 Kent House.

play equipment. The white walls and metal horizontal windows, which are the hallmark of this architectural style, have survived extremely well. The large balconies are very usable spaces and add considerably to the appearance of the scheme, which was listed in 1993 (Fig. 2.9).

1-3 Willow Road, NW3
1939, Erno Goldfinger.
U. Hampstead

These three houses overlooking Hampstead Heath are very significant to the history of British housing because their architectural style, which attempted to bring modernism to terms with the Georgian urban tradition, has since been so frequently copied. The houses are three storeys in height with the main living spaces at first floor level. This is emphasised externally by the projection of the framing around the large windows set in predominately brick elevations (Fig. 2.10).

Writing about the design in 1970, Erno Goldfinger said, "they are not eccentric, what I call Kasbah architecture – that very early

Figure 2.10 1–3 Willow Road: large first floor windows overlook the Heath.

international style, white walls and horizontal slit windows, which always looks avant garde because it never caught on, except with spec builders in the Cote d'Azur. I really tried to build a late Georgian or Regency terrace in a modern way" [1]. Despite this, it is a genuine building of the modern movement. The reinforced concrete frame offers open plans internally which can be readily sub-divided and modified. The only fixed point is the staircase with a plumbing duct in the middle.

The National Trust has acquired Goldfinger's house, which Avanti Architects have restored to enable it to be open to the public [2]. The three houses are Grade II* listed.

[1] *AJ*, 11/3/70, p. 597; [2] *AJ*, 28/3/96, pp. 41–44; *AJ*, 28/3/96, pp. 24–26.

St Anne's Close, Highgate West Hill, N6
1947–1948. Walter Segal. U. Kentish Town

This group of eight semi-detached houses designed by Walter Segal for himself and his

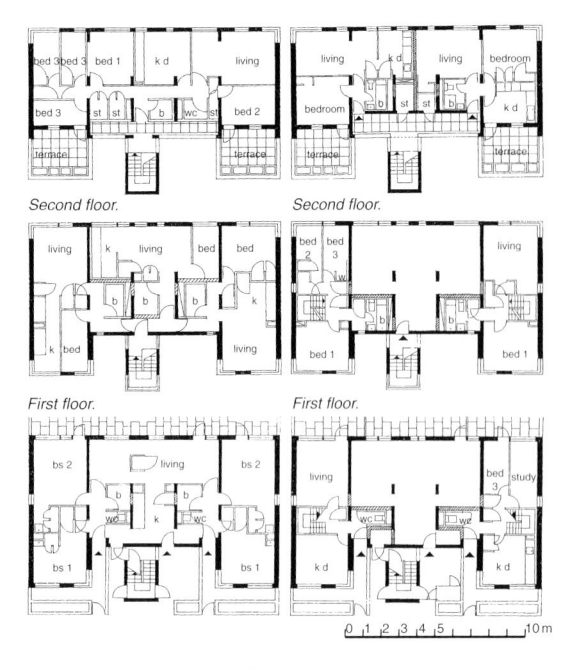

Figure 2.13 PSSHAK, Adelaide Road. Sample plans: solid lines show the support structure; hatched areas show demountable party walls; open blocks show the "kit" (reproduced with approval from *AJ*, 21/5/75, p. 1073).

Park Hill created an opportunity to develop the split-level principle. The mixture of houses, flats and maisonettes was arranged in terraces along the contours to take full advantage of the slope of the site and the superb views across Highgate Cemetery to Parliament Hill (Fig. 2.14). Every dwelling has a south-facing private open space screened from its neighbours. The scale of the buildings was kept low to not more than two-and-a-half-storeys, but a density of some 70 dwellings per acre (173/ ha) was achieved. A network of pedestrian streets and play-squares run between the terraces. These are overlooked from kitchens, allowing for the supervision of children and natural policing of streets. A high level of car parking was provided underground in lock-up garages. The white modernist image, which the Architects saw as an essential part of the concept, came from the predominate use of light-coloured concrete blocks (Fig. 2.15).

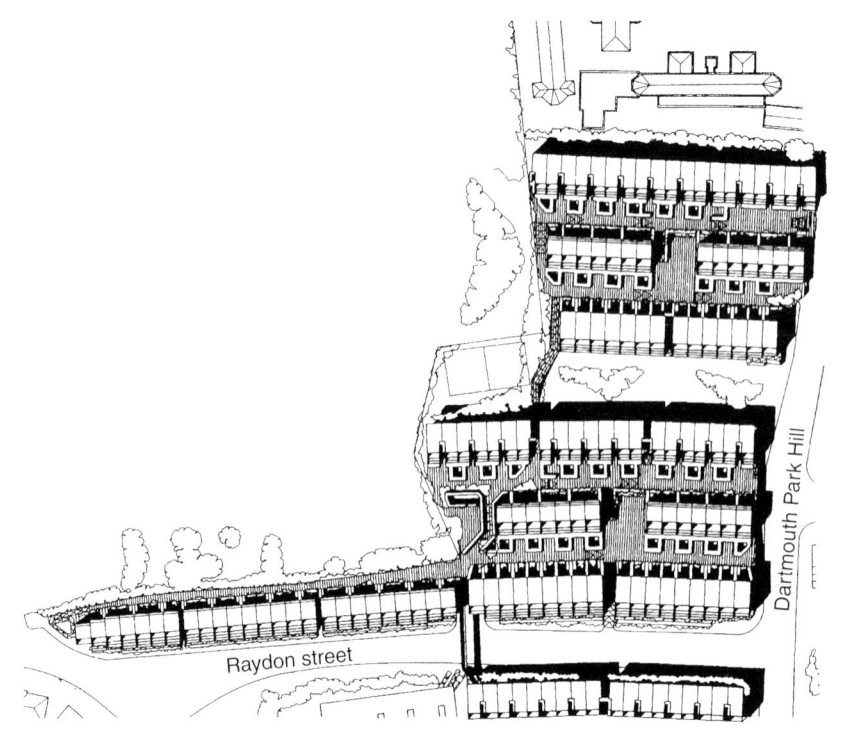

Figure 2.14 Highgate New Town, Phase 1: site layout.

Stage 2, Dartmouth Park Road/ Raydon Street was very different. By 1976, the Borough Council had written a new design brief which insisted that all families be housed at ground floor level in brick low-rise housing with pitched roofs. The scheme contains 107 flats and houses in two- and three-storey terraces, which were designed around the former street pattern. The housing was built in colourful brickwork with decorative light metal balconies to reflect the traditional housing in the area.

AD, 3/72, pp. 145–164; *AR*, 9/73, pp. 159–162; *AJ*, 10/8/77, pp. 236–238; *RIBAJ*, 11/79, pp. 483–489; *AJ*, 12/8/81, pp. 294–306.

Branch Hill, **Hampstead**, **NW3**. *1978. U. Hampstead*. This was much smaller than the other split-level schemes of this period. The development comprises 42 houses clustered tightly on a steeply sloping site in a woodland setting in one of the most select areas of London close to Hampstead Heath. Restricted covenants required that the buildings were to be in semi-detached form not higher than two storeys, but the design interprets these requirements in a most liberal manner.

The scheme was designed with rows of housing along the contours of the site with level changes within the dwellings. A series of pedestrian alleys and steps run between the dwellings across and down the contours. Gardens are formed on the roofs of dwellings below except for the lowest level of housing. From within the dwellings, the large areas of glass make it possible to fully appreciate the changing landscape of the site that varies with the seasons (Fig. 2.16). The house plans ingeniously separate the activities of parents and children by creating a communal zone in the

Figure 2.15 Highgate New Town, Phase 1.

Camden Gardens, NW1, Kentish Town Road, NW1
1993. Jestico + Whiles. U. Camden Town

Jestico + Whiles was commissioned by the Community Housing Association to design this rented housing scheme on a restricted site in Camden overlooking the Grand Union canal. Its 27 dwellings are distributed between a three-storey terrace of houses and flats along the side of the Grand Union Canal and three square "villas" facing Camden Gardens. These accommodate flats and maisonettes. The location of parking courts at the entrance between the villas gave the required 50 per cent provision and allowed space in the centre of the scheme for pedestrian use (Fig. 2.21).

The appearance of the terrace is characterised by the treatment of the external communal stairs. A large double-height curved trellis for planting supports two frameless glass canopies that give the whole area a light and transparent quality. A wide stair passes through the trellis to a deck of timber slats at first floor where a second staircase leads to the upper level. The villas were entered through freestanding portals of terracotta painted masonry. Light buff bricks are used throughout in a simple stretcher bond with raked pointing.

AJ, 9/3/94, pp. 45–55; AJ, 13/10/94, p. 30; B (Housing Design Awards), 27/10/95, p. 23.

Bruges Place mixed-use development, Baynes Road/Randolph Street, NW1
1987. Jestico + Whiles. U. Camden Town

Bruges Place demonstrates that light industrial uses and housing can be combined, provided access to both is carefully organised. The former Second World War bombsite was zoned by the planners for industrial use even though it was surrounded by housing. They preferred two-storey industrial development but the architects successfully argued that the urban grain of the area dictated the development should be of mixed use and four storeys in height (Fig. 2.22).

The scheme ultimately included 20,000 sq. ft. (2000 sq.m.) of industrial space in multiple units on the ground and first floors. Entrance to the ground floor part of the project is from a central mews from which access to the first floor is at the northern end. The residents of the 21 dwellings on two floors above the workspace park their cars in two side streets and gain entry via staircases and lifts in the south of the complex which overlooks the Regent's Canal. The stairs lead to landscaped courtyards at second floor level from where the housing is entered. The dwellings all have good views out from private balconies on the outer faces of the building. The yellow brick and orange banding is striking and contrasts well with the dark green joinery and metalwork. Much credit is due to the Architects' determination to see the site correctly developed.

AJ, 15/7/87, pp. 32–37, 41–54; B, Housing Design Awards 1989, p. 26; RIBAJ, 11/90, pp. 6–7.

Kings Cross Estate Action, Cromer Street, WC1
1996–2001. Tibbalds Monro (Gardner Stewart Architects/ Tibbalds Planning and Urban Design), Camden Building Design Services, AFH Shaw Sprunt, The Floyd Slaski Partnership, Hunt Thompson Associates. U. Kings Cross, Euston

It is easy to miss this significant project as a result of the new railway and commercial infra structure in and around Kings Cross and St Pancras railway stations. To the south of Euston Road, the £46 million Kings Cross

Figure 2.21 Camden Gardens: looking into the internal courtyard.

Figure 2.22 Bruges Place.

Estate Action project enabled over 1,000 council and housing association properties based on Cromer Street to be refurbished internally and externally over 5 years from 1996 to 2001. At the time it was one of the largest local authority building projects in London.

The housing included a mixture of pre-1919 brick tenements of fine architectural quality and post-1950s high-rise slab blocks. Several architectural practices were employed to ensure a variety of design approach. The post-1950s housing was colourfully over-clad to increase thermal capacity and reduce heating costs. The blocks were given new entrances, boundary walls, fencing and planting, which have completely transformed the area (Fig. 2.23). Considerable attention was given to increasing security by the provision of concierge-controlled access and door entry systems. A range of energy efficiency measures included new central heating and a combined heat and power scheme. The brick tenement housing was carefully and sensitively restored. Its freshly cleaned brickwork and painted metal balconies emphasise its architectural qualities.

The environmental improvement proposals build on the quality of the existing urban structure of streets and squares (Fig. 2.24). They include a self-enforcing 20 mph speed zone with speed tables and pinch points, the introduction of pedestrian/cycle routes and renewal have reduced considerably and the image of deprivation in the Kings Cross area has been greatly reduced.

AT, 9/97, pp. 57–58; *AJ*, 14/5/98, pp. 33–36; *Design Out Crime*, pp. 284–290.

Latitude House, Gloucester Avenue/Delancy Street/Parkway, Camden, NW1
2005. Alford Hall Monaghan Morris. U. Camden Town

This elegant limestone-clad housing development was built on the triangular site of a former garage. It contains 12 large two- and three-bedroom apartments arranged in three sub blocks, one of three storeys over a basement and the other two of four storeys (Fig. 2.25). The massing relates sensitively to the surrounding architecture, the lower part to the scale of the adjacent villas in Gloucester Crescent and the main part to the adjacent Edwardian terraces on Gloucester Avenue and Oval Road.

The southern elevation cantilevers at each floor, which ensures that the large terrace garden at ground floor level is not overlooked from apartments above. The setback to the building line at the northern end is used to flood light into the basement flat through a sunken patio garden and the middle setback is used as another hidden ground floor terrace. The three elevations seen from the road are faced with limestone whilst the rear is rendered. The floor-to-ceiling windows are large and set in black wooden frames. Each dwelling has a slightly different internal arrangement of rooms, which produces a variety of windows on the façades. The building is setback from the street behind a simple brick garden wall. The space between this and the building is surfaced with iroko timber slats, limestone paving and planting beds.

Figure 2.23 Kings Cross Estate Action: a new image for 1960s housing.

of pavements. The open spaces between the blocks were simply designed with low maintenance in mind. Children's play areas relate to their location, either within the semi-private housing spaces or in a square. The three urban squares, Regent, Argyle and Bamber Green have been upgraded. Generally all have higher railings, improved entrances, new seating and extensive planting. In one square, a multi-use games area (MUGA) was provided which is very popular. New street lighting and CCTV cameras were included in the environmental improvements.

Resident involvement, including the large Bangladeshi community, was very high and many people benefited from training initiatives. A local office was established and this still remains as the focus of a Community Trust. The project has strengthened a very diverse community, crime and fear of crime

Figure 2.24 Kings Cross Estate Action: environmental improvement plan by Tibbalds Monro (reproduced by courtesy of Gardner Stewart Architects).

AT 168, 5/06, pp. 68–73; BD, 10/2/06, p. 3; AJ, NHBDA Report, July 2006, pp. 58–59; Housing Design Awards 2006 Publication, pp. 24–27.

CITY OF LONDON

Golden Lane and Crescent House, Goswell Road/Baltic Street, EC1
1962. Chamberlin Powell and Bon.
U. Barbican

Against a wealth of talented architects including the Smithsons (pp. 12–13), Geoffrey Powell won this most prestigious architectural competition in 1952 for the development of a site on the northern boundary of the City of London which had been heavily bombed during the Second World War.

Golden Lane, with its 17-storey tower clad externally in yellow curtain walling, was much admired for its bold approach to the design of urban housing. It epitomised everything that was good about mixed development. The housing blocks were conceived as a framework to linked landscaped pedestrian courtyards formed by four- and six-storey

Figure 2.25 Latitude House.

blocks of flats and maisonettes. The tower stands as the centerpiece (Fig. 2.26). In the tradition of Le Corbusier's Unite d'Habitation, the roof of the tower was laid out as a terrace for the tenants of the upper floors. Its most distinctive feature – the over-sailing canopy on the roof – covers the water tanks, lift motor rooms, etc. The dwellings were very varied in size and type to cater for a wide range of people. The scheme has a wealth of community provision including shops, sports facilities, a swimming pool, a community hall, tennis courts and a crèche.

The project has retained much of its original quality. Writing in 2006, Architect Eric Parry, commented that it has "a generous and well used environment, that together with the carefully considered architecture of the flats, makes most recent schemes look clumsy and mean spirited" [1]. It is now Grade II listed.

Crescent House is Grade II* listed (Fig. 2.27). The design of the curved terrace is frequently likened to the brick and concrete idiom of Le Corbusier's Maisons Jaoul but adapted for its urban setting. Its façades are of bush-hammered concrete, brick and timber forming a profile of segmental curves. The stepping of the block to follow Goswell Road was particularly well handled.

[1] B, 10/11/06, p. 39; AJ, 20/3/52, pp. 354, 358–362; AD, 7/53, pp. 190–194; AR, 1/54, p. 52; AR, 1/56, pp. 34–37; AD, 9/56, pp. 294–298; AR, 6/57, pp. 414–425; AJ,

Figure 2.26 Golden Lane tower clad in yellow curtain walling.

27/6/57, pp. 947–948; AJ, 7/11/96, p. 25; AJ, 29/12/60, pp. 931–942; B, 10/11/06, p. 39; B, 10/11/06, p. 39.

The Barbican, bounded by London Wall, Beech Street and Moorgate, EC2
*1973. Chamberlin Powell & Bon.
U. Barbican, St Paul's, Moorgate*

At the end of the Second World War, the resident population of the City of London had declined to as few as 5,000 compared to some 125,000 a hundred years previously. This meant that whilst during the day the City bustled with half a million commuting workers, by evening it was reduced to a ghost town, a "City of cats and caretakers". The vision of the Barbican was to change this by building "a genuine residential neighbourhood, incorporating schools, shops, open spaces, and other amenities … even if this meant forgoing a more remunerative return for the land" [1].

The solution was perhaps the closest that British housing design has ever got to applying Le Corbusier's planning theories in the form of 125 m (415 ft) high triangular towers – the tallest in Europe when first built – soaring above interlinked courtyards of medium-rise flats (Fig. 2.28). Some 6,500 people now live in 2,113 flats with parking for 2,500 private cars underground below a pedestrian podium level. Built for the middle- to high-income group, the design avoids the balcony and deck access so favoured at the time for council flats. Entrance to the flats is by closely spaced lifts and staircases, which are rigidly controlled by concierge and door entry systems.

The buildings themselves are imaginatively sculptured and the spaces are well proportioned and landscaped. Yet, the overriding feeling is one of bleakness. The large areas of empty paving are hard and windswept and there are few people about. Even the presence of the Barbican theatre complex in the centre of the development makes little difference (Fig. 2.29). It may be "a haven of quiet but it is hardly a city. The vision was not fulfilled" [2].

AR, 1/54, p. 51; AR, 8/73, pp. 71–90; [1] Ibid., p. 71; [2] Ibid., p. 74; AR, 8/81, pp. 239–251.

CHAPTER TWO • LONDON

Figure 2.27 Crescent House, Golden Lane Estate.

Greenwich

Well Hall Estate, Ross Way/Phineas Pett Road, SE9
1915. LCC Department of Architecture. R. Eltham

The Housing and Town Planning Act of 1919 was considerably influenced by the programme of housing development carried out during the First World War to provide housing for munitions workers in London and elsewhere [1]. Raymond Unwin headed a team of architects in the Ministry of Munitions. The team included Frank Baines, whose Well Hall Estate in Woolwich was the finest achievement of the programme.

The scheme of 1298 houses was conceived and built at a great speed. Its design was firmly rooted in the tradition of Unwin's pre-war garden city ideology using a wide variety of materials and external finishes including timber framing, tile hanging, stone, brick and render. This was matched by a generous use of gables, dormers, overhangs, tunnels and various other projections and recessions "to produce an architectural ensemble that seemed centuries apart from an age of total war" [2] (Figs 2.30 and 2.31).

After the war, the Well Hall Estate attracted considerable attention from overseas and from civil servants preparing the "Homes Fit for Heroes" legislation. However, the average cost per dwelling was £622 [3], which was reduced by at least half in most local authority development that followed. Consequently Well Hall stands as a symbol of

Figure 2.30 Well Hall Estate, Eltham (redrawn from MoHLG, Design in Town and Village, HMSO, 1953, p. 69).

Figure 2.31 Well Hall Estate: great variety of house appearance.

AR, 1/57, pp. 42–43; AJ, 27/3/58, p. 458; AR, 2/59, pp. 108–120; AJ, 21/1/70, p. 138; *The Architect*, 7/71, pp. 36–42; AJ, 9/7/75, p. 54.

Thamesmead Phases 1 and 2, Abbey Wood, SE2
1972. GLC Department of Architecture and Civic Design. R. Abbey Wood

Thamesmead was the product of forecasts in the early 1960s that London needed 500,000 new homes within the next ten years. The GLC had just lost its bid to build a new town for 100,000 people at Hook in Hampshire. It therefore looked to less environmentally sensitive sites such as the flat marshland of Erith. The GLC's Masterplan of 1965 for the site envisaged a population of 60,000 people living in a mixture of council and private housing in a roughly 65/35 split. It was to be a self-sufficient community with its own shops, schools, pubs, health centre and other community buildings together with factories and workshops offering local employment. Traffic and pedestrian segregation was to be given a high priority in the planning of the development. The images of new housing built in an environment of canals and lakes were most impressive and many visitors came from home and overseas to see what a "city for the twenty-first century" looked like [1] (Fig. 2.34).

Public sector housing was constructed using the most advanced systems of prefabrication with a factory on the site. The first two phases, of 2,741 dwellings, were completed in 1972. A third of the dwellings were family houses with gardens mostly grouped around pedestrian courtyards. The 13-storey tower blocks of flats were designed for two and three people. To meet a local bylaw concerned with the possible flooding of the site, the whole scheme was raised above ground level with walkways forming a continuous

Figure 2.32 The Hall, Blackheath: Span housing preserved in its original 1950s form.

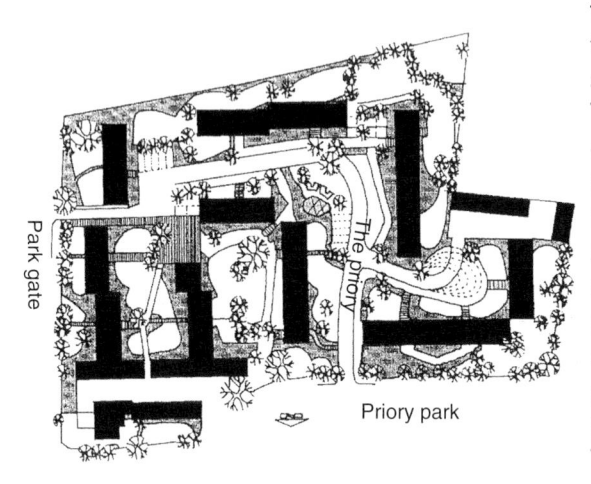

Figure 2.33 The Priory, Blackheath: site layout.

other Span housing in the area. This scheme is now Grade II listed.

Brooklands Park and Blackheath Park (1964) comprises nine houses with staggered pitch roofs that give clerestorey lighting. Two houses at right angles skillfully complete the composition.

Holmwalk (1980). This was the last of Span's housing to be built in Blackheath. The 10 two- and three-storey brick-fronted dwellings, arranged in four groups, have a delightful appearance when approached from the southwest corner of the site.

Figure 2.34 Thamesmead: lakeside terraces of concrete housing.

route through the tower blocks at first floor level. This effectively separated pedestrians from the streets below resulting in both levels lacking life and activity.

By 1972, the development had proved expensive and unpopular with residents, and the spirit to continue had gone. Thamesmead's problems were compounded by unemployment and poverty during the 1980s. The public transport connections with London remained tortuous, and the promised road link across the River Thames was never built.

Gallions Reach Urban Village (R. Plumstead). After the completion of the GLC housing, the design of Thamesmead took a very different direction. Gallions Reach is an Urban Village developed by a group of housebuilders on the land immediately to the north of the GLC development. Most of the housing has been for private sale with a proportion built by housing associations for rent and shared equity. The Thamesmead Eco Park project aims to exploit the latest thinking on environmental sustainability. A group of eco houses has been built together with a visitor centre.

AR, 9/70, pp. 158–160; AJ, 11/10/72, pp. 817–831; AJ, 18/10/72, pp. 879–896; RIBAJ, 1/88, pp. 60–67; RIBAJ, 1/98, pp. 60–67; [1] Ibid., p. 61.

Nightingale Heights, Nightingale Vale, SE18
1994. Hunt Thompson Associates. R. Woolwich Arsenal

This 24-storey tower block of 93 flats, built by the London Borough of Greenwich at the end of the 1960s, was part of a successful estate action bid for Phase 2 of the improvements to the Woolwich Common Estate in south-east London. The project is a good example of the potential for extending the life of high-rise housing. The block suffered from inadequate heating and insulation, high condensation, poor windows and a lack of security. There was a high level of tenant dissatisfaction, low morale, and the flats were hard to let, but there was a willingness on the part of the tenants to participate in resolving the problems.

The block was fully encased with a high-performance aluminium cladding system which incorporated aluminium clad timber windows (Fig. 2.35). Each balcony was enclosed to create a warm, dry conservatory. A new central gas-fired heating system serving all the dwellings was installed in the roof space, resulting in a substantial reduction in the heating costs. Security was improved by eliminating two of the three entrances and employing a concierge and a TV monitoring system. A common room was provided for the tenants, which leads off the lobby. The external space was enclosed and replanted, and private gardens were formed for the residents.

B (Housing Design Awards), 27/10/95, p. 27; AJ, 7/11/96, pp. 28–30.

Greenwich Millennium Village, SE10
*From 1999. Masterplan: Ralph Erskine, Hunt Thompson Architects, Hurley Robinson Architects.
U. North Greenwich*

This was the first project in English Partnership's Millennium Village programme aimed at improving standards of design and environmental sustainability. **The masterplan** for the 13 hectare (32 acre) site (Figs 2.36 and 2.37) envisaged a riverside development containing 1,079 flats and 298 houses. This would

Figure 2.35 Nightingale Heights in its white overcladding.

be developed by a consortium comprising Taylor Woodrow, Countryside Properties, Moat Housing Group and Ujima Housing Association. In addition, the masterplan proposed the following design and development principles:

- Housing grouped around courtyards to encourage a sense of community and be flexible, adaptable and extendible to accommodate changes in family size.
- Mixed commercial development, a primary school, health centre, shops, community buildings and workshops amongst the housing.
- 80 per cent reduction in primary energy consumption, 30 per cent in water demand, 80 per cent recyclable building and zero CO_2 emission. Housing to face south to maximise the benefits of orientation, and the scheme

Figure 2.36 The Millennium Village: Ralph Erskine's vision.

to have its own combined heating and power plant and recycling processes.
- Construction methods to be highly industrialised, with large sections of the dwellings made in factories with plumbing pre-installed.
- The use of cars to be discouraged in favour of a pool of hire vehicles on the site and public transport.

Bugsby's Way/Schoolbank Road, SE10. *Proctor and Matthews.* This phase (2a) has 189 residential units including 14 live/work dwellings and 47 affordable homes. They are arranged in three courtyard blocks, with an eight-storey apartment block and two- to three-storey family houses. The houses have modular facades with corrugated roofs that create a light-industrial aesthetic; however they still retain a domestic quality. The use of bright primary and other colours, cedar, aluminium and galvanised steel is a hallmark of the architects' work here and on other schemes (Fig. 2.38). The courtyards are

Figure 2.37 The Millennium Village: Ralph Erskine's site layout concepts.

superbly designed with sculptures and much planting.

Maurer Court, John Harrison Way, SE10. *Masterplan architects: Erskine Tovatt Architects, Production architects: EPR Architects.* Maurer Court is the antitheses of Erskine's masterplan vision (Fig. 2.39). It comprises three blocks of apartments accommodating a total of 199 one-, two- and three-bedroom flats and maisonettes. This includes seven affordable dwellings although 20 per cent is planned for the Millennium development as a whole. The density of development is 292 dwellings per hectare (118 dw/acre). A total of 292 car parking spaces are located in a two-storey basement car park for the scheme and for the hundred dwellings in the two adjacent blocks that form the neighbouring development. There are further spaces on John Harrison Way.

The scheme is characterised by the vaulted and varied roofline and colourful wall materials – bonded brickwork, white render

Figure 2.38 Millennium Village: new housing at Schoolbank Road.

and timber cladding – and steel balconies. The blocks enclose large gated landscaped courtyards containing communal seating areas and semi-private gardens.

The final phase of the Millennium Village up to the Dome, containing 1,500 dwellings, is being designed by Broadway Malyan working to the masterplan by Erskine Tovatt Architects.

AJ, 26/2/98, pp. 10–15; *AT Detail*, Issue 2, 1/02, p. 5; *AT Detail*, Issue 3, 4/02, p. 45; Birkbeck, D., and Scoones, A., *Prefabulous Homes: The New Housebuilding Agenda*, 2005, pp. 42–46;

B, 9/2/07, p. 24; www.buildingforlife.org

HACKNEY

Woodbury Down Estate, Stoke Newington, N16
1946–1948. LCC Architects' Department. U. Manor House

Woodbury Down (Fig. 2.40) was the first post-1945 experiment by the LCC into building

Figure 2.39 Millennium Village: Maurer Court reflects Erskine's housing design principles.

whole new communities. It had the first health centre and comprehensive school in England. The four tall blocks were the first high-rise flats to be built in concrete by the LCC. Previously, the height had been limited to five storeys but by using lifts, the block height could be increased to eight or nine storeys. The high horizontal balconies were designed as fire escapes. These, with the flat roofs and distinctive wide eaves, suggest an inter-war Viennese housing influence [1].

EH, p. 4; [1] Ibid., p. 4.

Lea View House, Springfield Road and Jessam Avenue, E5
1987. Hunt Thompson Associates, R. Clapton

In the late 1980s Lea View became synonymous with the regeneration of council housing estates. Built in 1939, it contained 250 flats and maisonettes which had become difficult to let, plagued with crime, vandalism and racial tension, and the vast majority of residents wanted to move elsewhere.

To tackle the issues, the residents launched a campaign, the outcome of which was the

Figure 2.40 Woodbury Down Estate: 1951 demonstration housing for the future.

appointment of architects to work with them from an office on the site. The key features of the improvements included accommodating large families at ground floor level in two- and three-story maisonettes. These have their own front entrance and private front and rear gardens. Access to the upper floor flats was via new lift towers, which were the scheme's iconic features (Fig. 2.41). Access to the courtyard was restricted to improve privacy and security.

The quality of the scheme and the process of development considerably enhanced the environment and empowered the residents. Crime and vandalism were virtually eliminated and there was a new sense of community spirit.

AJ, 20/7/83, pp. 52–55; *AR*, 4/85, pp. 60–61; *B*, Housing Design Awards 1987, p. 77; *RIBAJ*, 6/85, pp. 53–55

Mothers' Square, Sladen Place, Clarence Road, E5
1990. Hunt Thompson Associates. R. Hackney Central, Hackney Downs

Mothers' Square was developed on the site of the former Mothers' Maternity Hospital by a partnership between the Hackney Health Authority, Newlon Housing Trust and Access Homes Housing Association for mixed-tenure housing and neighbourhood medical facilities.

The design enclosed the site with a continuous unbroken three-storey neo-Classical building, with raised four-storey elements at key points. In the central space is a perimeter road around a central green (Fig. 2.42). The architects' initial proposal was for a more permeable through road but the local planners rejected this. Most of the central space is taken up with car parking, but pergolas and landscaping reduce its impact and help to make it feel secure and safe for children's play.

The housing association development comprises 21 family houses and 6 one- and two-bedroom flats for rent. In addition, there are 24 shared equity one- and two-bedroom flats, and warden-assisted sheltered flats for elderly people. All the dwellings have their living rooms looking into the square, which the architects claim is what the people like. To meet the "Care in the Community" legislation, which was coming into force in the late 1980s, a nursing home for elderly confused people was included. Hackney Health Authority was most anxious that this part of the project should not be segregated, and consequently, it too looks into the square. It is connected at the rear to a small day hospital that also serves a new home for adults with mental illness at nearby Clarence Road.

AJ, 8/8/90, pp. 34–44; Aldous, T., *Urban Villages*, pp. 34–35; *Voluntary Housing*, 2/95, pp. 15–16.

CHAPTER TWO • LONDON

Figure 2.41 Lea View: characterised by its new stairs and lift towers.

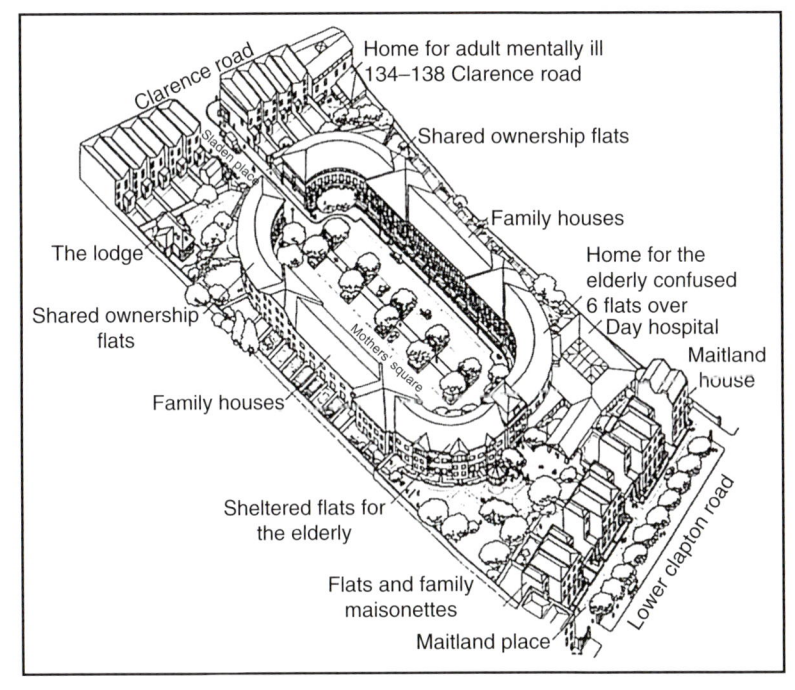

Figure 2.42 Mothers' Square.

Holly Street Estate Regeneration, Dalston, E8, Hackney
1997+. Levitt Bernstein Associates. R. Dalston Kingsland

Hackney is one of London's most deprived Boroughs. In 1991 a Comprehensive Estates Initiative (CEI) was formed to tackle the problems on five of the council's worst 1960s estates – Holly Street, Nightingale, Clapton Park, Trowbridge and New Kingshold. To achieve this, partnership arrangements were established between the local authority, central government, housing associations,

83

Figure 2.47 Nile Street.

on one side of the building and triangular on another – provide outdoor space for most of the flats as well as having a visually attractive effect on the exterior (Fig. 2.47) [1]. The building is clad in green copper on the Nile Street and Provost Street elevations and light timber panels in the courtyard and other elevations.

BD, 28/4/06, p. 11; AJ, 22/06/06, p. 34; *Inside Housing*, 23/6/06, p. 53; [1] Based on description by Peabody – www.peabody.org.uk

HAMMERSMITH AND FULHAM

Old Oak Estate, Wulfstan Street, W12
1909 to post 1945. LCC Architects' Department (A.S. Souter). U. East Acton

The 1890 Housing of the Working Classes Act enabled the LCC between 1890 and 1913 to build new housing for some 25,000 people. One of the largest developments was the Old Oak Estate built on a 54 acre (22 ha) site, where from 1909 to 1914, 304 houses and five shops were built (Fig. 2.48).

It was the first scheme to follow the new design principles embodied in the 1909 Town Planning Act that had largely been written by Raymond Unwin. At Old Oak, this was interpreted in a layout of U-shaped terraces grouped around small public gardens or greens with their end gables facing on to the streets. Access to many of the dwellings was by footpath only, which produced savings on the amount of road required.

There were many similarities in the design to Hampstead Garden Suburb, particularly Unwin's concept of "street picture". Terraces varied in length and appearance, and steep tiled roofs overhung the bedrooms with low eaves and dormers, and bedroom windows were frequently positioned in front and rear facing gables. Most of the external walls were built in brick but the occasional gable was picked out in half-timbering or tile hanging (Fig. 2.49).

Swenerton, M., *Homes Fit for Heroes*, pp. 16–18.

Thames Reach, 80 Rainville Road, Hammersmith, W6
1987. Richard Rogers Partnership. U. Hammersmith

Richard Rogers has only rarely designed grouped housing but this scheme at Thames

CHAPTER TWO • LONDON

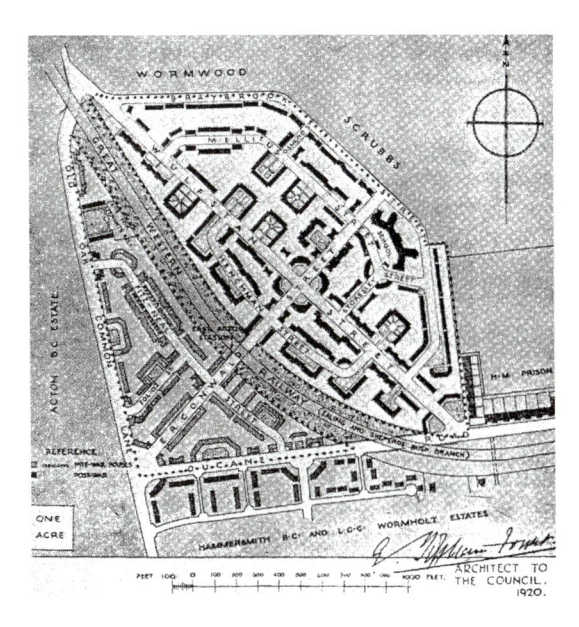

Figure 2.48 Old Oak Estate (from London Housing, LCC, 1937, p. 136).

Figure 2.49 Old Oak Estate.

Reach, on a site overlooking the river near the Hammersmith Bridge, is outstanding. The design is "bold and contemporary" [1] (Fig. 2.50). It is housing at the luxury end of the market, which presented a design opportunity not normally available to most architects.

The scheme comprises three linked five-storey pavilions each with two flats per floor and two double-height penthouses with roof terraces. The southern-most block is non-standard, with an extra storey. The riverside elevation is totally glazed to take advantage of the views. A strong "nautical" feel comes from the profusion of metal balconies located between and at the ends of the pavilions.

On the entrance side, each pavilion has its own staircase and lift approached along a "gangplank" from a well landscaped courtyard where visitors' car parking is located. Parking for the residents is off this courtyard in an underground communal car park. The roadside elevation is a complete contrast to the lightness of the riverside front. Built in purple brick, the curved staircase and lift towers present a feeling of great solidity.

[1] *B*, Housing Design Awards 1989, pp. 46–47; *AJ* 4/1/89; and 11/1/89, pp. 33–49.

Beaufort Court, 49 Lillie Road, SW6
*2003. Fielden Clegg Bradley Architects.
U. West Brompton or Fulham Broadway*

This project was another contribution by the Peabody Trust in the early 2000s to the development of modern methods of housing construction. It is a mix of flats and maisonettes, including residents' hall and landscaped areas. A blue astro-turfed court with facilities for basketball and football is situated above the basement car park (Fig. 2.51).

It was first in the UK to use structural bathroom pods in a process that brought together into one scheme three off-site prefabrication

89

Figure 2.50 Thames Reach.

Figure 2.51 Beaufort Court, Lillie Street.

processes – steel load bearing systems, steel panels and prefabricated bathrooms. The result was completely dry construction except for ground works. The pods were built in the contractor's factory in Milton Keynes to designs produced at an early project team meeting between the architect, the contractor, Peabody and other specialists.

Birkbeck. D., and Scoones, A., *Prefabulous Homes: The New Housebuilding Agenda* (2005) Constructing Excellence; www.peabody.org; www.buildingforlife.org

---

Fulham Island, between Fulham Broadway, Jerdan Place, Farm Lane and Danston Place, SW6
2003. CZWG Architects. U. Fulham Broadway

Fulham Island is a mixed-use development of housing, offices, shops and restaurants by the Manhattan Loft Corporation. The site is in an intensely urban location and the design demonstrates how an imaginative mixture of elevational treatment from combining refurbishment and redevelopment can uplift a neighbourhood as a whole (Fig. 2.52).

The scheme was designed in four blocks around the perimeter of the site with an underground car park beneath a central courtyard garden. The housing includes 20 two- and three-bedroom apartments, two penthouse duplexes in the five-storey block and 10 flats in the refurbished building at the eastern end of the site. One car parking space per dwelling was provided and an overall density of 60 dwellings per hectare (24/acre) was achieved. The new curved walls, roofline, balconies and colour of materials all make up the vibrancy of the design. Added to this is an array of decorative panels of brightly coloured Belgian brickwork and, along the curving façade of the five-storey building, a seven-course plinth of glazed brick laid so that no two bricks of the same colour – grey, lilac blue, lime green, yellow, turquoise, terracotta and white – are adjacent.

AT 145, 2/04; www.buildingforlife.org

HARINGEY

White Hart Lane, Risley Avenue, Lordship Lane, N17
1904–1912 and 1921–1928. LCC Department of Architecture (W.E. Riley). U. Wood Green

---

White Hart Lane was built on 177 acres (72 ha) of land, which made it the largest of the LCCs cottage estates built before 1914. Unlike the Garden City form of Old Oak Estate (pp. 88–89), the phase of White Hart Lane built before the First World War followed a grid layout which was more familiar to the speculative builders of the day (Fig. 2.53). To achieve a density of 27 dwelling/acre (67 dw/ha), narrow frontage house plans – as little as 12–15 ft (3.7–4.6 m) wide – were developed. This was abhorrent to Raymond Unwin who strongly advocated using only the more expensive wide frontage types.

Nevertheless the appearance of the scheme takes its cue from the Garden City movement. The houses have long roofs, low eaves, porches, two-storey projecting bays and elaborate chimney stacks, and a great variety of materials were used. At the junction of Risley Road and Awfield Avenue, the houses were setback around the intersection in true Garden City style. Behind the houses at Risley Avenue, Tower Gardens, Shobden Road and Wilfield Avenue, a large green area

Figure 2.56 Spa Green Estate (photo by Christopher Colquhoun).

Figure 2.57 Bevin Court.

to develop the Segal construction method (pp. 108–111), seek ecological solutions and promote client empowerment. The houses were narrow fronted using a construction arrangement that was half-Segal and half-conventional. Only the front and rear walls were timber-framed. The party walls between the dwellings were Thermalite blockwork with a plaster finish. This called for the self-build group to include a bricklayer and a plasterer, which had not been necessary on previous Segal schemes where wet trades were eliminated.

The houses are tightly grouped with gardens screened by high timber fencing (Fig. 2.58). Five of the residents opted for their gardens to be communal which made good use of the small amount of private space between the dwellings. These are overlooked from spacious timber balconies at first floor level.

The second site at **Sussex Way** comprises a row of three, single storey, L-shaped bungalows built within the perimeter brick wall of a former estate playground. These are much more recognisable as Segal houses, but hidden behind the wall, which makes them difficult to find.

AT, 2/97, pp. 26–33.

Royal Free Square, Liverpool Road, N1. 1992
1992. Pollard Thomas and Edwards and Levitt Bernstein Associates. U. Highbury and Islington

---

The Royal Free Hospital on Liverpool Road was designed by Charles Fowler in 1848. The site and all its listed buildings was acquired jointly in 1986 by Circle 33 Housing Trust and the New Islington and Hackney Housing Association who appointed two architectural practices to collaborate in producing designs for half of the site each (Fig. 2.59).

The development provides housing for families, couples, single people, elderly people, and there is accommodation suitable for people with physical disabilities including wheelchair use. The design combined a skilful mixture of new development with the conversion of the listed hospital buildings into housing. On the Liverpool Road frontage, converted matching pavilions emphasise the gateway into the project. This leads to the focus of the development – a square of housing around a communal garden that has the feel of the eighteenth and nineteenth century squares in the area around the site (Fig. 2.60).

At the Upper Road end of the site, the development is almost entirely new houses and flats except for the former water tower, which was converted into housing for young people. Most of the development here is two and three storeys in height with narrow streets. All family houses have private gardens and all flats have a patio or balcony except where prohibited by the listing of the old buildings. Part of the Upper Road end of the scheme also includes a new psychiatric Day Care Centre, built as part of the Care in the Community programme.

The central square garden is enclosed by railings and gates, which were designed by the new residents and their children in collaboration with the sculptor, Jane Ackroyd. The urban quality of the scheme is outstanding especially the treatment of the block-paved pedestrian/vehicular areas. The series of spaces for vehicles and pedestrians has been hailed as an excellent example of homezone design that does much to reduce the possibility of crime in the environment [1].

AJ, 15/7/92 pp. 20–23; AJ, 11/93, p. 31; B (Supplement) 5/94, pp. 12–13; [1] *Design Out Crime*, pp. 149–152; [1] ODPM/Home Office, *Safer Places* (2004), pp. 54–55.

Figure 2.58 Self-Build Housing at Nicholay Road.

Kensington and Chelsea

Kensall House, Ladbroke Grove, W10
1936. E Maxwell Fry. U. Kensall Green/ Ladbroke Grove

Kensall House was perhaps the most significant working-class housing scheme built in the modernist manner before the Second World War (Fig. 2.61). It was built on the site of an old gas works by the Gas Light and Coke Company to house its workforce, and the circular foundations of one of the gasometers were cleverly reused as part of the construction of the nursery school built with the scheme. The two long six storey, curving blocks were arranged on an approximately north–south axis so that the morning sun could penetrate the bedrooms and the afternoon sun the living rooms. The scheme included communal features that were innovative at the time, such as a laundry and a residents' social club.

CHAPTER TWO • LONDON

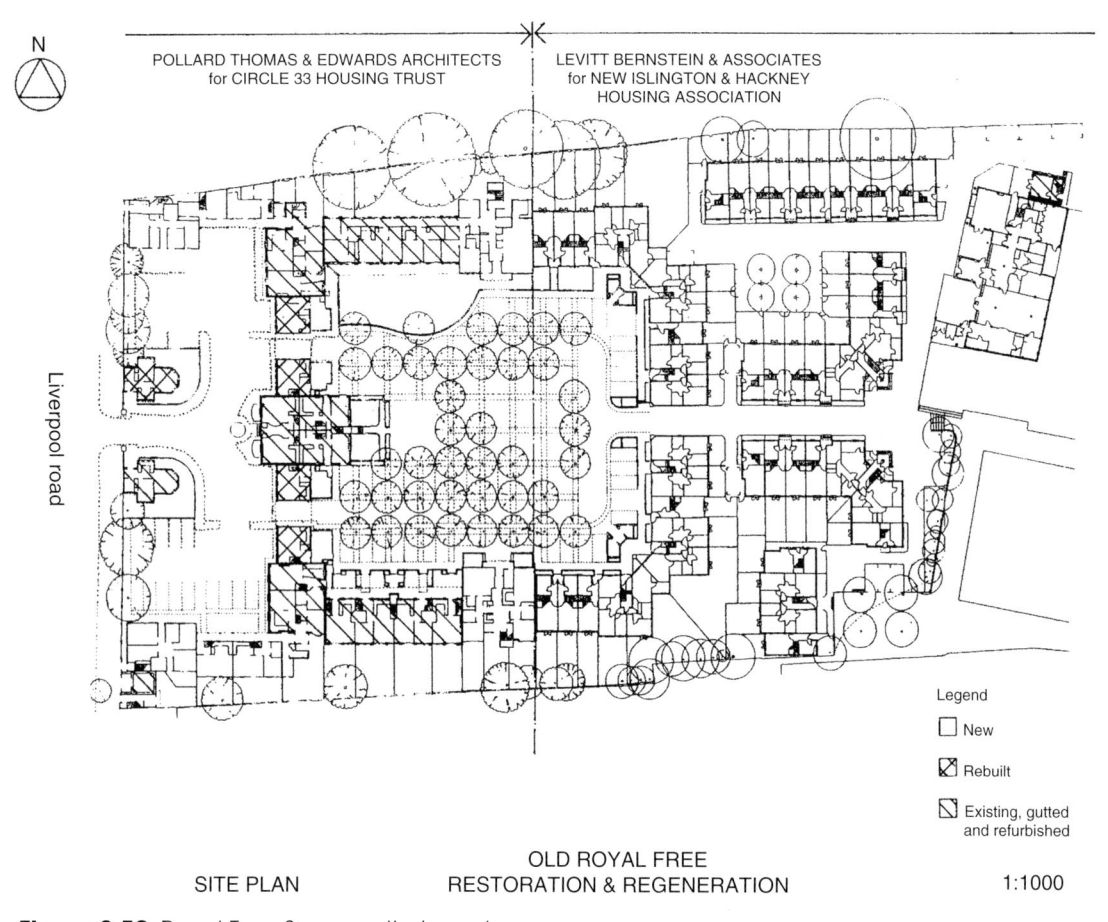

SITE PLAN — OLD ROYAL FREE RESTORATION & REGENERATION — 1:1000

POLLARD THOMAS & EDWARDS ARCHITECTS for CIRCLE 33 HOUSING TRUST

LEVITT BERNSTEIN & ASSOCIATES for NEW ISLINGTON & HACKNEY HOUSING ASSOCIATION

Legend
☐ New
☒ Rebuilt
◩ Existing, gutted and refurbished

Figure 2.59 Royal Free Square: site layout.

The external walls are finished in white render and despite its age, the scheme still looks well.

CIOH, *Taking Stock*, 1996, p. 21.

Trellick Tower, Golborne Road, W10
*1972. Ernö Goldfinger.
U. Westbourne Park*

Trellick Tower was one of the two tower blocks designed by Ernö Goldfinger during the 1960s. His earlier **Balfron Tower** (Grade II listed) at St Leonard's Road, Poplar, E14 (*DLR All Saints*, AJ, 22/5/68, p. 1133), built in 1965, was effectively a prototype for the far more sophisticated **Trellick Tower**. It was Goldfinger's last major building and the culmination of his philosophy on high-rise housing (Fig. 2.62). The development comprises 217 flats, six shops, an office, youth and women's centres, doctors' surgery and a basement community centre built as a nursery. It was a concept that owes much to Le Corbusier's Unité d'Habitation in Marseilles but the sophistication of the plan, the careful attention to every detail and the precision of the bush-hammered concrete are features that

Figure 2.60 Royal Free Square: urban housing of great quality.

make it stand out. The 31-storey block is linked by a slim, sculptural, semi-freestanding tower incorporating lifts, stairs and refuse shute with a projecting boiler house on the 32nd and 33rd floors.

The accommodation is very varied. Each third corridor floor contains 6 one-bedroom flats in each wing, with a storey of two-bedroom flats above and below reached off the same level. The 23rd and 24th floors contain 5 two-storey maisonettes and two flats.

Trellick Tower is stoutly defended against its critics by many of the residents. They praise the spacious interiors that are over the Parker Morris minimum areas of the day. They enjoy the exceptionally wide bay frontage (6.75 m/22 ft 2 in), which helps the proportions of the rooms; and they like the large south-facing balconies, which form a distinctive pattern across the facade. However, this popularity was not always the case. By the late 1980s, problems of vandalised lifts

CHAPTER TWO • LONDON

Figure 2.61 Kensall House, Ladbroke Grove: a rare example of inter-war modern movement design.

and public areas, the lack of open space and suitability then of the development for children had reduced the tower to part of a sink estate into which the poorest residents of the Royal Borough of Kensington and Chelsea were decanted. Life was almost intolerable. However, in the early 1990s the block was refurbished by the Council which has made it much more secure. It is now Grade II* listed and English Heritage wrote in support of this by saying, "no smart Kensingtonian living in stucco comfort gets to see London as do the residents of Trellick Tower. The views are inspirational and in the right light, almost spiritual" [1].

[1] *EH*, p. 4; *AJ*, 25/11/87, pp. 28–29; *AJ*, 19/1/73, pp. 79–94; Glancy, J., High rise arisen, *The Guardian*, 22/11/97, p. 71.

World's End, Kings Road/ Cremorne Road, Chelsea, SW10
1977. Eric Lyons, Cadbury Brown, Metcalf & Cunningham. U. Fulham Broadway

Conceived from 1961 and constructed between 1967 and 1977, World's End was one of the most celebrated housing schemes of its day. Here was the architect of the much admired low-rise Span housing addressing the

101

with the brutalist concrete approach that was so common of the 1960s. The scheme was devised as a complete "metropolitan village" with its own schools, community centre, shops and offices, and it incorporated high-quality landscaping into the design of the courtyard.

Sadly, the scheme faced the same serious maintenance and security problems as other high-rise development but in 1994, after extensive consultation with residents (80 per cent Council rented and 20 per cent owner-occupied), measures were taken to improve the worst of the problems including sensitively designed re-roofing which retained the original aesthetic of the scheme (*Architects: Norman and Dawbarn*).

AJ, 20/4/77, pp. 733–744; *Housing Review*, September/October 95, p. 102; AT, 9/1999, pp. 54–58.

St Mark's Road/St Quintin Avenue, W10
1980. Jeremy Dixon. U. Ladbroke Grove.

This scheme of 44 flats and houses superbly captures the scale and character of the surrounding Victorian terraces of North Kensington by grouping three dwellings behind each front gable (Fig. 2.64). At the lowest level is a single aspect, two-person semi-basement flat and above are two narrow frontage houses entered up a small flight of steps. The houses fronting St Marks Road are angled which helped the architect resolve the prominent design of the corner with St Quintin Avenue where there are single-person flats and community rooms. The rear gardens back onto a parking street.

The design of the front facades incorporates large timber-framed entrances and bay windows, which, with the white coping to the gables and front walls, gives the scheme its distinctive character. The rhythm of large

Figure 2.62 Trellick Tower: Erno Goldfinger's vision of urban living.

problems of designing high-rise housing on a site in such a prominent location between the King's Road, Chelsea and the River Thames.

His solution was a scheme of 742 flats in seven towers and a series of five-storey podium blocks set around two large courtyards (Fig. 2.63). The towers and blocks were highly sculptured with generous balconies, and they were brick clad which contrasted

Figure 2.63 High-density housing by Eric Lyons at Worlds End Chelsea.

brick gate posts capped with large pyramid coping hides the bin stores. These combine with the railings and stairs to separate the houses from the street in the best English street tradition.

AR, 12/80, pp. 342–347.

LAMBETH

Pullman Court, Streatham Hill, SW2
1935. Frederick Gibberd.
R. Streatham Hill

Figure 2.64 St Mark's Road housing.

During the inter-war years flats for sale or rent became popular with middle class people in London. These were intended mainly for single, childless and retired people who wished to live in a pleasant location close to transport links and public facilities. Although the flats themselves were often small, they were marketed as luxurious and labour saving and they had a degree of stylish living attached to them. Designs frequently leaned towards the new modernist architecture of white rendered walls, flat roofs and horizontal windows, and Frederick Gibberd's Pullman Court was one of the best of these (Fig. 2.65).

The scheme comprises 218 flats built on a site of just under 3 acres (1.2 ha). The flats fronting Streatham Hill are in three storey blocks set well back to preserve the existing trees. Behind these and forming two linked linear courtyards are five- and seven-storey blocks. The flats were designed to offer varying sizes from one to three rooms. The three-roomed flats had two double-bedrooms and were thought to be suitable for families. The five- and seven-storey blocks were served with lifts, which opened on to external galleries leading to the individual dwellings.

The buildings were constructed with a reinforced concrete frame and panel walls. The external walls were to be painted every 5 years and a permanent steel cradle rail was installed at roof level for this purpose. The flats were centrally heated from a single plant beneath the seven-storey block. To attract the purchasers, a swimming pool was provided in the furthest courtyard.

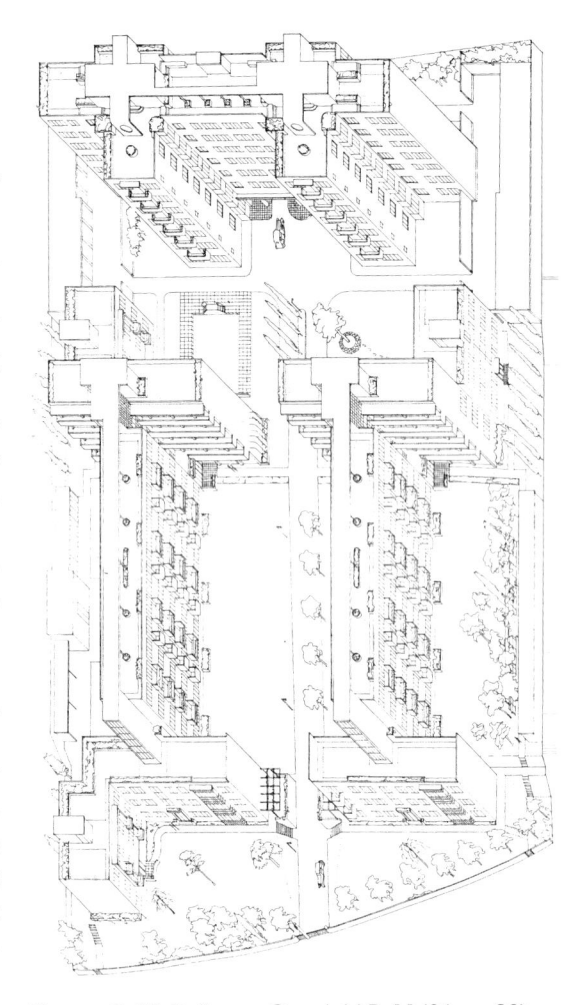

Figure 2.65 Pullman Court (*AR*, 11/36, p. 28).

Ravetz, A., *The Place of Home*, p. 43; AR, 1/36, pp. 28–30.

Coin Street Community Builders, Upper Ground, SE1
1994 to present day. Lifschutz Davidson; Haworth Tompkins Limited. U. Waterloo/London Bridge

---

"The battle of Coin Street" has become a legend of how a local community can use its power to change the minds of politicians and developers. Faced in the early 1980s with the threat of a giant office and commercial development, the Coin Street Community Builders (CSCB) successfully lobbied to secure the 5.3 hectare (13 acre) site for housing, open space and community enterprise. This was achieved with the help of the Mayor of London – Ken Livingston – who assisted them with the purchase of the land at a token price.

They became a Company and formed a separate legally registered housing association – the Coin Street Secondary Housing

Co-operative – which was able to secure funding for housing development from the Housing Corporation. This led to the formation of separate co-operatives to take on the management of each of the schemes as they were developed. The residents joining the co-operatives were nominated by Lambeth and Southwark Councils on a 50–50 basis, provided they were working in the area and agreed to be members of their respective co-operative. CSCB developed commercial activities to further its social aims. Most significant was renting out commercial space, the proceeds from which were added to Housing Corporation grant to build further development. This enabled a standard of affordable housing far beyond that grant-funding alone could achieve. In turn, co-operative residents and the wider community fueled corner shops, community centres and childcare facilities which also added to CSCB's community objectives.

CSCB's first project was 56 traditionally designed low-cost dwellings for the Mulberry Housing Co-operative on a site overlooking the first area of open space in the Bernie Spain gardens. This was followed by three most remarkable projects.

Palm Co-operative, **Broadwall** (*1994*). *Lifschutz Davidson*. This project, which comprises 25 dwellings, was the subject of a limited architectural competition. It contains 11 three-storey houses with gardens designed as a long terrace with towers of flats at each end. The nine-storey tower at the River end contains one-bedroom flats on the basis of one flat per floor served by double lifts. The architects' intention for the exterior was to use materials that "grow old gracefully". No fewer than nine were used – red brick, treated hardwood, zinc, copper, painted metalwork, bright metalwork, white soffit panelling, stone copings and timber trellises. These were beautifully composed with large windows from which there are superb views (Fig. 2.66).

Oxo Tower Wharf (*1996*). *Lifschutz Davidson*. This project, which included the renovation of the famous Art Deco Tower, provided 78 one- to three-bedroom flats for low-cost rent on the third to seventh floors. Below are commercial areas consisting of shops and workshops. Above, the building has been capped by a new floating roof structure, which accommodates very smart restaurants.

"**Iroko**" **project** (*2001*). *Haworth Tompkins Limited*. The design of the latest project was also won by the architects in competition. It is a mixture of affordable rent and private/shared housing comprising 32 large four- and five-bedroom family houses, 18 smaller maisonettes and nine flats, grouped on three sides of a large courtyard garden. Underneath is a 260 space commercial car park that provides cross-subsidy for the affordable housing above. Ground floor dwellings have private back gardens looking onto the communal garden. The wide spacious balconies on upper levels are shaded from the sun by timber screens and have translucent panels between to provide privacy.

AR, 5/81, pp. 273–276; AT, 10/94, pp. 40–48; B (Housing Design Awards), 27/10/95, p. 6; AJ, 13/6/96, pp. 24–45; AR, 2/97, pp. 56–60; B, 28/11/97, p. 50; Cunningham, J., "Winners in the Oxo game", *The Guardian*, 11/9/96, pp. 6–7; AT, 4/02, pp. 21–33; *Inside Housing*, 19/1/07, pp. 32–34. *Note*: Part of the development falls within the L.B. Southwark.

PRPZEDfactor, Brixton Water Lane, Brixton, SW2
2006. PRP Architects/Bill Dunster Architects ZEDfactor. U. Brixton

---

This scheme of 12 one- and two-bedroom flats for key workers was developed by the

Figure 2.66 Coin Street: high-quality co-operative housing with the Oxo Tower in the distance.

Presentation Housing Association. It demonstrates how the thermally efficient BedZED design principles (pp. 41, 131–132) can be applied to everyday housing in urban locations and achieved at reasonable cost by ordinary building contractors.

The scheme was designed as a joint venture between PRP Architects and Bill Dunster Architects. Their aim was to make the detailing and construction as simple as possible, but the structure was designed with extra-wide insulated wall cavities and double or triple glazing to meet the higher environmental standards that will be imposed on all new homes in 2010 as part of the tightening of the building regulations and carbon emission reduction. Unlike BedZED, there are no photovoltaic cells and wind turbines.

The flats are all fronted on the south side with 2 m deep conservatories, which enables occupants to use the space positively (Fig. 2.67). Property consultant, F.P. Savilles, advises that this adds £10,000 to the value of each flat [1]. The flats are heated and ventilated using solar, wind and renewable biomass energies which were designed to keep the total energy bill to as little as £75 per year. The roof is entirely covered in water-powered solar collectors, which provide space heating and domestic hot water. In summer, the solar-heated water reaches 60°C and supplies all the hot water needs. In the winter, water reaches only 25–30°C. This is circulated in plastic pipes within the floor screeds to provide space heating, which is important in the north-facing bedrooms. Top-up heating and hot water for the scheme as a whole comes from a wood pellet-burning boiler connected to a hot water tank.

[1] B, 04/11/05, pp. 58–62; B Supplement, The Sustainability Awards 2006, p. 27; AJ, 4/5/06, p. 42; R&R, 5/1/07, p. 25; www.buildingforlife.org

Angell Town estate regeneration, Brixton Road/Boatemah Walk, Brixton, SW9 7JP

2006. Master planner: John Thompson and Partners. Architects: Burrell Foley Fischer LLP, Greenhill Jenner Architects, Ann Thorne Architects Partnership, Mode 1 Architects, Levitt Bernstein Associates Limited. Urban design support from Oxford Polytechnic. U. Brixton

Angell Town, completed in 1978, was a council estate of four- and five-storey blocks connected by high-level bridges. From the start, the estate suffered from crime and unsociability, which was so great that taxi drivers refused to enter [1]. There is now little remaining of the original Angell Town following a £67 million Estate Action programme started in 1998. This enabled most of the blocks on the estate's edges to be refurbished with new ground level entrances and staircase towers, together with the removal of the bridges between blocks. The blocks in the centre of the development were replaced with two- and three-storey houses fronting a permeable pattern of trad-itional streets. The estate now contains 632 dwellings (previously 878) for affordable rent, of which 370 is new housing and 262 are refurbished flats (Fig. 2.68).

Car parking for the new housing was provided at the ratio of one space for every two dwellings. This is located mostly on-street and is well overlooked from houses. Previous garage sites were redeveloped with commercial units, which provide a focus for the community and income for the independent residents' organisation, the Angell Town Community Project (ATCP). ATCP is an influential member of the project steering group. It participated in the selection of architects and worked closely with them [1].

The new housing at Boatemah Walk was named after Dora Boatemah who founded ATCP in 1978 and was a driving force behind

Figure 2.67 PRPZed Eco Housing, Brixton.

the estate's regeneration. The three-storey block (Anne Thorne Architects Partnership) of 18 flats curves in the manner of a Regency terrace (Fig. 2.69). It is of timber-framed construction and has an Eco-Homes rating of Excellent. This is achieved with double the standard of insulation of standard homes, timber construction from sustainable sources, the use of toxic and non-toxic materials, rainwater harvesting, water efficient dual-flush toilets using 90 per cent recycled grey water, passive air extraction from kitchens and bathrooms and solar panels in the roof. The technology is proving successful but the engagement of future residents in the design process was vital – "There's no point having all these environmental features if people don't use them – if they haven't bought into sustainability (through participation in the design)" [1].

AT 158, 5/05, pp. 24–29; [1] The Guardian, 26/7/06, p. 8; www.buildingforlife.org

LEWISHAM

Segal self-build housing
1980+. Walter Segal, Jon Broome, Brian Richardson, Architype

Walter Segal had already enjoyed a successful career, when in the early 1960s he designed and constructed a temporary timber house in his garden at Highgate whilst his house was being renovated. This was the beginning of

CHAPTER TWO • LONDON

Figure 2.68 Angell Town, Brixton: street housing and courtyard parking.

the "Segal" method of house building, which was to occupy him until his death in 1985. Segal never liked describing his houses as "system houses". He was more concerned with their architectural philosophy and their radical approach to building techniques. He considered the building industry to be technologically and economically backward. The structure of its organisation was archaic and inefficient and its methods of production chaotic. Unlike most industries, it had never changed with industrialisation.

The aim of Segal's methods was to use materials, which could be obtained easily and required minimal cutting. Ready-made components should be used wherever possible. He preferred the timber post-and-beam structure with columns 10–12 ft (3–4 mm) apart which, he considered, gave maximum planning flexibility. His structure stood on ground slabs, which enabled different site levels to be accommodated and facilitated the easy distribution of services. The plans varied according to the users' needs within the constraints of the modular construction system and the sewer positions, which dictated the location of the bathrooms.

The first sites made available by Lewisham Borough Council were considered almost impossible to develop but Walter Segal rose to the challenge. They are as follows:

- 11/13 Elstree Hill, Bromley (R. Ravensbourne)
- Longton Avenue, SE26 (R. Sydenham)

Figure 2.69 Boetemah Walk, fine curved terrace.

- 30/31 Brockley Park, SE23 (R. Catford)
- Walter's Way, SE23 (R. Honor Oak Park)
- Segal Close, SE23, 1981 (R. Catford/Catford Bridge) (Fig. 2.70).

Funding for the schemes was devised through an equity sharing rent/purchase/leasing scheme and everyone was guaranteed a Council mortgage (from Lewisham) to cover the cost of the lease. After completion, the self-builders were responsible together for maintenance.

AJ, 23/3/66, pp. 763–769; *AJ*, 30/9/70, pp. 769–780; *AJ*, 17/12/80, pp. 1183–1205; *AJ*, 20/6/84, pp. 35–38; *AJ*, 5/11/86, pp. 31–68; *AJ*, 7/11/96, pp. 48–50; *AJ*, 25/5/95, p. 45.

Regeneration of the Pepys Estate, Foreshore Street, Deptford, SE8 3DG
2005. bptw partnership. U. Surrey Quays

Built in the 1960s and 1970s by the London Borough of Lewisham, the Pepys Estate reflected the enthusiasm of that time for high-density housing with brick facades to soften the architectural image. Unfortunately the long, dark internal access corridors and other design features proved problematic. During the 1990s an Estate Action SRB-funded

CHAPTER TWO • LONDON

project attempted to deal with the problems, but this proved ineffective; so in 1998, the programme was halted before completion. It was then decided to bring in the Hyde Housing Association, demolish seven blocks, which had not been altered and replace them with new housing.

The architects developed their design through extensive resident participation and negotiation with English Heritage who were interested because the site was close to important listed buildings associated with the former Deptford Royal Naval Yard. The residents wanted to retain open space whilst English Heritage insisted that the block fronting the river should follow the existing building line and be raised on piloti to reflect the amenity of the riverside walk. In the end most other blocks were built on the footprints of former housing.

The project contains 169 new houses and flats designed to a density of 142 dwellings per hectare (60 dw/acre). The accommodation includes a mixture of social for rent and shared-ownership housing in the form of one-, two- and three-bedroom flats and 7 four-bedroom houses. The use of timber-framed construction was adopted as a modern method of construction. This increased the design period but reduced building time. It was also considered more environmentally sustainable than traditional methods of construction.

Of particular merit is the quality and robustness of the design of roads and parking which was based on homezone principles with traffic calming and direction by bollards, different levels, variety of paving surfaces and planting (Fig. 2.71). Car parking was provided at a ratio of 60 per cent and located at the front of, and overlooked by, the new housing.

B, 12/5/06, p. 22; B, 12/5/06, p. 22; *The Guardian*, 18/4/07, p. 4; www.buildingforlife.org

Figure 2.70 Segal Close: an early self-build scheme by Walter Segal, Jon Broome and Brian Richardson.

MERTON

Watermeads, London Road/ Rawnesley Avenue, CR4: Mitc
1977. London Borough of Merton Architects Department, Borough Architect, Bernard V. Ward. R. Mitcham

Watermeads was perhaps the most successful of the perimeter housing schemes built by the London Borough of Merton in the late 1960s and 1970s (pp. 19–20). It was built on a four hectare (10 acres) site overlooking the River

111

Green. The layout is based on a permeable grid pattern of streets, off which are small courtyards of housing (Fig. 2.74). The block-paved streets are designed as tree-lined avenues and the result is a very robust urban environment. The housing fronting the former docks were designed in the form of pavilions and many of the old cranes were preserved (Fig. 2.75).

A series of "village codes" was produced to guide the design. These proposed landmark projects in key locations to introduce design variety. One of these was the imposing "Crescent", located at the eastern edge of the development. Similarly in 2001 the Peabody Trust invited small London practices to participate in an architectural competition to design shared-ownership housing on three sites of which two were eventually built.

Evelyn Road (2004). *Niall McLaughlin Associates.* This is a small three-storey development with an eye catching front elevation of curtain walling with iridescent colour film overlaid with a clear polycarbonate to reflect different light (R&R, 24/06/05, p. 9; www.peabody.org).

Boxley Street (2004). *Ash Sakula.* These 4 two-bedroom flats are particularly suited to non-co-habiting couples, that is, with a dual income but not a couple. The flats are a block of four, clad in translucent silver and gold fibreglass with a transparent, corrugated exterior wall, filled with colourful wires.

Figure 2.74 West Silvertown site layout by Gardner Stewart Architects. See also DETR, Places Streets and Movement, 1998, p. 45, HMSO, London (Crown Copyright).

Residents feel like they are living in a real-life work of art – "and you would never think they were part of London's affordable housing push" (description from Peabody Trust – www.peabody.org).

AJ, 7/11/96, pp. 36–37; *Planning Week*, 6/2/97, pp. 14–15; *RIBAJ*, 11/96, p. 11; *RIBAJ*, 3/98, pp. 31, 33, 78–79.

Richmond-Upon-Thames

Parkleys, Ham Common, TW10
1956. Eric Lyons. R. Richmond + local bus

This was Eric Lyons's first large private housing development for Span. It helped set an architectural style for housing that became very common – in both private and public sector housing, but unfortunately rarely with the same success.

Parkleys was aimed at first time buyers and Eric Lyons recognised the importance of designing to the same budget as speculative developers providing the same accommodation. The dwellings were quite small but were popular. Consequently there has been little change and extensions are rare. The scheme looks very much as it did when completed, with flat roofs, tile and timber cladding, open layouts, etc., all as Eric Lyons intended (Fig. 2.76).

The site was a former nursery garden, which contained some fine trees and plants, most of which Eric Lyons was able to incorporate in his

Figure 2.75 West Silvertown Urban Village.

designs. The scheme is a mixture of terraced houses forming partially enclosed inter-linking courtyards (Fig. 2.77) and three-storey flats set amongst the fine trees. Car parking is in small groups close to the dwellings.

AJ, 20/1/55, p. 72; *Architecture and Building*, 8//55, pp. 289–294; *A&BN*, 27/11/57, pp. 715–724; *AR*, 2/59, pp. 108–120.

Langham House Close, Ham Common, TW10
1961. James Stirling and James Gowan. R. Richmond + local bus

---

Stirling and Gowan's flats built in the gardens of Langham House – a large Georgian house – had a great influence on British housing design in the 1960s and beyond (Fig. 2.78). The Grade II* listed project contains 18 flats in three-storey blocks, and its appearance owes its origins to the Dutch De Stijl movement of the 1920s and to Le Corbusier's Maisons Jaoul in Paris (1956). English Heritage consider it important as an early and highly influential example of "New Brutalist" architecture, used to great effect in a speculative development … in particular the combination of brick and exposed shuttered concrete, in what was considered an "honest use of materials" [1].

During the 1960s the brickwork panel and full-height windows with wide window transoms at knee height were to be seen

Figure 2.76 Span housing at Parkleys, Ham Common, preserved in its original form.

CHAPTER TWO • LONDON

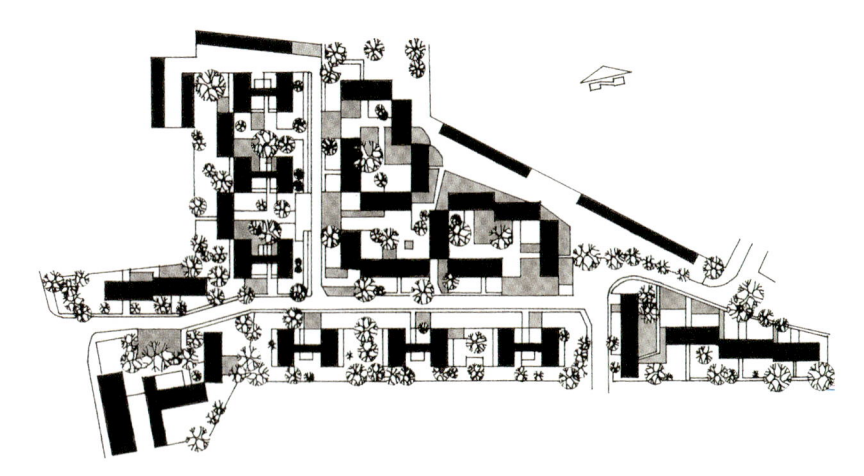

Figure 2.77 Parkleys: site layout.

Figure 2.78 Langham House Close, Ham Common.

117

Figure 2.80 Setchell Road: successful late 1970s high-density/low-rise housing.

windows to studio apartments give the pavilions a character quite different to anything else in London Docklands (Fig. 2.84).

AR, 4/89, pp. 52–54; AJ, 2/11/88, pp. 52–57; L'Architecture d'Aujourdhui, 12/89, pp. 106–107; RIBAJ, 3/89, pp. 38–41.

The Lakes (1997), *Shepheard Epstein Hunter (with N Pishavadia of Persimmon Homes)*, comprises 275 town houses built on the site of the partly filled in Norway Dock and designed in the form of villas and terraces around the water's edge. In many instances,

CHAPTER TWO • LONDON

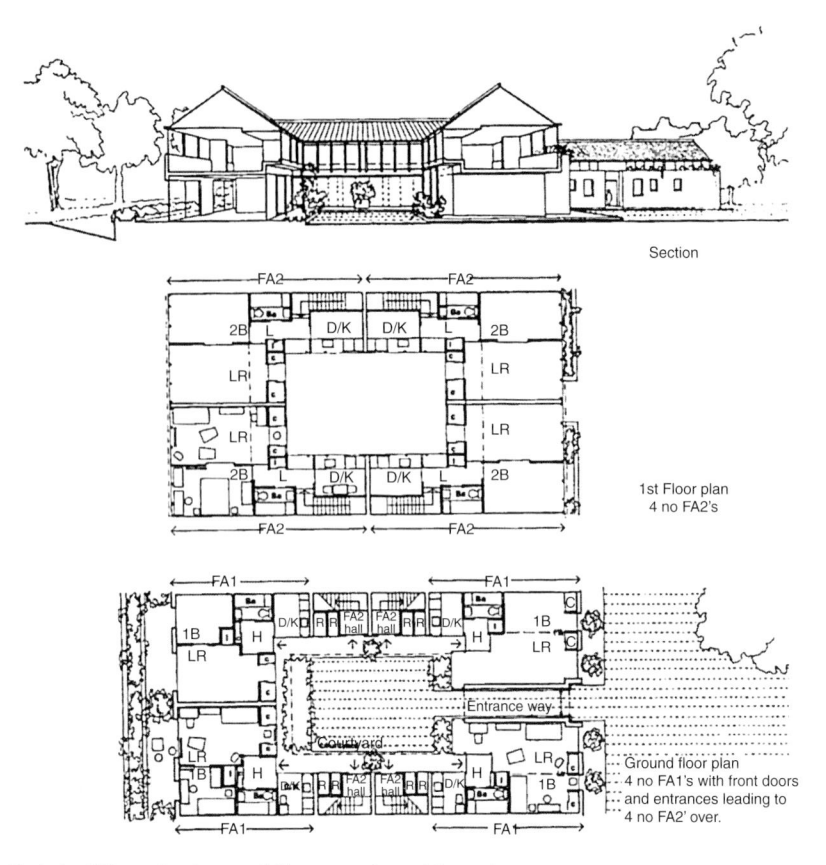

Figure 2.81 Setchell Road: plans of the courtyard housing.

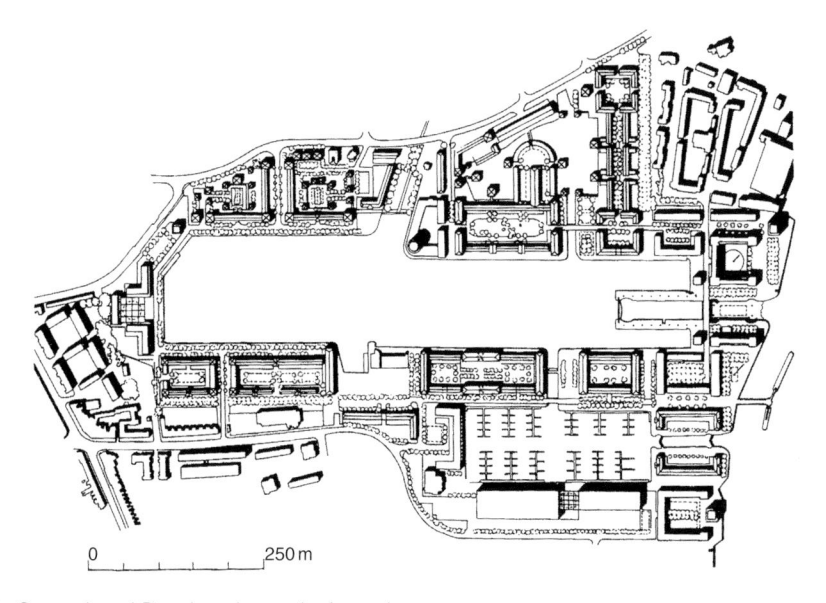

Figure 2.82 Greenland Dock: urban design plan.

121

Figure 2.83 Greenland Passage.

Figure 2.84 Finland Quays.

Figure 2.85 The Lakes.

the houses are accessible only across timber bridges (Fig. 2.85).

B (Homes Supplement), 14/6/91, p. 10; B (Brick Awards), 11/97, pp. 52–53; RIBAJ, 6/91, p. 56; RIBAJ, 3/98, p. 34.

South-east of Tower Bridge, SE1
LDDC. U. London Bridge/Tower Hill

The stretch of Waterfront development from Tower Bridge to London Bridge and Rotherhithe to the east has some of the finest streets in Docklands and some of the best of the LDDC housing.

Horselydown Square, **Shad Thames** (1989). *Julyan Wickham Associates*. "Horselydown Square makes an excellent bit of city" [1]. It was the first scheme to introduce new urban spaces relating to the existing building form and pattern of use in the area. It is mixed-use comprising shops on the ground floor and a combination of offices and 76 flats on the four floors above. The scheme is designed around two squares, entered at positions that reflected existing pedestrian routes across the site to the river. The north-west approach, close to Tower Bridge, is framed by two partially glazed drums which signify "entrance" (Fig. 2.86). The architecture contrasts sharply to the warehouses around but the distinctiveness of the new spaces gain much from the exuberant use of colour – a combination of blue, red and rich terracotta.

AJ, 16/5/90, pp. 49–51; RIBAJ, 3/98, p. 31; [1] AT, 7/99, p. 65 (Edward Cullinan).

The Circle, **Queen Elizabeth Street** (1989). *CZWG*. This development creates a strong sense of streetscape and is a focal

Figure 2.86 Horseleydown Square: entrance from Tower Bridge.

point in a grid of streets. The development has a mix of uses with shops, offices, restaurants and a health club plus a swimming pool on the ground floor. Above are 302 apartments that range from 38–50 sq.m. studios to three-bedroom penthouses of over 100 sq.m. Parking for 400 cars is in two levels of basement. The residential accommodation is in four segments each served by pairs of lifts and approached by lobbies on either side of the street. The central circle acts as an approach and setdown to the entrances. The walls facing the circle were finished in ultramarine coloured glazed bricks, which creates the impression of a blue canyon. Complete with the equestrian statue in the centre of the space, it is one of London Dockland's special places (Fig. 2.87).

AJ, 17/10/90, pp. 26–40, *Blueprint*, 7/90, pp. 34–37; *RIBAJ*, 2/98, p. 32.

China Wharf (1988). *CZWG*. China Wharf reflects the stylish reputation of its architects. The building nestles ingeniously into a tight site amongst a number of sober Victorian warehouses, most of which have been converted into housing. The ground floor contains offices and above are seventeen flats, each planned in a scissors form so that every flat has a river view.

The scheme has three elevations, each responding to its immediate location. The facade to Mill Street is clad in London stock brick with blue engineering brick details to match its warehouse neighbours. The courtyard facade has small windows turned away from directly looking over New Concordia Wharf. The river facade has large areas of glass and each apartment has its own balcony. To provide privacy, the central in-situ concrete panel was introduced with wings and flanges, making it read like a ship's construction. The whole of this was then painted in red B.S. 04 E 51.

AR, 4/89, pp. 28–37.

Vogan's Mill, **Mill Street** (1989). *Michael Squire Associates*. Vogan Mill rises like a beacon up to its 16th storey penthouse. The tower replaces an existing grain mill built in 1813; it combines with listed former warehousing to provide 65 two- and three-bedroom luxury flats. The slim tower contains one flat per floor and is best viewed from the river where the whiteness of its modernity, with its cut-away corners and curving roof, makes it stand out above the darkness of the old warehouses (Fig. 2.88).

AJ, 16/5/90, pp. 38–41.

Gainsford Street Halls of Residence (1990). *Conran Roche*. Designed for the London School of Economics, this modest six-storey building is built in pale yellow brick but enlivened on the Gainsford Street frontage by the inclusion of nautically inspired balconies. The building accommodates 280 students in a series of six-bedroom flats planned around a basic core of kitchen and bathroom facilities.

AJ, 16/5/90, pp. 25–26.

The Anchor Brewhouse (1990). *Pollard Thomas and Edwards*. This is one of London's most picturesque sites next to Tower Bridge, which has been beautifully transformed into housing and offices (Fig. 2.89). Originally built in 1789 and rebuilt in 1891 after a fire, the

Figure 2.87 The Blue Circle.

Figure 2.88 Vogan's Mill rising above China Wharf and other buildings at St Saviour Dock.

Figure 2.89 The Anchor Brewhouse.

building was a Courage's brewery. It now provides a variety of dwellings ranging from tiny studio flats with bedrooms at mezzanine level to an enormous multi-level apartment under the cupola. The external appearance has been sensitively restored to its former condition. New levels have been inserted which give some rooms truly exciting views. The major change to the outside of the building was the provision of a vertical glass bay which has been inserted into the previously blank west end of the complex overlooking Tower Bridge. This adds to the space quality giving wonderful views out through the bridge.

AR, 10/90, pp. 81–84.

New Concordia Wharf, Mill Street, EC2 (1981–1983). *Pollard Thomas and Edwards in succession to Nicholas Lacey and Partners.* This project pioneered the conversion of the warehouses in this part of Docklands. The courtyard of buildings was formerly part of St Saviour's Flour Mill established in 1882, and re-built in 1894/1898 after a fire. The mill complex is specially known for its water tower and chimney. The conversion into mixed-use development, principally housing, has carefully preserved the existing fabric of the buildings. The long facade to St Saviour's Dock has deeply recessed new windows in keeping with the character of the building and metal balconies were fixed across the former loading bays. The timber jetty was renewed to its original pattern and crossing the entrance to the dock there is a delightful new footbridge designed by Whitby and Bird and Nicholas Lacey and Partners (1995).

AJ, 12/2/98, pp.27–28.

Figure 2.90 Woolfe Crescent, Surrey Quays.

Woolfe Crescent, Canada Street, off Quebec Way, Surrey Quays, Rotherhithe, SE16
*1989. CZWG Architects.
U. Surrey Quays*

The majority of Surrey Quays is suburban but with a very high-quality landscape infrastructure that can be best appreciated from the top of Stave Hill. Wolfe Crescent is one of the few exceptions to this. Built on a 0.8 hectare (2 acre) site fronting Albion Channel, which is all that remains of the extensive former Surrey Docks, the development contains 53 apartments and 26 houses. It has two principle elements – a large crescent of houses terminated by four-storey apartment buildings and five small freestanding octagonal blocks of apartments (Fig. 2.90).

Four of these octagonal blocks stand on the channel front enclosed by the crescent. The fifth is on the east corner of the site. This arrangement enables most of the flats and houses to have a view of the watercourse to which the scheme relates. The brick octagonal buildings with their corner windows, basket balconies and domes are best seen from the well landscaped walkways alongside the Channel.

B, 11/9/87, pp. 59–61; *RIBAJ*, 7/89, p. 5; *AT*, 1/90, pp. 22–25.

Riverside Apartments (formerly Princess Tower), Rotherhithe Street, SE16
1990. Troughton McAslan and Tim Brennan Architects. U. Rotherhithe

This eight-storey tower is one of the landmarks along the River Thames (Fig. 2.91), its

Figure 2.91 Riverside Apartments, formerly Princes Tower.

design is unashamedly of the modern movement with reference to the designs of Eric Mendelsohn and Serg Chermayeff in the inter-war years. The bow windows, horizontal strip windows and white cladding are supported on a steel frame that is an update of the experimental concrete and steel of early modernism. The client required a two-storey penthouse at the top of the building that included a sun terrace and glass observation room on the roof. The building is best viewed from the river.

AJ, 16/7/86, pp. 20–23; AJ, 12/2/98, p. 39.

Friendship House, 3 Belvedere Place, Borough Road, SE1
2004. MacCormac Jamieson Prichard. U. Borough

The London Hostels Association is a charity founded in 1940 that provides low-cost rental housing particularly for young, single people working in London for the first time or undertaking an educational course. This project has 160 bedsitting rooms and ancillary communal accommodation on a site with limited road frontage overshadowed by a high viaduct carrying trains to London Bridge station.

Figure 2.92 Friendship House.

The entrance is off a narrow opening on Borough Road (Fig. 2.92). Within the site, the scheme is wrapped around the perimeter enclosing a secluded garden with a pool that reflects light into the rooms around and creates a sense of calm away from the noise from the railway and surrounding roads [1]. There is a wooden bridge over the pool positioned on an axial pedestrian walkway that connects all the principle common areas and the courtyard to the entrance and reception. The building backs up close to the railway viaduct and a wall clad in zinc shingles is an effective sound barrier.

Bedsitting rooms are mostly single en suite but some are double bedrooms. Nine rooms were designed for people with physical disabilities. The communal accommodation includes two lounges looking into the garden, a garden room, an Internet room, TV room and a quiet room. Self-catering kitchens are provided at the corners of the buildings for groups of 10 residents who provide their own food and utensils. There is also a laundry and vending machines.

[1] Housing Design Awards 2005 Publication, pp. 16–19; *B*, 22/7/05, p. 53; www.london-hostels.co.uk

---

6 Barons Place, Webber Street, SE1
2004. Proctor and Matthews Architects. U. Waterloo

Barons Place, situated behind the Old Vic Theatre, was another recent experimental modular housing development built by The Peabody Trust (see also pp. 84–87 and 89–91). It is three-storey, low-cost housing for working people who need accommodation for a short period of time not exceeding 5 years. The

AJ, 14/4/5, pp. 5, 14; *BD*, 14/7/6, p. 4; *The Guardian Environment*, 17/5/06, p. 9; [1] www.peabody.org.uk; www.buildingforlife.org; Housing Design Awards 2007 Publication, pp. 62–63.

Tower Hamlets

Boundary Street Estate, Arnold Circus, E2
1896–1902. LCC Department of Architecture. U. Shoreditch

The Boundary Street estate is the oldest surviving development of rented housing built by a local authority. The estate of 1,002 flats was built in 20 tenement blocks on slum clearance land. The streets were laid out as tree-lined avenues radiating from a small circus with a bandstand (Fig. 2.95). The radical development also included schools, workshops and community facilities on the site, following the principles of the Arts and Crafts movement, of which some of the LCC architects were members. The scheme was coordinated by Owen Fleming, and six different architects worked on the design of the buildings. It was first occupied mostly by white-collar workers as the rent was too high for poorer people but this changed in later years.

B, 3/1/86, pp. 20–21; *AJ*, 8/5/97, p. 12; www.buildingforlife.org

Lansbury Estate, East India Dock Road, Poplar, E14
1951. LCC Department of Architecture. DLR All Saints

The concept of millennium villages is not a new phenomena for one of the features of the

Figure 2.95 Boundary Street Estate: one of the earliest LCC housing developments.

1951 Festival of Britain was the live model of architecture and planning – the new Lansbury estate. The site was a "comprehensive development area" of 50 hectares (124 acres) that had suffered severe bomb damage during the war. The development was conceived as a neighbourhood of 9,500 people, complete with schools, shops, churches and all the facilities necessary to create a community. The brief called for low-rise housing of human scale, in not more than six storeys, designed to a maximum overall density of 136 persons per acre (336 p.p.ha.). The buildings were to be built in yellow brick, preferably London stocks, and to have slate roofs to carry on the local tradition of London's East End.

Many prominent private architectural practices were involved in its design. This included Frederick Gibberd who designed the shopping centre and market place with its famous landmark tower – the first new post-war pedestrian shopping precinct in London (Fig. 2.96). The Lansbury live exhibition was not a success. Architects and architectural writers were not impressed with the quasi-vernacular architecture that was described as worthy, dull and somewhat skimpy.

[1] AJ, 6/9/51, pp. 275–304; AJ, 3/7/74, pp. 23–42; [1] Ibid., p. 40.

Cluster Blocks, Usk Street/Claredale Street, Bethnal Green, E2
1952/1960. Fry Drew, Drake and Lasdun/Sir Denys Lasdun & Partners. U. Bethnal Green

Sir Denys Lasdun was a twentieth century British architect of great distinction with many fine buildings to his name including the National Theatre. His aim in designing housing was to improve on what was being built by local

Figure 2.96 Lansbury Estate: live housing model for the 1951 Festival of Britain.

authorities. He was interested in the Smithson's concept of cluster housing (pp. 12, 15) and during the 1950s he designed two such schemes at Usk Street and Claredale Street. The Bethnal Green council was one of the most progressive housing authorities in London but was constrained by a limited amount of land. Lasdun's concept was therefore of considerable interest.

His intention was to create a "vertical street" in a core structure connected by bridges to four towers set at angles to each other. The core contained services and communal amenities – clothes drying platforms, lifts stairs and refuse chutes, which are all noisy elements. The dwellings themselves were akin to semi-detached houses but placed on top of each other. They were seen to be very private and quiet with only their entrance halls, WC's and internal stairs and bathrooms facing on to the access balconies.

Usk Street comprises 24 maisonettes in an eight-storey block formed of four smaller towers set at different angles to each other with six units per double floor. These were linked to the central lift tower and staircase with bridges. The dwellings were served by a district heating system in the basement. The 16-storey Keeling House at Claredale Street contains 56 two-storey maisonettes and 8 single-storey flats linked to a core containing stairs, lifts and activity areas (envisaged as places for children's play). This pattern of semi-detached maisonettes is expressed in the rhythm of the elevations, in which solid balconies alternate with the narrow horizontals of the bedrooms in between (Fig. 2.97).

From the very beginning, both blocks suffered vandalism, crime and anti social behaviour but listing to Grade II and Grade II*, respectively, by English Heritage, has supported improvement and tenure change. A third tower by Lasdun, Trevelyan House, built as part of the Greenways Estate with the Usk Street tower, has also been listed Grade II.

Figure 2.97 Cluster Blocks at Claredale Street.

AR, 1/54, p. 49; AD, 2/56, pp. 125–127; AD, 2/58, p. 62; AR, 5/60, pp. 305–312; AJ, 6/12/61, p. 90; AR, 1/77, pp. 52–58; AJ, 6/7/95, p. 8.

Roy Square, Narrow Street, E14
1988. Ian Ritchie Architects. DLR Limehouse

Narrow Street is one of London Docklands most historic streets on the north bank of the River Thames. Roy Square established new ground in creating private housing of urban quality. The predominantly four-storey housing is grouped around a rectangular court, which is entered from a flight of stairs off Narrow Street. The form of this central

CHAPTER TWO • LONDON

Figure 2.98 Roy Square: internal courtyard.

space and the large rectangular metal bay windows on the dwellings are reminiscent of courtyards in the Berlin's 1984 IBA housing exhibition, although the pools at each end linked by a narrow channel and lush planting give the court a decidedly Moorish flavour (Fig. 2.98).

The external face of the scheme presents a lively frontage to the surrounding streets. The architects sought to respect the area's Georgian character and to design the housing as pavilions linked by lower recessed blocks containing stairs and lifts. This is now a familiar pattern for housing in London Docklands, which clearly succeeds in this scheme.

AJ, 5/89, pp. 35–36; AR, 4/89, p. 46; AJ, 8/2/89, pp. 24–29; L'Architecture d'Aujourd Hui, 12/89, p. 114; BB, Autumn/92, p. 8.

Shadwell Basin, Wapping Wall, E1
1988. MacCormac, Jamieson, Pritchard & Wright. DLR and U. Shadwell

New Shadwell Basin dates from 1854–1858 and is overlooked by St Paul's Church built in 1820–1821 by John Walters. The 169 dwellings built on three sides of the Basin represent in style and density a fine attempt at producing a contemporary dockside housing form that echoes the key qualities of the early nineteenth century brick warehouses that once characterised the area. In this respect, it is different to other LDDC schemes of its time (Fig. 2.99). The terraces and flats are not single blocks like warehouses but a series of five-storey brick pavilions linked with metal and glass loggias, all unified by painted iron balustrades. The Venetian arched ground floor

Figure 2.99 Shadwell Basin.

on the waterfront elevation, reminiscent of the Albert Dock in Liverpool, creates a most attractive base to the design.

Most of the development is apartments, but on the north-eastern side of the basin are three-storey houses designed in the same style complete with colonnade and arches. In the centre of the northern side of the basin, there is a gap in the run of housing around the basin, created by the LDDC to allow a view of the church.

AJ, 25/9/85, p. 52; AR, 2/87, pp. 51–54; AR, 4/89, pp. 47–49; RIBAJ, 3/89, pp. 38–41.

Cascades, Westferry Road, E14
1988. CZWG. DLR Heron Quays

The Cascades, situated on a bend of the River Thames close to the West India Dock and Canary Wharf, has one of the most distinctive housing forms in the River Thames skyline.

Built by Heron Homes, the 168 apartment scheme stands on a 2.3 acre (0.93 ha) site bounded on two sides by water. It comprises a 20-storey block of apartments and one of six-storeys plus three shops on the ground floor (Fig. 2.100).

Building upwards, instead of outwards, provided space for landscaped gardens, a health centre and swimming pool. It also offered spectacular views. The great 45° slope incorporates the fire escape beneath a canopy of corrugated steel and glass, which extends over the swimming pool to form a skylight. The cladding is a stock brick with blue engineering brick bands. The architects claimed to have respected the location through incorporating in the design a whole range of portholes, funnels, lighthouse balconies and tower.

AR, 2/89, pp. 30–33; *L'Architecture d'Aujourd Hui*, 12/89, p. 112; *RIBAJ*, 10/88, pp. 30–33; *RIBAJ*, 3/89, pp. 38–41; *RIBAJ*, 12/89, pp. 28–33.

Compass Point, Sextant Avenue, Manchester Road, E14
1986. E14. Jeremy Dixon.
DLR Island Gardens

Compass Point was built during the later 1980s boom period for London Docklands. Its design reinterprets many traditional building forms, some of which Jeremy Dixon used in other schemes illustrated (pp. 102–103, 154–156). The stepped gables are distinctively Flemish, whilst the white bow windows reflect nineteenth century English sea-front housing. Behind the riverfront housing are a number of paired villas and terraces of high urban quality built on an axis at right angles to the river. The main street, Sextant Avenue, contains the largest villas and culminates at the far end in a crescent with a small gap through to give access to Manchester Road. At the other end, the views of the river are framed by two gateway buildings

Figure 2.100 The Cascades: a landmark on the River Thames.

(Fig. 2.101). The spaces created in the scheme – streets, mews, crescents – are enhanced by the care taken with the design of the hard paving and landscaping.

AR, 2/87, p. 33; *AR*, 4/89, p. 46.

Winterton House, Tower Block Refurbishment, Watney Market Estate, E1
1996. Hunt Thompson Associates.
DLR Limehouse

It is well worth taking a stop at Limehouse on the Docklands Light Railway to view the 25-storey Winterton House as an illustration

Figure 2.101 Compass Point: looking towards the River Thames.

of creating new life for a warn out tower block (Fig. 2.102). The building's original steel frame had been developed by British Steel in the 1960s to be as economic as possible. The former cladding was of lightweight GRP, and the floor was of hollow pots. On its own, the frame could not support available cladding systems and heavier concrete floors, which were required to improve the sound insulation. In addition, the block had many of the typical problems of 1960s high-rise housing. The jointing between the cladding panels was poor, the windows could only be replaced externally and there were asbestos problems. This led to the building being vacated and occupied by squatters.

The proposal to clad the building in brick came from the brief, which required a 50-year life before the first major maintenance. Consequently the building was stripped back to its frame and concrete core. A new external wall of brickwork was built, which, along with 150 mm of quilt and high-performance double glazed windows was designed to be highly energy efficient. The brickwork strengthens the existing steel frame to which it is connected by a steel jacking structure at roof level.

Northwood Tower, Wood Street, Walthamstow, E17 (1992). *R. Wood Street, Walthamstow*. Hunt Thompson Associates were architects for another tower block over-clad in brick for the London Borough of Waltham Forest.

AJ, 7/11/96, pp. 46–47; *AJ*, 7/11/96, pp. 46–47; *AJ* (Supplement), 12/6/97, pp. 12–14; *BD*, 22/8/97, p. 12; *B* (Brick Awards), 28/11/97, p. 48; Northwood Tower: *AJ*, 5/2/92, pp. 39–41.

CHAPTER TWO • LONDON

Burrell's Wharf, 262 West Ferry Road, E14
*1995. Jestico + Whiles.
DLR Island Gardens*

The planning brief in 1987 from the LDDC for this spectacular riverside site called for the preservation of the Grade II listed shipyard buildings built by Brunel in 1830, which had been owned for a 100 years by Burrells, the paint manufacturers. The complex now comprises new residential apartments, retail shops, workspace, a large leisure facility with a swimming pool, squash court, indoor running track, gymnasia, library, pool room, restaurant and spa baths (Fig. 2.103).

High-density development was necessary to offset the substantial infrastructure costs. The layout took on an axial form with most of the buildings at right angles to the River Thames except for two major riverfront buildings, which frame the central square. This way, most dwellings have a glimpse of the water. Vehicular access to the commercial development is from the north whilst access to the housing and the underground car park beneath the central square is off the riverside drive. The result is a large successful development of fine new buildings integrated with Brunel's workshops within an urban design framework of considerable strength and integrity.

B, Housing Design Awards, 27/10/95, p. 22; *RIBAJ*, 11/90, pp. 42–43.

Dundee Wharf, Three Colt Street, Limehouse, E14
1997. CZWG. DLR Westferry

This tall, striking project, built by Ballymore Properties, is a powerful landmark at a bend in the River Thames. A rather extraordinary false oil-rig structure which appears to lean out off the front of the building adds to the

Figure 2.102 Winterton Tower refurbishment.

variety and sense of fun in the building' design (Fig. 2.104). In front is a very fine footbridge designed by YRM/Anthony Hunt Associates and completed in 1995.

B, 28/11/97, p. 52; *RIBAJ*, 3/98, p. 33.

Tower Hamlets Housing Action Trust (HAT)
1994 + Architects as indicated

Tower Hamlets HAT was established in 1993 following a ballot of the residents of three Council estates – Lefevre Walk (Parnell Road),

139

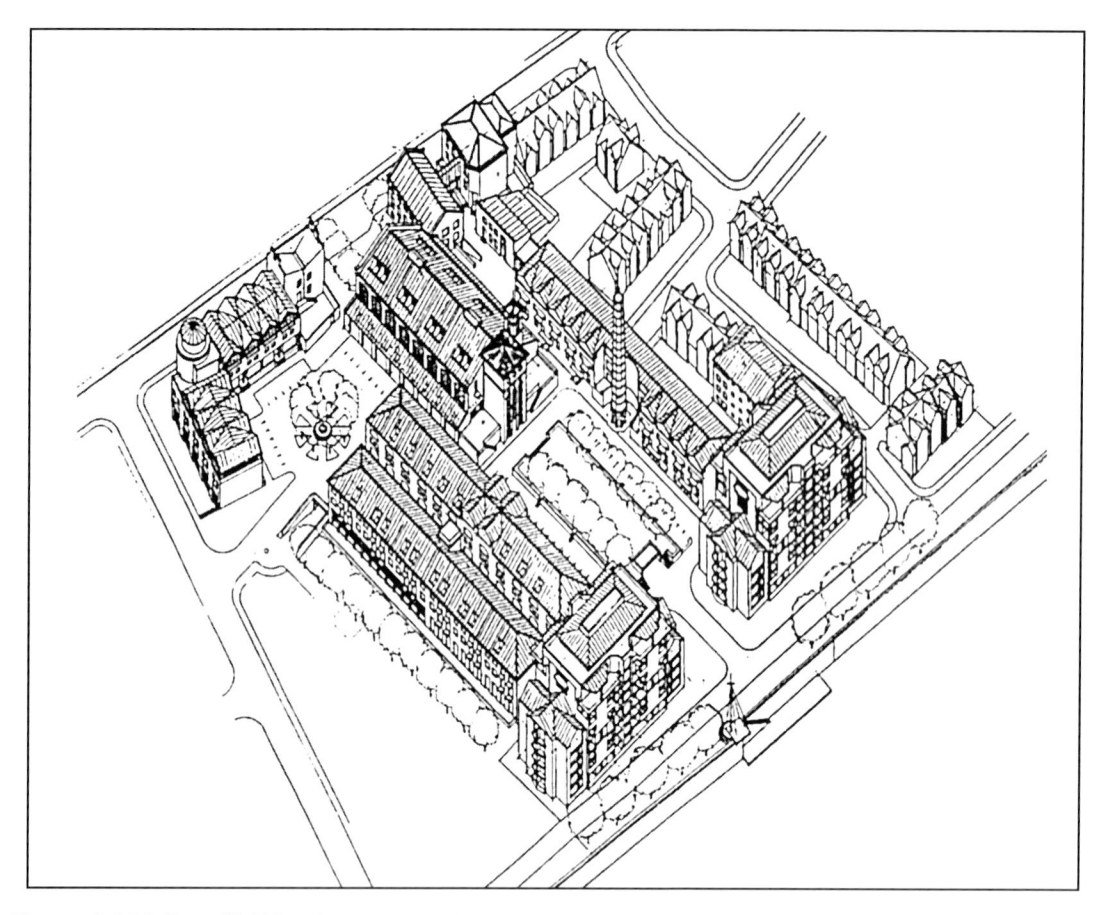

Figure 2.103 Burrell's Wharf: axonometric drawing.

Monteith (Old Ford Road) and Tredegar Road, which were built in the late 1960s and early 1970s. These high-density estates all displayed the physical problems associated with system built estates of the time. The masterplan produced in 1994 proposed the demolition of most of the housing and its replacement with over 1,100 new low-rise dwellings, approximately 50 percent of which would be houses with gardens.

The masterplan objectives were to be achieved with extensive resident participation. Important was a sustainable succession strategy, which involved the formation of a Community Based Housing Association (CBHA) and a Community Trust to take over the long-term ownership and management of community facilities developed by the HAT. Originally it was envisaged that the development would be totally publicly funded but this proved to be an enormous commitment for the Government. Therefore, the HAT entered into arrangements with Circle 33, and a newly formed subsidiary, Old Ford Housing Association, for them to take over the development function and to raise private finance to cover the shortfall of government allocation.

The development included the following projects.

Cherrywood Close, Coborn Road, E3 *1996. Thomas Pollard and Edwards. U. Bow Road.* This scheme was the first to be completed by the Tower Hamlets HAT. It comprises 11 two- to four-bedroom houses, 23 two- and three-bedroom mews housing and 6 one-bedroom flats. The site, which had been a railway station and then a builder's yard, was bought by the HAT to start the process of decanting people to reconstruct their estates. Its narrowness was cleverly overcome by using wide frontage houses with all rooms facing south onto large walled gardens. Where the site was wider, short terraces of three-storey town houses formed a landscaped square (Fig. 2.105). The use of wide frontage houses permitted considerable variety of internal arrangements, and porches, bay windows, verandas and conservatories could be selected by the tenants from a menu of options.

Monteith Phase 1, Parnell Road, E3 *1997. AFC Shaw Sprunt. U. Mile End.* Built on a site overlooking the Hertford Union Canal and Victoria Park, this was the first of five phases in the redevelopment of the Monteith Estate comprising terraced housing and a block of flats overlooking the canal. Its communal areas have been designed to be light and have views of and access through the south-facing courtyard to the canal and park. The low pitched roof has been designed to create the impression of it floating over the structure below (Fig. 1.19).

Figure 2.104 Dundee Wharf with its distinctive oil-rig structure and the bridge.

BowZED zero carbon housing, Tomlins Grove, E3
2004. BDaZEDfactory. U. Bow Road

In this scheme, Bill Dunster related the Bed-ZED technology (pp. 41, 131–132) to a building with high levels of masonry thermal mass. The four-storey building contains four apartments. The two lowest floors contain two bedrooms and the second floor one. At the top level is a studio apartment. This diminishing size of apartments creates a stepped section and a cascade of balconies and conservatories on the south elevation (Fig. 2.106).

Inside there are few immediate signs of the technology that replaces space heating. Instead is a combination of measures that include:

- South-facing living rooms with a large amount of glazing, terraces and conservatories highly imaginative whilst fitting well into its traditional surroundings (Fig. 2.110).

AR, 10/90, pp. 59–63; RIBAJ, 12/91, p. 35; B, 11/91 (Housing Design Awards), pp. 38–39.

Wandsworth

Cottage Estate Roehampton, Dover House Road, SW15
1922. LCC Architects Department. R. Barnes

Roehampton is most noted for the 1950s Alton Estate (pp. 147–149) but close to it is an LCC cottage estate of some historical significance built as part of the "Homes fit for heroes" programme. The estate developed quickly and as a result it set the standard for new interwar LCC housing.

The layout placed the houses on either side of tree-lined streets and around greens (Fig. 2.111). Land at the back and between blocks was designated for allotments. The layout achieved a density of 15.8 dwellings per acre (39 dw/ha). As this was higher than the Tudor Walters' maximum special permission had to be sought from the government. Culs-de-sac were not used for fear that they would cause the housing to degenerate into slums. The appearance of the houses followed the example of Hampstead Garden Suburb. In the early stages, the architects used good quality materials, including clay tiles, and inventive detailing – arches, stringcourses, decorative brickwork, etc. Regrettably after the government housing cuts of 1921, these could no longer be afforded which reduced the quality of the later phases.

Swenerton, M., *Homes Fit for Heroes*, pp. 162, 181.

Figure 2.110 20b Bistern Avenue: circular balconies mark the entrance.

secluded site. The design echoes the Modern Movement, but unlike the white buildings of the 1930s, the building is painted in dramatic colours, with terracotta walls and blue stairwells, which work well in the street scene. Large trees have been retained in front of the flats, almost touching the balconies in places. The flats are on either side of a central covered stairwell in which the rhythm of the circular corner balconies is repeated. The solution is

Figure 2.111 Cottage Estate, Roehampton.

Alton Estate, Roehampton, SW15. (East) Portsmouth Road, (West) Roehampton Lane
LCC Architects' Department – Alton East 1952–1955 (including Oliver Cox, A.W. Cleeve Barr and Rosemary Stjernstedt under Robert Matthew); Alton West 1954–1963 (Bill Howell and Colin Lucas). Elderly people's bungalows 1955–1958. R. Barnes

In the late 1940s and 1950s London was experiencing an acute housing crisis and an urgent need for new housing. The LCC championed mixed-development and its most ambitious schemes were at Roehampton using a range of houses and flats to suit all ages and household size.

The different design of the two phases, East and West, reflected the liberal attitude of the Architect to the Council, Leslie Martin, who allowed teams to develop a personal style. **Alton East** contained 744 dwellings on an 11 hectare (28 acre) site. The dwellings included 10 eleven-storey blocks mixed with four-storey maisonettes and two-storey houses. The site was formerly gardens to a number of Victorian houses and in order to preserve the mature trees, buildings were placed on the footprint of the former villas. The tower blocks were clad in cream bricks (Fig. 2.112), which contrasted with the red brick, pitched roofed houses and maisonettes set on the slopes below. The design was the product of a highly sociable approach to housing which owed its inspiration to 1940s Swedish design.

The later **Alton West** phase is a larger development comprising 1,867 dwellings on a

Figure 2.112 Alton East tower blocks influenced by Swedish design.

site of nearly 40 hectares (100 acres) overlooking Richmond Park. The scheme comprises a mixture of 12-storey point blocks, five- to six-storey slab blocks, maisonettes, terraced housing and bungalows (Fig. 1.6 + cover). The influence of Le Corbusier is easy to see. The five large slab blocks set picturesquely into the slopes of the site are clear descendants of the Unite d'Habitation at Marseilles. Most significant was the use of pre-cast elements that set the agenda for system building in Britain for the next 15 years.

In total contrast are **two groups of bungalows** for elderly people **at Minstead Gardens** and **Danebury Avenue**. These were important to the formula for mixed development in the 1950s and they nestle quietly amongst the trees virtually untouched and complete with flat roofs and chimneys stacks (Fig. 2.113).

The 10 tower blocks in Alton East have been listed Grade II, whilst the five slab blocks in Alton West and the two groups of bungalows are Grade II*.

AR, 1/54, pp. 52–57; AR, 7/59, pp. 21–35; AJ, 30/3/77, pp. 594–603; Scoffham, E.R., *The Shape of British Housing*, pp. 64–70; EH, p. 5.

Figure 2.113 Alton West: charming bungalows unaltered since the 1950s.

Montevetro, Battersea Church Road, SW11
1999. Richard Rogers Partnership and Hurley Robertson Associates. U. Fulham Broadway

---

Montevetro stands on a prominent bend of the River Thames next to the Grade I listed St Mary's Church (Fig. 2.114). The building is aligned north–south diagonally across the site, allowing for the creation of a new public park and riverside walk from which there are splendid views across the river to Chelsea. The apartments are grouped around four lift and stair towers into five blocks that slope down from 20 storeys at the north end of the building to four at the south end. The 103 apartments are mainly two-bedroom flats but with some one- and three-bedroom flats and two-storey penthouses in the space beneath the sloping roof. All living rooms and kitchens face west and overlook the river with bedrooms on the eastern side. There is a two-storey leisure centre/security building and 170 parking spaces located in a single floor of underground parking and a single-storey structure behind the leisure centre.

Figure 2.114 Montevetra by Richard Rogers.

Montevetro is a building of its time and it fits the location. It particularly enhances the setting for the church. Writing about the project in 2000, Richard Rogers commented, "Montevetro is the right scale for the Thames, which is a big river. Too many opportunities have been lost in London and elsewhere, because we are afraid to learn from the past. When Wren rebuilt St Paul's, he didn't replicate the old cathedral but designed something of its own day" [1].

[1] *AT*, 4/2000, pp. 50–59.

Westminster

Churchill Gardens Estate, Grosvenor Road, Lupus Street and Claverton Street, SW1
1949. Powell and Moya. U. Pimlico

Churchill Gardens provided much early post-Second World War experience of high-density housing. Under the guidance of its Town Clerk, Mr. Parker Morris, Westminster City Council in 1946 promoted an architectural competition, which was won by Philip Powell and Hidalgo Moya. The site was an area of obsolete terraced houses badly damaged by the wartime bombing. The brief called for high-density housing appropriate to the site, which resulted in the construction of 1,661 flats and houses.

The design rejected the traditional form of the Pimlico streets in favour of the European modernist thinking of seven- to nine-storey blocks of flats set in green space at right angles to the River Thames (Fig. 2.115). Many of the flats were wide frontage to be light and airy. The north–south axial arrangement maximised sunlight penetration, a principle first developed by Walter Gropius for his 1930s Seimensstadt Housing in Berlin. Four-storey blocks of flats built between the rows of higher blocks created a series of courts in which there were trees, lawns, gardens and children's play areas. Along the frontage of Grosvenor Road were two terraces of three-storey town houses.

The buildings are concrete frame structures clad in yellow brick and with glazed staircases and distinctive rooflines. Originally the walls of the recessed balconies were painted with bright colours in the theme of Le Corbusier's Unité. A district heating scheme took surplus

Figure 2.115 Powell and Moya's Churchill Gardens Estate.

heat pumped as hot water through a tunnel beneath the river from the Battersea Power Station. It was then stored in a huge circular glazed heat accumulator tower (which can still be seen) before distribution to the blocks.

The first phase of the development won a Festival of Britain Award in 1951 and all of phase 1a (Gilbert, Sullivan, Chaucer, Coleridge, Pepys and Shelley and the accumulator tower) are listed Grade II*. English Heritage comments that the Gilbert and Sullivan blocks are the most exciting – "The horizontal grid of galleries and balconies is carefully contrasted with the vertical grid of the window mullions, whilst the bands of glazing give a translucent quality to the blocks". [1]

[1] *EH*, p. 4; *AR*, 9/53, pp. 176–184; Richards, J.M., *An Introduction to Modern Architecture*, p. 160; Scoffham, E.R., *The Shape of British Housing*, p. 56; *AJ*, 4/7/96, pp. 28–58.

26 St James place, SW1
1961. Sir Denys Lasdun & Partners.
U. Green Park

This eight-storey block of luxury flats overlooking Green Park was built on the site of two Georgian houses that had been destroyed during the Second World War. It reflected all the hopes of the new modernist architecture in the early 1960s, here applied for the first time since 1945 to the top end of the private sector housing market. Lasdun's intention in the design "was to produce a building of the time which would, in terms of urban renewal, concern itself with the relationship between buildings of historic interest and modern architecture" [1].

The external architectural treatment is a direct expression of the internal spatial organisation, including the split levels and extra high living rooms (Fig. 2.116). The structure is reinforced concrete clad with Baveno grey granite with white vitreous mosaic on the soffits. The internal levels are expressed externally by the bands of granite. The penthouse is set back behind a terrace and has a cantilevered roof slab over. The deep overhanging balconies, with thin metal balustrade, have a functional purpose in shading interiors from the summer sun.

The prominent architectural writer of the time, Ian Nairn, considered it "a triumphant justification of putting completely modern buildings right next to the eighteenth century. It is a real tour-de-force and only a few British Architects could have brought it off" [2]. The building is now listed Grade II*.

[1] *AD*, 11/61, pp. 510–517; ibid., p. 511;
[2] *AJ*, 29/6/61, p. 968; *AJ*, 15/1/64, p. 153; *RIBAJ*, 7/61, pp. 355–361; Jones, E., and Woodward, C., *A Guide to the Architecture of London*, 1992, p. 256.

Figure 2.116 26 St James Place: landmark design by Denys Lasdun.

125 Park Road, NW1
1970. Farrell Grimshaw Partnership.
U. St John's Wood/
Baker Street

This 11-storey tower was designed in the "high-tec" fashion of the mid-1960s [1]. It was built by the Mercury Housing Association, which was a co-ownership society with one-third of its finances for development coming from the Housing Corporation and two-thirds from a Building Society. It was Farrell and Grimshaw's first major new building.

The stringent funding from the Housing Corporation determined a minimal approach. Each floor has 2 one-bedroom and 2 two-bedroom flats and there are 4 one-bedroom penthouse flats and a caretaker's flat. The square floor plan was based on the simple idea of building around a single central core containing one internal staircase and ventilated by a shaft. There were no structural walls between the core and the perimeter walls, merely columns, which maximised the amount of windows for habitable rooms and offered flexibility in the division of internal space. This concept was further emphasised by the continuous glazing and banding of corrugated anodised aluminium sheeting curved on the corners (Fig. 2.117). The building is Grade II* listed.

[1] Jones, E., and Woodward, C., *A Guide to the Architecture of London*, 1992, p. 101; *AD*, 10/70, pp. 483–490; *AJ*, 20/1/71, pp. 130–133; *AD*, 2/73, pp. 93–94; *Techniques et Architecture*, 4/73, pp. 50–51.

Lillington Gardens, Vauxhall Bridge Road, Pimlico, SW1
1968–1972. Darbourne and Darke. U. Pimlico

Figure 2.117 125 Park Road.

Lillington Street, built by Westminster City Council, brought about a major shift from the Corbusian image of the 1960s to a brick aesthetic within a high-density/low-rise design framework. Its vibrant red brick matched Street's 1861 Church of St James the Less, which overlooks the site (Fig. 2.1). The effect was to influence public sector housing in Britain for the next 10 years. The brief required accommodation for some 2000 people together with sheltered housing for 90 elderly people, two doctors' surgeries, three public houses, 10 shops, a community hall, a public library and a number of ancillary uses. The DOE was anxious to use the first phase of the scheme to set new standards and granted extra funding to achieve the quality of detail and finish.

The first phase of 350 dwellings at Charlwood Street contains three-, six- and eight-storey blocks laid out around the perimeter of the site. Wings of housing push out into the central space to create a series of lushly planted inter-connecting courts. Access to the dwellings is off decks at two levels. These look on to the courts and continually changed direction, opening out into wider spaces at intervals. The partially covered decks are brick paved and softened with planting on the outer edge. The use of narrow-fronted split-level scissor dwelling plans contributed to a high density but this was also made possible by a low car parking ratio of 0.6 per dwelling. The dwellings were smaller than Parker Morris standards but they had large balconies and a high degree of individuality.

153

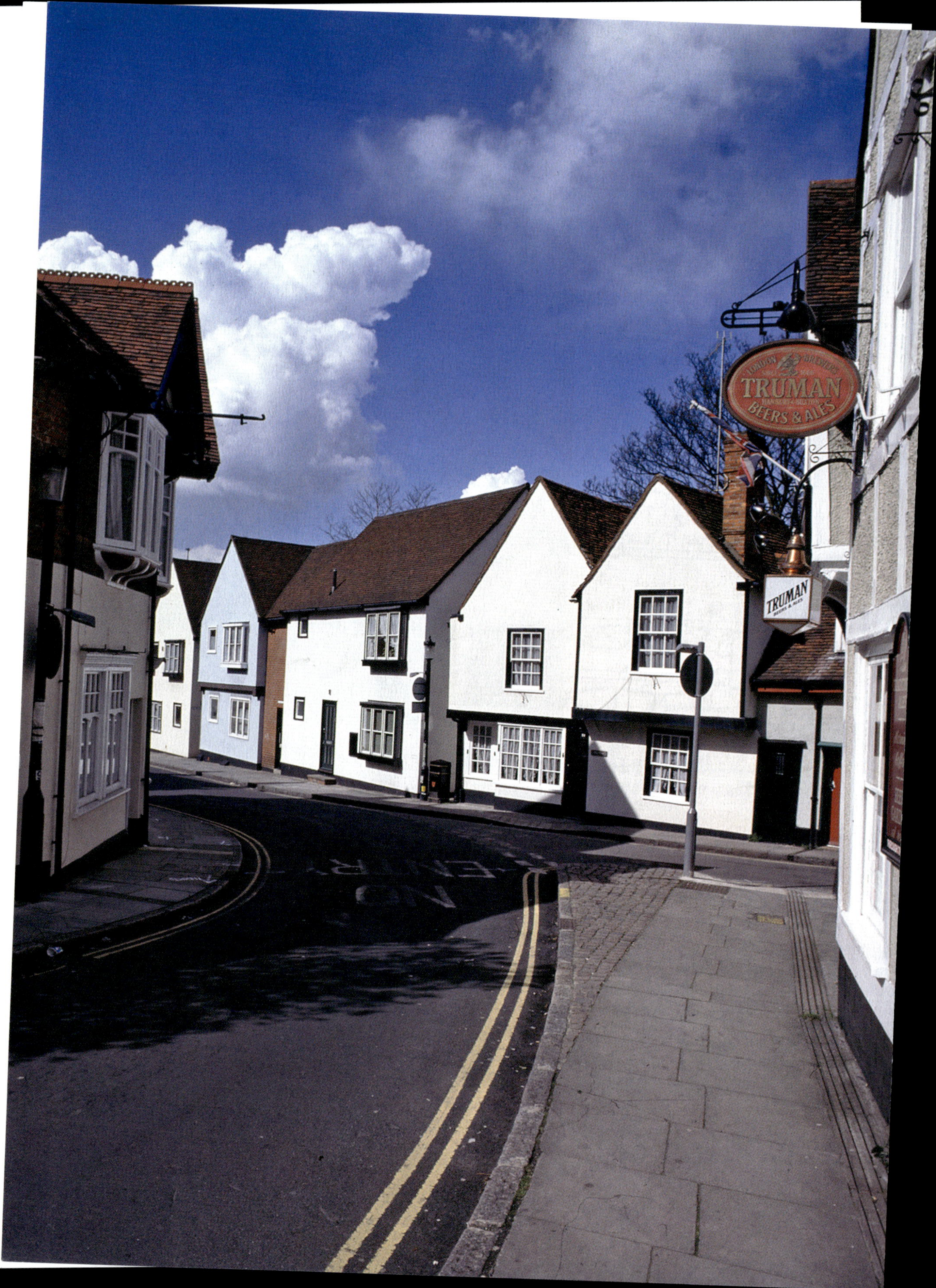
TRUMAN
BEERS & ALES
TRUMAN

The English Regions

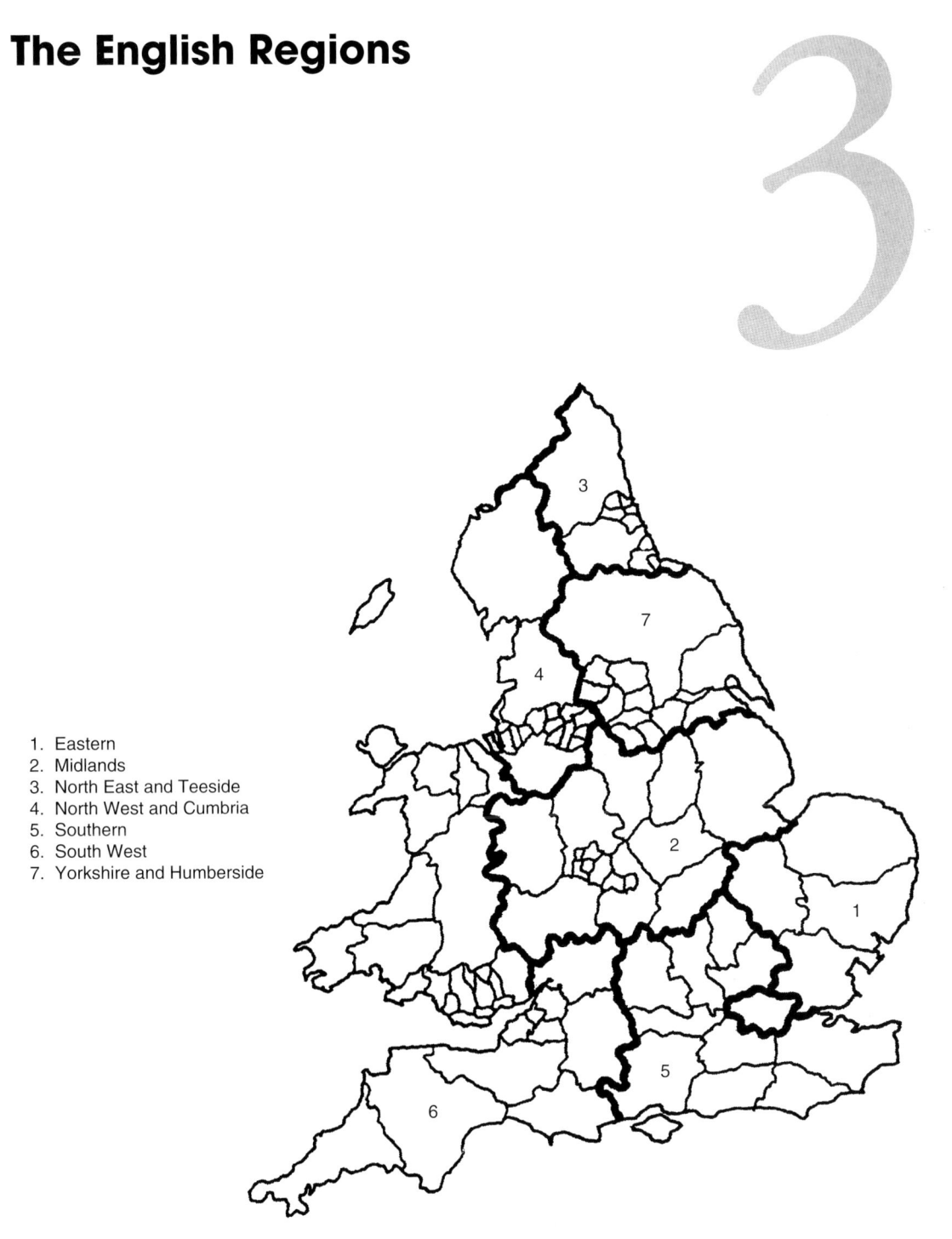

3

1. Eastern
2. Midlands
3. North East and Teeside
4. North West and Cumbria
5. Southern
6. South West
7. Yorkshire and Humberside

Figure 3.2 The English Regions.

Figure 3.1 The Dutch Quarter, Colchester (p. 171).

Eastern England

Cambridgeshire

The Quadrangle, Highsett, Hills Road, Cambridge, CB2
1960. Eric Lyons and Partners. R. Cambridge

This is one of the best works of Eric Lyons and Span Developments Limited, which richly deserves its Grade II listing. It contains three distinctively different groups of housing. The "quad", which fronts the main road, mirrors the traditional Cambridge college courtyard combining flats, maisonettes and garages (Fig. 3.3). The views through to the rear gardens, though now with semi-open screens and gates, are an important part of the composition.

At pedestrian entry points into the courtyard there are wide garages at ground floor level. The construction is cross wall with concrete floors. The architectural treatment of the buildings, with flat roofs, deep white painted fascia, tile hanging and horizontal bands of windows with an irregular pattern of side casements and pivoted top-lights, set a trend which was to be extensively copied in both private and public sector housing design for many years.

Behind the quad housing is an L-shaped group of simple two-storey terraces of flat-roofed houses with porches. They are designed in typical Span style with panels of brickwork alternating with areas of white painted timber and glass. The third group is three-storey town houses built in a pale yellow brick.

Figure 3.3 Highsett, Cambridge: quad courtyard housing by Eric Lyons and Span.

These face the street, or are built at right angles with footpath access (Fig. 3.4).

EH, p. 10; *AR*, 1/58, pp. 74–75; *AR*, 2/59, pp. 108–120; *The Builder*, 21/1/61, p. 114; *AD*, 5/62, p. 234; *Architect and Building News*, 28/9/60; *Housing Review*, 11–12/60, pp. 186–188; *AJ*, 29/9/65, pp. 4, 10.

Supported housing, Peterborough and District
1970–1980s. Matthew Robotham & Quinn

During the 1970s and 1980s Matthew Robotham & Quinn used the East Anglian vernacular in a most imaginative way to produce bright, modern design solutions for a number of supported housing projects. The mixture of roof heights, dormers, low eaves and traditional materials created a village quality. The detailing of the traditional materials, especially the brickwork and tiling, is particularly outstanding.

Sudbury Court, Stonald Road, Whittlesey, Peterborough, PE7 *1977. R. Peterborough.* This scheme of 32 single-person flats and bungalows for elderly people, a warden's house and a common room, was built in a suburb of Peterborough by the Nene Housing Association. An additional five family houses were included to provide variety and to help overcome any institutional feeling.

AJ, 2/11/79, pp. 1096–1097.

Tuckers Court Sheltered Housing, South Street, Stanground, Peterborough, PE1 *1988. R. Peterborough.* This sheltered housing scheme for elderly people, built by the Minster Housing Association, demonstrates a masterly integration of organisation and elevation, carried through to the smallest detail.

Figure 3.4 Highsett, Cambridge: "timeless" town house design.

Figure 3.5 Tuckers Court sheltered housing for elderly people.

Most flats are accessed off a linear internal street covered by a pitched roof with exposed timber trusses. The upper floor flats have their own staircase, which can accommodate a stairlift. A delightful feature of the corridor is how at intervals it looks out onto small garden courts. The white rendered walls with diagonal and stained wood feature windows and contrasting stained balcony timber, together with the natural clay tiles is a colourful way of relating to the vernacular tradition of the English Fenlands (Fig. 3.5).

B, Housing Design Awards 1989, pp. 50–51; Colquhoun, I., and Fauset, P., *Housing Design, an International Perspective*, pp. 180–183.

Southbrook Field, Church Lane, Papworth Everard, Nr Huntington/St Neots, CB3 *1987. R. St Neots.* Papworth Village Settlement is a charity and housing association whose objectives are the rehabilitation, training, employment and housing of physically handicapped people and their families. Established in the 1920s it has grown into a thriving community where physically disabled people are fully integrated into the village.

The scheme was designed to offer independence and privacy for 33 people with physical disabilities who may be confined to wheelchairs. The housing is grouped around three courts. Common room, warden's office, kitchen, laundry and guest bedroom are sited centrally (Fig. 3.6). Sixteen carports were provided with covered access to the dwellings through "cloisters". The main dwelling type is a self-contained single-person flat with separate sitting room, bathroom and bedroom.

AR, 1/86, p. 65; *Housing Design: an International Perspective*, pp. 209–210.

Bishop's Walk, Ely CB7
2003. Hawk and Dovetail; Conservation Architect and Urban Planner: Derek Latham Architects

This is a fine example of new housing in a sensitive conservation area that was positively promoted by the local authority. Having purchased the land, East Cambridgeshire District Council

CHAPTER THREE • THE ENGLISH REGIONS

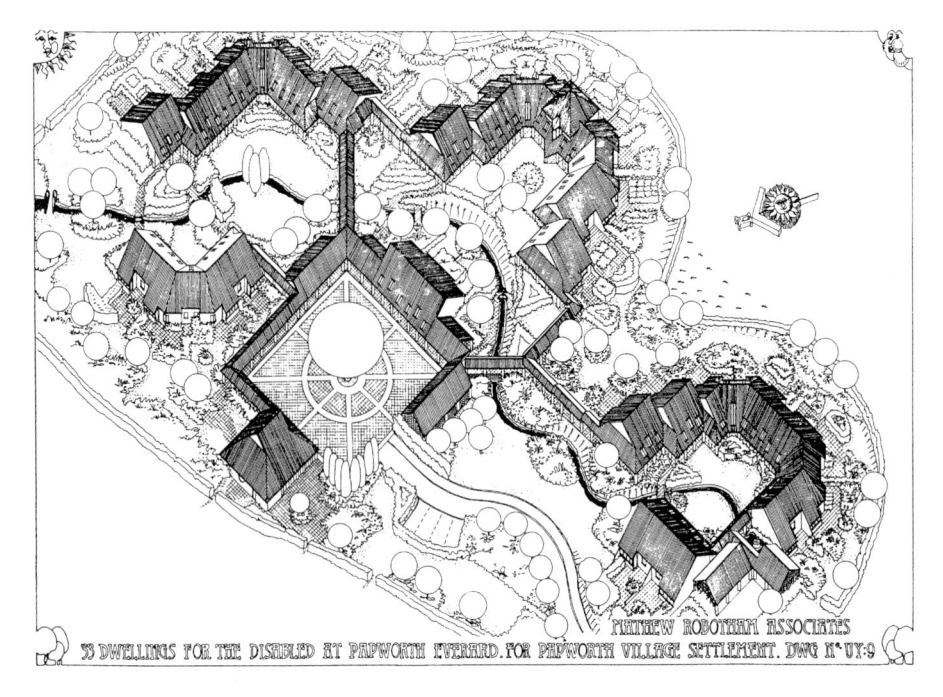

Figure 3.6 Papworth Village Settlement: housing for people with physical disabilities.

appointed architect planner Derek Latham Associates to produce a layout and design guide for a development/design competition and tender. Local residents participated in preparing the design guide through community planning workshops, which resulted in the inclusion of a large park on part of the site.

The scheme, built by Hopkins Homes, comprises 79 dwellings including 50 four-bedroom town houses and 29 one-bedroom flats. Parking is provided at a ratio of 1 space per dwelling. The narrow-fronted houses, some of which are exceptionally large, provide a high-density solution (34 dw/ha – 14 dw/acre). Some have integral garages. The variety of building heights, elevations and materials within each terrace gives each dwelling an individual appearance. There is a wide range of spaces in the layout including a large green, streets and rear parking courts overlooked by apartments at first floor level to increase natural surveillance (Fig. 3.7).

www.buildingforlife.org

Accordia (Phase 1), Brooklands Avenue, Cambridge CB2

Phase 1: 2006; whole project due to finish 2010. Architect and Masterplanner: Fielden Clegg Bradley; Architects: Alison Brooks and Macreanor Lavington; affordable housing (implementation) Dewjoc Architects. R. Cambridge

This is a superb project on a 9.5 hectare (23.5 acre) site that previously accommodated a government office complex. It cut new architectural ground for Cambridge, an academic city more used to "neo-Georgian, Surrey vernacular" than modern innovative design [1]. The masterplan was prepared by Fielden Clegg Bradley for developer, Countryside Properties. This proposed 378 dwellings (166 flats and 212 houses) at a density of 67 dwellings per hectare (27 dw/acre) excluding the large amount of open space in the plan. Thirty per cent of the housing is to be affordable homes for rent and shared ownership.

Figure 3.7 Bishops Walk, Ely: town houses framing a green.

Phase 1 comprises 72 houses for sale and 101 affordable dwellings. Fielden Clegg Bradley brought in two other architectural practices to introduce design variety and a fourth practice developed the design of the affordable housing for the Wherry Housing Association. Aberdeen Avenue, with its attractive belt of trees, forms a central axis to the site. The larger houses and apartments are around the perimeter, enclosing smaller houses and apartments within the site. The housing fronting Brookland Avenue at the entrance has four very distinctive semi-detached houses designed by Alison Brook (Fig. 3.8). These have copper roofs that sweep over a highly glazed family space below. The large four-storey town houses facing the trees with mews studios behind were designed by Macreanor Lavington.

Figure 3.8 Accordia: houses by Alison Brook at the far end.

Figure 3.9 Accordia, Houses with "chimneys" overlook a green space.

There is a variety of terraced house forms across the site but the most notable is the three-storey, three- or four-bedroom type designed by Fielden Clegg Bradley. Each house has an outdoor space at every level. The lowest accommodates gated parking under the house, which provides a sense of openness in the tightly arranged mews streets. Both first and second floors have terraces, and tall chimneys link all three floors at the rear of the house. One of these terraces and chimneys face on to a large green that leads down to the Hobson Brook and a wildlife area (Fig. 3.9). Also overlooking the green is a green oak-frame apartment building with generous balconies designed by Fielden Clegg Bradley and a Victorian House that is now occupied by English Heritage.

The affordable housing has a common link with the sale housing through height, massing and materials. Regrettably it is somewhat tucked away and lacks features that make the sale housing so attractive.

[1] *AJ*, NHBDA Report 7/2006, pp. 8–9, 54–55; *BD*, 5/5/06, pp. 1, 12–17; *AT*, 5/06, pp. 40–45; *B*, 12/5/06, p. 22; *RIBAJ*, 6/06, pp. 32–38; *AJ*, 22/6/06, p. 11; *AJ*, *B*, 21/7/06, pp. 24–25; *B*, Regenerate supplement, 9/06, pp. 48–49; www.buildingforlife.org

ESSEX

Crittall Workers Housing, Silver End, Nr Braintree, CM7
1926–1932. R. Braintree/White Notley

The construction of this most remarkable group of housing designed in the art-deco style was the creation by one person, Francis Crittall, whose factory manufactured (and still does in Braintree) metal windows and doors. Started in 1926, his intention was to create a village of the future, which he thought would result in a more productive work force through better living standards. His son, Walter Crittall was the person behind the design. He was influenced by the Bauhaus movement, white modernism, flat roofs and metal windows that looked to the future. The main street of art-deco houses is most impressive (Fig. 3.10).

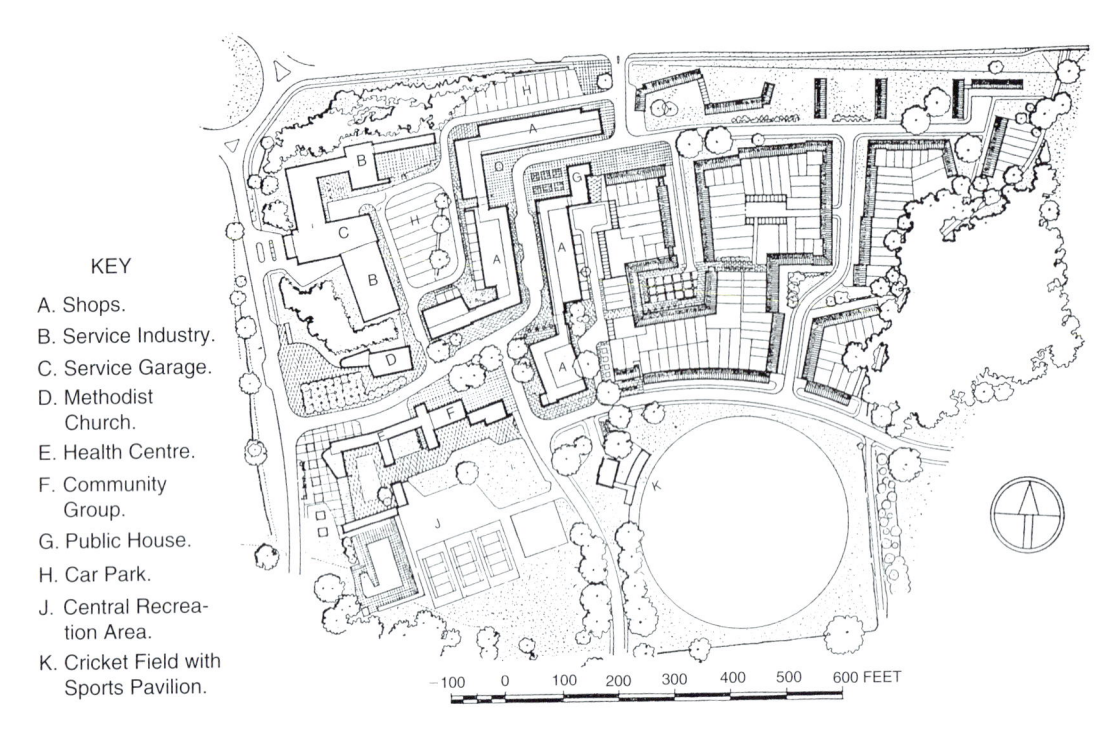

KEY
A. Shops.
B. Service Industry.
C. Service Garage.
D. Methodist Church.
E. Health Centre.
F. Community Group.
G. Public House.
H. Car Park.
J. Central Recreation Area.
K. Cricket Field with Sports Pavilion.

Figure 3.12 Part of Mark Hall neighbourhood, Harlow (from Design in Town and Village, HMSO, 1953, p. 30).

Figure 3.13 Town houses overlooking the village green at Mark Hall, Harlow.

garages with living rooms and kitchens at first floor level (Fig. 3.13). The living room windows were emphasised externally with a projecting concrete surround, a motive used by Erno Goldfinger at Willow Road (p. 55).

The scheme won a MoHLG Housing Design Award in 1953. It is Grade II listed.

AR, 5/55, pp. 311–315.

Bishopfield and Charter Cross, Harlow New Town, CM20
1963. Neylan and Unglass, R. Harlow Town

The design of this scheme was based on research into courtyard housing undertaken at Cambridge University by Leslie Martin and Lionel March (pp. 19–20). It was the subject of an architectural competition in 1961 won by Michael Neylan who adopted the L-shaped patio houses as the basis for his design. This form of house had been successfully used by Jorn Utzon in his 1960 Kingohusene estate at Helsingor in Denmark and it was thought to offer a high degree of privacy. At Bishopfield it

CHAPTER THREE • THE ENGLISH REGIONS

Figure 3.14 Bishopfield, Harlow.

was combined with narrow pedestrian lanes similar to those in traditional Turkish villages – hence the name by which the estate became known – "The Kasbah" (Fig. 3.14).

The brief set three principle design criteria – a density of 20 dwellings per acre (45 dw/ha), 100 per cent car parking and the layout had to take account of the site which was a hill isolated by roads from neighbouring developments. The scheme provided 239 houses, flats and maisonettes. At the top of the hill was the "podium" – a platform beneath which was garaging for cars. Its roof was a pedestrian concourse encircled by a ring of flats. Stepping down the hill were fingers of patio houses, which were separated by wedges of open space.

In its early days Bishopfield was well liked and there was a strong sense of community but this was not to last. Regrettably newcomers did not have the same memory of the early years and the scheme declined as crime and anti social behaviour increased.

AJ, 25/5/61, pp. 765–772; AJ, 3/11/71, pp. 967–968; AR, 7/66, pp. 39–42.

Dutch Quarter, West Stockwell Street, Colchester, CO1
1977. Colchester Borough Architects Department. R. Colchester

The Dutch Quarter in Colchester received its name from sixteenth century Huguenot refugees. They left behind a tightly knit area of timber framed cottages, pressed close together amongst the winding lanes in the centre of Colchester. In the 1950s, some of these cottages were demolished by the Council but fortunately in the mid-1970s the remaining were renovated and the vacant sites redeveloped with 47 houses and flats for rent.

The layout took its cue from the existing street pattern with the buildings kept close to the back edge of pavement. Development built on the backlands of the site was grouped around landscaped courts connected to the main streets by alleys. The form of the housing reflects the old buildings with projecting upper floors, steeply pitched roofs and white plastered walls (Fig. 3.1). The scheme was

171

very important to the early promotion of the Essex Design Guide.

AJ, 26/10/77, pp. 780–781.

Brentwood Place, Sawyers Hall Lane, Brentwood, CM15
1975–1979. David Ruffle Associates. R. Brentwood

This scheme of 64 private houses is close to the centre of Brentwood. It was a forerunner of the Essex Design Guide and it is now possible to see the success of the original concepts. The houses are grouped in a series of courts, mews and private drives (Fig. 3.15), with access off a single spine road. The design seeks to reflect the character of a historic Essex townscape, and it employs a wide range of external materials and colours, which have mellowed with time. Groups of houses are linked by garages and screen walls that are covered with overhanging planting.

Figure 3.15 Brentwood Place: early Essex Deign Guide housing.

opportunity to experiment with the design of roads and footpaths (Fig. 1.16). Most of the housing was for private ownership with only 7 per cent housing association rented housing.

South Woodham Ferrers, CM3
Started 1973. Masterplan by Essex County Council. R. Woodham Ferrers

---

South Woodham Ferrers was the first built example of a Country Town. It was planned to have a population of 18,000 and responsibility for its coordination has been entirely in the hands of Essex County Council Planning Department. Over 4,500 houses have now been built together with schools, public houses, churches and other communal facilities together with its town centre. Most controversial is the "period look" of the centre that was implemented in line with the Essex Design Guide principles. Regrettably the centre is beginning to look somewhat tired.

The new housing development gave the planning department and others plenty of

---

Abode and Cala Domus, Newhall, Harlow, CM17
Masterplanner: Roger Evans Associates; Architects: (Abode) Proctor and Matthews Architects; (Cala Domus) PCKO Architects. R. Harlow Mill

---

Newhall, on the outskirts of Harlow, was the vision of the landowners – to create a 2,800 dwelling development on 81 hectare (200 acre) of former farmland. It was to be "an architect inspired sustainable community" [1], and they commenced the design by superimposing street plans of Florence, Bath and other memorable historic towns onto the site map to see graphically what could be achieved. The completed masterplan gave strict guidelines on design, stating, "pastiche and fake architectural devices will be avoided" [1]. A pallet of materials and colours was developed by a colourist who related them to the natural materials in and

CHAPTER THREE • THE ENGLISH REGIONS

Figure 3.16 Abode: stylish housing in a new neighbourhood at Newhall, Harlow.

around the site. Twenty-five per cent of the housing was to be affordable.

Abode (2003), the second phase of development, contains 82 dwellings ranging in size from single-bedroom apartments to five-bedroom houses of 57 sq.m. (1087 sq.ft.), designed to a density of 43 dwellings per hectare (17 dw/acre). It is tightly knit around spaces, which have a Home Zone feel with a continuous hard surface between the buildings and no separate footpaths. The parking ratio is 1.7 spaces per dwelling plus 15 visitor spaces. These are provided in a mixture of integral garages, open parking beneath dwellings and spaces within the homezones. The elevations are full of colour and treated with a variety of massing, detail, materials and colour (Fig. 3.16).

Cala Domus (2005) is distinctive and colourful with glazed balconies, brickwork, render, pressed metal panels, welsh slate on straight roofs and standing seam zinc on curved roofs. The scheme contains 74 four dwellings in a mixture of houses, flats and maisonettes, designed to a density of 38 dwellings per hectare (15 dw/acre). It is grouped along streets and around a large green (Fig. 3.17). Car parking is provided on the basis of 2:1 for houses and 1:1 for apartments. Its highly varied two- and three-storey roofline is capped by the landmark Chase Tower, an apartment block that resembles a windmill except that the blades have been replaced by photovoltaic panels to generate electricity for lighting parts of the building.

173

Figure 3.17 Cala Domus, Newhall.

AJ, 23/6/05, p. 44; *B*, 21/4/06, p. 10; *Green Places*, 11/05, p. 8; *BD*, (Housing supplement), 30/6/06, pp. 17–18; [1] www.buildingforlife.org

---

Outlook, The Garrison, Campfield Road, Shoeburyness, Southend-on-Sea, SS3
2006. Hawkins Brown. R. Shoeburyness

This impressive housing development demonstrates the quality of design that should be sought in the regeneration of the Thames Gateway, if it is to be successful.

The site is just a short walk from Shoeburyness railway station, from where direct trains run to London. The scheme is approached through former army barracks (closed down in the 1980s) now redeveloped for housing. It consists of four blocks of 30 two- and three-bedroom high-spec apartments. All the blocks face south-east and enjoy a spectacular view of the Thames Estuary (Fig. 3.18). In his *BD* article on the design of the scheme Jes Fernie writes that each of the four blocks "was conceived as a mass, cut into in such a way as to break down the facades and play a visual game of shifting planes. The castellated profile is a nod to the history of the site and an attempt by the architects to create a dialogue with the flat horizon it faces" [1]. He also refers to the interest of the architects in sculptor, Jim Partridge's work in wood, which led them to design the buildings as "a series of storage boxes that had been washed up by the sea" [1].

The buildings are raised on brick plinths and service areas such as stairs and lifts

CHAPTER THREE • THE ENGLISH REGIONS

Figure 3.18 Outlook, Shoeburyness.

are also in brick. Otherwise the composition of timber cladding, glass balconies and large metal windows and doors create highly sculptured sea view elevations. All timber was procured from forestry stewardship certified sources and, where possible, natural and self-finishing materials were used in preference to applied finishes. Car parking is in the plinths and entered at the sides of the buildings.

[1] *BD*, 21/7/06, pp. 12–15; *B*, 16/2/07, p. 84.

Norfolk

Rural Housing at Ditchingham, near Bungay, NR35, and Loddon, nr Norwich, NR14, South Norfolk
1947–1963. Tayler and Green (Private Transport Essential)

The listing in 1998 of post-war housing by English Heritage drew attention to a number of almost forgotten rural housing developments built from the late 1940s to the early 1960s for the former Loddon Rural District and other Councils in South Norfolk area by architects Herbert Tayler and David Green. A number of the schemes were illustrated in the early government Housing Manuals published after the Second World War. The housing was widely admired and copied and has remained popular with their tenants.

The schemes were small simple groups of houses and bungalows. At close level they are full of delightful brick pattern work, tiles, wavy bargeboards, white painted windows and a "distinct sense of comfort and place" [1]. Some brickwork is colour-washed; elsewhere it is covered with trellising which has retained its original freshness. Frequently the schemes are dated in decorative brickwork. The use of pantiles and "crinkle-crankle" walls all came from the architects understanding of the local vernacular. The schemes of most note are:

Windmill Green, Ditchingham (1947–1949, 1965). Simple colour-washed terraces of houses placed around three sides of a green.

Agnes Hood Terrace and Scudamore Place, Ditchingham (1951, 1958–1965). Two groups of housing for elderly people built across the road from each other. The

175

Figure 3.19 Tayler and Green at Davy Place, Loddon.

earlier scheme is a simple terrace. The later has parallel rows of bungalows linked by crinkle-crankle walls and with a prominently designed corner where there is a day centre and warden's house (Fig. 1.4).

Church Road, **Bergh Apton**, near **Loddon**, **NR15** (1956). Housing around three sides of a small green built in subtle pink and black colour-washed brickwork with bargeboards and diaper patterns.

Davy Place, **High Bungay Road**, and **Low Bungay Road**, **Loddon** (1963). A small development of elderly people's bungalows with a day room and a warden's house. It contains fretted bargeboards, bottle ends and contrasting brick patterns (Fig. 3.19).

Housing at **Forge Grove** and **Kenyon Row, Gillingham, South Norfolk, NR34**. 1955, 1957 by Tayler and Green is also Grade II listed.

[1] Bannister Fletcher, p. 1380; EH, *Something Worth Keeping? Housing and Houses: Rural Housing*, pp. 8–9; AJ, *Masters of Brickwork*, Supplement, 12/12/84, pp. 28–31.

CHAPTER THREE • THE ENGLISH REGIONS

Figure 3.24 Martlesham Heath: housing overlooking the green in the Heathfield hamlet.

The Midlands

Birmingham

Post-war Prefabs, 394–427 Wake Green Road, B13
1945. Birmingham City Council. R. Birmingham Small Heath

The temporary emergency housing manufactured in redundant aircraft factories between 1944 and 1948 proved to be of exceptional value (pp. 7–8). Around a dozen different types were developed and they were expected to last for around 20 years. This little group of 16 prefabs in Birmingham is of the "Phoenix" variety (Fig. 3.26). They demonstrate the quality of achievement at such a difficult time in history and now they are Grade II listed.

Ravetz, A., *The Place of Home*, pp. 96–98; *EH*, p. 4.

Enveloping of Pre-1919 Housing, Balsall Heath, B5/B12 and other locations
1978–1990. Birmingham City Architects' Department

In 1978 Birmingham City Council embarked on a most ambitious programme to improve the fabric of its pre-1919 bylaw street housing. By 1981, the Council had enveloped 1700 dwellings and the programme continued at a high level until the introduction of means testing in the 1989 Local Government and Housing Act. Whilst there was a tendency for enveloping to over-unify the appearance of the housing, it nevertheless gave a huge

Figure 3.25 New housing at Brindleyplace, Birmingham (p. 183).

Figure 3.26 Post-war prefabs, Birmingham: to many they were "little palaces".

Figure 3.27 Enveloping of pre-1919 terraced housing in Birmingham.

environmental uplift to many parts of the inner city in Birmingham (Fig. 3.27). The programme proved that enveloping costs less than clearance and redevelopment and it avoids unsettling the community. It therefore made economic and social sense as well as being good for the physical environment.

Goodchild, B. *Housing and the Urban Environment*, Blackwell Science, 1997, pp. 158–161.

Brindley Place Urban Regeneration, Birmingham B16
Various Architects and Designers.
R. Birmingham New Street

Brindley Place was part of Birmingham City Council's drive to regenerate the central area and bring international status to the city. It was close to the new International

Convention Centre, Symphony Hall and other city centre public buildings and spaces and it became the first mixed-use, canal-side development of its type in the United Kingdom with offices, housing, shops, cultural facilities, restaurants, cafes and public spaces. The housing was located to overlook part of Birmingham's extensive canal system (see Fig. 3.25 on page 182) and the opportunity for people to live in the city centre proved highly popular.

AT, 11/99, pp. 40–41.

CASPAR I, 100 Charlotte Street, Birmingham B3
1999. Alford Hall Monaghan Morris. R. Birmingham Snow Hill

The concept of CASPAR (City-Centre Apartments for single people at Affordable Rents) was developed by the Joseph Rowntree Foundation (JRF) in the late 1990s and early 2000s. It reflected a concern for the declining inner cities and the growing need for affordable housing for young single people and couples close to the city centre workplace. The site at Charlotte Street was ideal for this purpose. It backs on to the Birmingham and Fazeley Canal which can be seen from all the new apartments.

The design comprised two parallel four-storey blocks of flats on either side of an atrium glazed at each end with what appears to be a floating roof above. The atrium is criss-crossed by stairs and angle steel bridges giving access at the various levels to the flats. The front entrance to the atrium is on Charlotte Street (Fig. 3.28) and secure car parking is located below the building and accessed at the rear, but if a resident has no car, a rent rebate is granted.

Despite JRF insisting on the flats costing less than £50,000 each (without subsidy) they were larger than normal practice (c. 50 sq.m.). This accommodated the lifetime homes requirement of the brief for easy adaptation for disability or old age. Each flat has a hall, living/dining room and bedroom and most have balconies. Most face into the courtyard on one side and the street and canal on the other and benefit from thorough light and ventilation.

AT, 4/2000, pp. 22–31.

Castle Vale Housing Action Trust, High Street, Tangmere Drive, Farnborough Road, Abingdon Way, Watton Green, B35
1993–2005. Masterplan: Hunt Thompson Associates. R. Birmingham New Street (No. 67 bus from Corporation Street)

The Castle Vale Estate was built between 1964 and 1969 on 200 hectares (600 acres) of land on the north-east edge of Birmingham near the junction of the M6 and M42 motorways. It was Birmingham's biggest post-war estate with almost 20,000 people in 5,000 dwellings plus two shopping centres, schools, churches and other social and community facilities. The housing comprised 34 tower blocks plus maisonettes and low-rise housing. Almost 1,500 dwellings had been purchased by their owners under the right-to-buy legislation introduced after 1979. From the 1970s, social and economic decline set in with unemployment at 26 per cent. Crime levels, vandalism and anti social behaviour grew, which was aggravated by physical and design problems with the housing.

The Housing Action Trust (HAT) was set up in 1993 following a ballot of the tenants in which there was 93 percent support. Since then the regeneration has resulted in the demolition of 2,200 dwellings, including all of the tower blocks except two which were too close to existing schools. One of these was converted into vertical sheltered

Figure 3.28 Caspar 1, Birmingham: affordable housing for young people.

housing for elderly people and the other into housing for young homeless people; 1,500 new dwellings were built and 1,333 houses improved. A large new central park was created. The old shopping centres were demolished and replaced with new shops at High Street with a library and offices for the Community Housing Association and a new Sainsbury's supermarket. The new housing around Abingdon Way is a mixture of 2–4 storeys built in brick, whilst the later housing on Farnborough Road is rendered in a variety of primary colours giving it a bright modernist feel (Fig. 3.29). Eleven experimental eco houses were built on Watton Green, off Tangmere Drive.

The regeneration of the estate was accompanied by economic and social regeneration initiatives including job creation, training opportunities and raising the education attainment level. The HAT was wound up in 2003 but its work is being continued by the resident-led Castle Vale Community Housing Association. There is a development trust running community enterprises, a credit union, an environmental trust, a community care partnership and a community radio station. A residents' satisfaction survey undertaken in 2005 indicated that there were still problems, particularly from low income, but residents felt that crime and vandalism had reduced as a result of the new development.

Figure 3.29 Castle Vale HAT, colourful housing at Farnborough Road.

Information from the Castle Vale Community Housing Association; Monument, A., *No longer Notorious. The Revival of Castle Vale* (2005) Castle Vale Community Housing Association; *R&R*, 7/10/05, pp. 22–23.

Park Central, Bath Row, Birmingham, B15
Zone 1 2005; whole development 2013.
Gardiner Stewart Architects.
R. Birmingham Five Ways

In 1999, the majority of Birmingham's council tenants voted against the transfer of their housing to an alternative landlord. However, the tenants of what was then the Lee Bank estate demanded that their 2,800 dwelling estate, built in the 1960s, be modernised even if this meant a transfer. Their housing was eventually transferred to a charitable social landlord specially established for the estate – the Optima Community Association (OCA). Funded by a £50 million grant from the Estate Renewal Challenge Fund and nearly £300 million of loans and investment from the private sector, OCA embarked on one of the country's largest physical and socio-economic regeneration programmes, and in 1992, Crest Nicholson became a Development Partner.

The masterplan proposed replacing 1,350 dwellings with 1,670 new properties and refurbishing 1,200 flats in tower blocks. Key principles of the plan were:

- Radical estate renewal to create sustainable mixed-tenure, mixed-use community. New housing to include social, shared ownership and private for sale housing distributed so that the different tenures were not evident. Existing tenants could choose to live near former neighbours as long as they select a suitably sized dwelling.
- A high-quality park in the centre of the development.
- Commercial development to include offices, a hotel, large super market and corner shops.
- Uplift in sales values to be put into improving product and environment.
- Team working and innovation following the Egan principles of partnering.

Figure 3.30 Park Central, Birmingham.

- An extensive socio-economic programme to train and support the existing and new community and create new long-term employment through the commercial development.

The housing was designed to an average density of 155 dwellings per hectare (63 dw/acre), which was considered appropriate for a site so close to the city centre. The layout of streets is permeable (Fig. 3.30) and car parking was provided on a 60 per cent basis for apartments and 100 per cent for houses. Some mews housing has integral garages. The distinctive red and blue brickwork evolved from a study of Birmingham's urban terraces and warehouses. The housing has an eco rating of "very good" and carbon emission of two and a half times lower than schemes running on electricity. The development will be connected to combined heat and power at a later phase of the development and will be completed in 2013 with a 22-storey eco tower.

B, 10/3/06, pp. 52–57; Property Week, 23/7/04, pp. 72–73; *B*, *Regenerate* (Supplement) – Regeneration Awards 2005, pp. 25, 45; *B*, (Supplement): 2006 Regeneration Awards, p. 19, 35; Regenerate, 2/07, p. 27; www.buildingforlife.org

NORTHAMPTONSHIRE

Sustainable suburb (site B): Upton, Northampton, NN5
2006. Masterplan EDAW and the Prince's Foundation. Architects: Lead project designer: Working Group (Ben Pentreath); Architects: Cusato Associates and others. R. Northampton (1.8 miles distance)

Upton is part of the large urban expansion planned for south-west Northampton, which in turn, is part of the Milton Keynes–South Midlands growth area. English Partnerships

drainage, nearby workshop roofs and the access road, and sand filtered. A septic tank and reed-bed deal with black waste, discharging it into the aquaculture lake. Compost toilets are installed and waste is recycled on the site. The proposals also included for the co-operative to grow its own food on the 10 hectare (24 acre) site, which is large enough to achieve total self-sufficiency. The glass front opens onto a large lake containing fish and a reed-bed system that feeds into it at one end.

B, ECOTech, No. 1, 3/02, p. 40; www.hockertonhousingproject.org.uk

Castle Boulevard, Nottingham, NG7
2005. Letts Wheeler, R. Nottingham

This is a fine street housing scheme of 38 apartments on a site, which lies at the foot of a large escarpment that formed part of the original defenses of Nottingham Castle. The design brief required the protection of the caves and making them publicly accessible, preserving the view of them from the Boulevard and creating an appropriate setting for the monument.

To achieve these aims the housing is in the form of six large "villas" which are in scale with nearby Victorian housing. These are built close up to the back edge of the footpath to provide space at the rear, and in between are three large courtyards through which it is possible to see the caves. The street façade has a strong rhythm of brickwork and double-height glazed bays (Fig. 3.33). The three central blocks are linked by recessed transparent stairwells that also allow views through to the escarpment behind. In addition a larger gap in the frontage opens up a dramatic pedestrian entrance to the site, set below a glazed bridge. The side and rear elevations were designed to give good views of the escarpment from inside the apartments.

The dwellings are a mixture of one- to three-bedroom apartments with the living area of the two-level upper apartments set within the roof. Eight of the apartments are live/work spaces.

AT, 5/05, pp. 70–75; B, 11/11/05, pp. 4–5.

Figure 3.33 Urban housing, Castle Boulevard, Nottingham.

CHAPTER THREE • THE ENGLISH REGIONS

Figure 3.34 The Byker Wall, Newcastle upon Tyne. (p.194).

North-east England

GATESHEAD

Staiths South Bank, Tyne Bank, off Team Street, Gateshead, NE8 2LS
Phase 1: 2005; whole project: 2010. Masterplanner and Designer: Hemingway Design; Masterplanner and Architect: IDP Architects (Formerly Ian Darby Partnership); Masterplanner and Landscape Architect: Glen Kemp. R. Newcastle Centra/Dunston

When Wayne and Gerardine Hemingway criticised the "Wimpeyfication" and "Barrattification" of Britain, housebuilder George Wimpey invited them to work alongside architects Ian Darby Associates to produce a masterplan and housing designs for a site that in 1990 had been part of the Gateshead Garden Festival. The outcome was a most original design that offers a new approach to the traditional practices of the volume house builders (Fig. 3.35). The project will eventually comprise around 700 dwellings. Phase 1 contains 158 dwellings for affordable market sale on a 3.4 hectare (8.5 acre) site. It has a wide range of house types including "Tyne" flats with individual staircase access to apartments on the first floor.

The housing is laid out in small clusters of around 20 dwellings on three sides of communal landscaped gardens (Fig. 3.36) which have brick barbeques, children's play areas, outdoor seating, and the occasional table tennis table. Every house has a parking space but no garages were built. Refuse is collected from centrally located bin storage and there are recycling facilities. Bicycle parking and bicycle stores are also provided. The project benefited from being part of the government's homezone programme launched in 2001 (see pp. 38–39). One of the first things Wimpey did was to plant an avenue of trees through the site to the river. Access from this road into the site is along shared pedestrian/vehicular

Figure 3.35 Staithes South Bank, Gateshead (photo: Tim Crocker, Architectural Photography, by courtesy of Wayne Hemingway).

CHAPTER THREE • THE ENGLISH REGIONS

Figure 3.36 Staithes South Bank: site layout (drawing: Glen Kemp, Landscape Architect).

routes serving on-street parking in front of housing and in discreetly located parking courts. Traffic speed is calmed by trees and shrubs sometimes positioned in the middle of a pedestrian/vehicular route. The streets gradually become narrower and the pavement wider as the bias towards the pedestrian becomes more obvious. A management company was set up by George Wimpey to maintain the environment, including the communal gardens and the administration of the car parking, for which an annual charge is payable by the residents.

The scheme is not recognisable as a normal Wimpey product. It has a wealth of elevation variations from using a variety of colour of brick, render, timber and mono-pitched roofs. The internal design also offers variety. Purchasers can chose between open plan living with fewer internal walls or a more traditional layout, or if they decide to live upstairs to take advantage of the river view then the bedrooms can be located downstairs.

B, 22/7/05, p. 53; *B*, Regenerate – regeneration Awards, *2005*, p. 33; Housing Design Awards 2005 publication, pp. 28–31; *B*, 26/8/05, pp. 15, 36–40; www.buildingforlife.org

MIDDLESBOROUGH

Central Area Housing, Grange Road/Hartington Road, TS1
1986. Dixon Del Pozzo.
R. Middlesbrough

Situated close to the centre of Middlesbrough, this scheme was developed jointly by Middlesbrough Borough Council, Sanctuary Housing Association and North Housing Association. It is an excellent model of high-density housing that is well suited for its urban location.

Figure 3.37 Central area housing, Grange Road Middlesbrough.

The scheme comprises a mixture of two- and three-storey housing incorporating flats, houses and shops. The layout was designed in the form of curved terraces, which neatly creates a series of interwoven streets, courts and pedestrian spaces (Fig. 3.37). Vehicular penetration is very high with car parking organised in small groups amongst the excellent landscaping. Despite its location, there are few signs of vandalism. The buildings are all robustly designed with a good balance between brickwork and painted timber panelling. The external works have stout railings, walls and fences.

RIBA Northern Region Housing Group, *Housing North*, p. 12.

NEWCASTLE UPON TYNE

The Byker Redevelopment, Conyers Road, NE6
Completed in stages from 1971 to 1982. Ralph Erskine, Vernon Gracie & Associates. R. Newcastle Central Station. M (Metro): Byker Station

Byker was one of the last of the large local authority housing schemes to be built. It is Grade II listed and has special place in British housing. Ralph Erskine's idea of tenant involvement in the design process was a significant forerunner for architects interested in self-help and community-participatory projects. The pop-in, where he had his office, served as a one-stop consultancy service for residents.

Located 1 mile east of the centre of Newcastle, the scheme comprised 2,200 dwellings on a south-westerly slope with excellent views across Newcastle and the Tyne Valley It is large and high density yet it has a considerable amount of two-storey family housing and a great deal of architectural variety. A small pilot group of 48 houses at Janet Square provided the architects with essential feedback from the tenants. A substantial part of the "wall" on the northern perimeter of the site followed. It contained small units, which were intended for households without children, mainly elderly people.

The outer face of the wall is a masterly design of brick, whilst the inner face is an abundance of colourful timber balconies (see Fig. 3.34 on page 191). The wall was to shelter the courts of housing with gardens from the noise that was expected to be generated by a proposed motorway, which was ultimately not built (Fig. 3.38). Car parking provision of 1.25 spaces per dwelling was provided and extensive tree and shrub planting took place in the early years to hide it. Children's play areas and seats and tables were located in the pedestrian areas. One of the most successful elements is the sheltered housing schemes for elderly people (Fig. 3.39). No-one visiting Byker will come away without sensing the thrill of Newcastle City Council's brave commitment.

Ralph Erskine also designed timber framed houses for sale at **Lakeshore**, **Killingworth** (completed in 1970). *R. Newcastle Central Station + M: Four Lanes End.*

AJ, 16/5/79, pp. 1011–1021; AR, 12/74, pp. 346–362; AR, 7/97, p. 23; AJ, 4/4/76, pp. 731–742; AJ, 9/5/79, pp. 961–969; AR, 12/81, pp. 334–343; AJ, 24/3/05, p. 12; RIBA Northern Regional Housing Group, *Housing North*, p. 25.

Private Housing, Jesmond and North Newcastle.
1962–70. R. Newcastle Central Station + M.

There are a number of outstanding private housing schemes in the northern suburbs of Newcastle, built in the 1960s by A. Cragie and Son Ltd, which were influenced by Eric Lyons and Span. Most of the schemes have since never been altered or added to by their owners, but where they are different to Span developments is that this has been achieved without the establishment of a maintenance company, and there was no commitment upon the house owners except an annual payment for grounds maintenance.

Fenwick Close, **Buston Terrace**, **Jesmond**, **NE2** (1962–1964). *Brian Robson. M: Jesmond.* The existing Victorian house on the site was converted to provide two large family houses with 5 two-storey family houses and two smaller bungalows being built in the grounds. The houses are remarkable for their copper-covered hyperbolic parabolic roofs, which gave clerestory lighting within the deep house plan.

Avondale and **Ferndale**, **Rectory Road**, **Gosforth**, **NE3** (1968). *Waring and Netts Partnership. M: Milford Road.* These houses were built on the adjoining gardens of two large detached Victorian villas. The double courtyard evolved from the separate acquisition and development of the two sites (Fig. 3.40).

Wyncote Court/Jesmond Park Court, **Jesmond Park East**, **NE7** (1970). *Waring and Netts Partnership. M: Jesmond.* This scheme, which comprises 35 houses and 50 flats, consists of two-storey terraces cleverly arranged to retain the existing trees and set them within a series of well landscaped courts. The design accommodates the motorcar in small groups within garage courts and ensures

Figure 3.38 Byker redevelopment: site layout (from RIBA Northern Region, *Housing North*, p. 25, by courtesy of the RIBA Northeast Region).

Figure 3.39 Byker: low rise family housing and high rise sheltered housing for elderly people.

Figure 3.40 Avondale and Ferndale, Gosforth: high quality private housing of the 1960's.

a quiet and pleasant pedestrian environment (Fig. 3.41).

EH, p. 10; RIBA Northern Regional Housing Group, *Housing North*, pp. 6, 23; *AJ*, 15/11/67, p. 1253.

NORTHUMBERLAND

Collingwood Court, Oldgate, Morpeth, NE61
1988. Jane and David Darbyshire, R. Morpeth

Located on a most attractive riverside site in the Morpeth Conservation Area, this private sheltered housing scheme for elderly people was the subject of a designer/developer competition promoted by Castle Morpeth District Council. The brief insisted on the retention of the existing trees and the leafy riverbank. The scheme is approached through an elegant high archway (Fig. 3.42), which opens onto a series of inter-locking courtyards with two-storey buildings and landscaped gardens (Fig. 3.43). Each dwelling is independent and most have south-facing living rooms that look into the courtyards. As in most private sheltered housing schemes there is little demand for community provision and as a result only one small room and ancillary accommodation has been provided next to the warden's office.

Figure 3.41 Wyncote Court/Jesmond Park Court.

Figure 3.42 Collingworth Court, Morpeth: sheltered housing for elderly people.

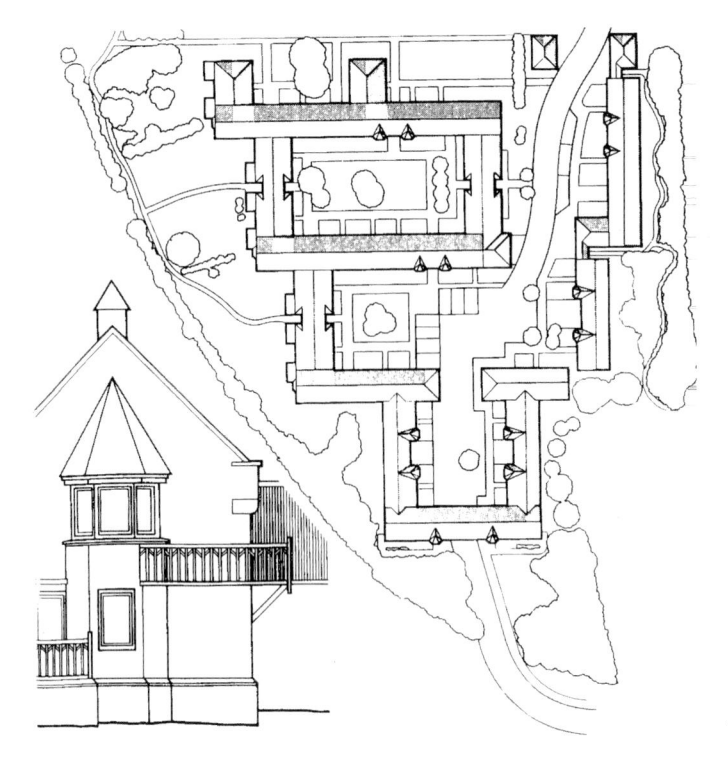

Figure 3.43 Collingworth Court: typical elevation and site layout.

The building materials were chosen to blend with the character of Morpeth – a blend of slop-moulded facing bricks with reconstructed stone dressings and second-hand slate roof coverings, complemented with good detailing and external joinery.

B, Housing Design Awards 1989, p. 14–17; *RIBAJ*, 12/89, p. 9.

Northumberland Village, Monkseaton (between Percy Avenue and Beech Grove). NE26
1990. Jane Darbyshire & David Kendall Ltd, Wimpey Homes and North Tyneside Council. M: Monkseaton

---

Northumberland Village, built in 1880 as a children's home and hospital, is close to the centre of Monkseaton in the north of Newcastle upon Tyne. It was purchased in 1986 by the District Council to prevent commercial development and sold on to Wimpey Homes for housing development. The scheme contains 29 flats of which 54 are sheltered dwellings for elderly people.

There were five Victorian villas on the site with large front gardens; four were converted into semi-detached houses and one was demolished to make way for 76 new flats on the vacant land. The former extensions at the rear of the villas were removed and new double garages with bedrooms above in steeply pitched roofs added at the front. This significantly improved the appearance of the houses from the street. A large administration block, built in 1938, was converted into sheltered flats, a small block of 1960s flats was upgraded and the existing Davis Court flats were given a face-lift with a change of colours and balconies.

The new and old buildings blend well into a series of open and enclosed courtyards off the central spine road. Existing trees have

Figure 3.44 Northumberland Village, Monkseaton: superb use of tiling.

been retained and car parking is located in small well screened groups. Most impressive is the retention and additional use of red/orange wall tile hanging in delightful traditional English patterns (Fig. 3.44).

B, Housing Design Awards, 1991, pp. 11–13; *RIBAJ*, 12/91, p. 33.

SUNDERLAND

Washington New Town
1964–1989. Chief Architect, Eric Watson. (Masterplanners) Llewelyn Davies, Weeks, Forestier-Walker and Bor. (Private Transport Necessary)

The 1965 masterplan for Washington New Town was based on a grid of main roads at approximately 1 mile intervals. Each grid square contained two or three "villages" (after Durham miners' pit villages) of 4,500 people in which two thirds of the housing was for social rent and one third for private sale. The villages had their own primary school, open space, small shopping centre of six or so shops, a pub and a community centre. Secondary schools, churches and other community facilities were located at link points between villages.

During the period 1970–1990 Washington Development Corporation Architects received numerous RIBA, Housing, and Civic Trust Awards for their housing design. There was great concern to reject Radburn layouts and find new ways of accommodating the motor-car in residential areas and, whilst Runcorn and Telford New Towns pioneered the first shared access ways, Washington's architects were interested in "mews" and "mixer courts" in high-density, low-rise layouts. A common feature is the long continuously curving terrace of mixed heights, ranging from single to three storeys (Fig. 3.45).

Fatfield Village (Fallowfield Way), NE38 (1980). Took on the form of a hillside village (Fig. 3.46).

Lambton Village (Malvern Road), NE38 (1982). The centre contains a meeting hall, shops, a public house and clock tower. A sheltered housing scheme for elderly people was designed around covered cloisters.

Ayton Village (Dunlin Drive), NE38 (1984). A series of avenues lead to mews

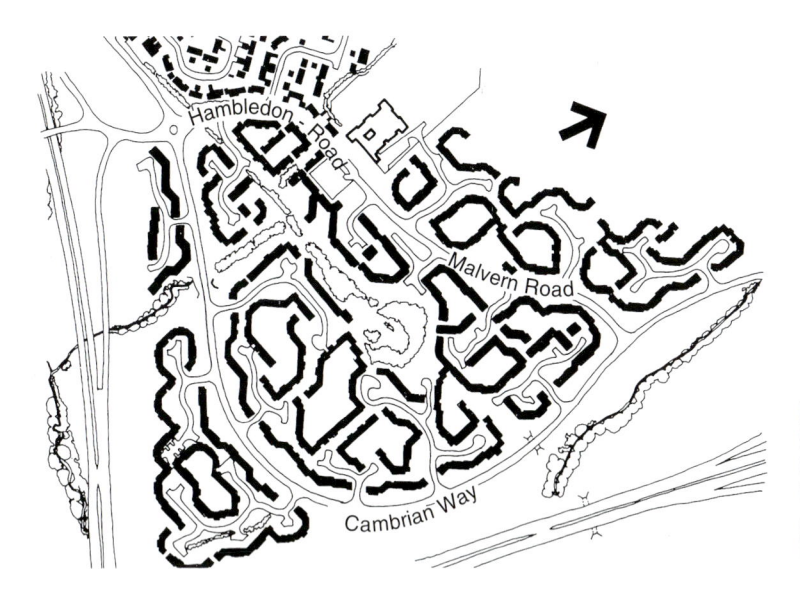

Figure 3.45 Washington New Town: Lambton Village Plan layout (from RIBA Northern Region, *Housing North*, p. 36, by courtesy of the RIBA North-east Region).

Figure 3.46 Washington New Town, Fatfield Village.

courts of mainly houses with coloured panels in upper storeys.

In complete contrast at **East Bridge Street**, **Shiny Row**, **Mount Pleasant**, **DH4** (1980). The Corporation improved two terraces of miners cottages built in the form of "Tyneside" flats with individual staircase access to first floor flats. The houses were restored to their original appearance and there were extensive improvements to the external environment and the banks of the River Wear.

DOE Housing Awards publication, 1978, p. 19; DOE Housing Awards publication, 1980, p. 50; RIBA Northern Regional Housing Group, *Housing North*, pp. 36–39.

Figure 3.47 Beetham Tower, landmark tower in Manchester. (p. 227).

CHAPTER THREE • THE ENGLISH REGIONS

North-west England

CHESHIRE

Hamilton Close, Parkgate, Wirral, CH64
1960. Nelson and Parker, R. Neston

Located in a leafy suburb, this cul-de-sac contains five exquisitely designed detached houses with pyramidal copper roofs and over sailing cedar-clad upper floors. The appearance of the houses has changed very little since they were built and the quality of the design can easily be seen (Fig. 3.48).

EH, p. 10.

Black Road, self-build housing improvement, Macclesfield, SK11
1974–1975. Rod Hackney Associates. R. Macclesfield

The old terraced houses on Black Road were built in 1815 to accommodate textile mill workers. By the 1960s they were in poor condition with outside privies, damp walls and rotting stairs; demolition appeared inevitable. The residents, many over 65 years of age, were actively opposed to moving out of the neighbourhood. So they asked Rod Hackney, then living at 222 Black Road, to speak for them.

Figure 3.48 Hamilton Close: unique private houses from the early 1960s.

203

His first task was to get Black Road reclassified as a General Improvement Area by proving the cost of improvement would be less than demolition and rehousing the occupants. To qualify for a housing improvement grant, the residents would have to buy their house and raise the money to do so. They were agreeable to keep the costs down by undertaking some of the building work themselves. This gave a clear advantage to refurbishment but considerable political campaigning was still required before consent and funding was given by the local authority.

Subsequently, 55 families began the hard task of reconstructing their homes to suit individual requirements (Fig. 3.49) building out single- or two-storey extensions for kitchens and bathrooms. The back yards were converted into a mixture of well-planted communal and private areas.

A second scheme at Black Road quickly followed after which Rod Hackney developed schemes in many places throughout the country. His experience suggests that housing rehabilitation is not so much an architectural problem as a matter of organisation, management and funding which requires a large measure of good will and trust between all the parties.

AJ, 20/2/85, pp. 995–1002; *AJ*, 5/10/77, p. 630; *AJ*, 29/10/75, p. 876; *AJ*, 12/11/75, pp. 995–1002; *AR*, 4/85, pp. 57–61; *Architecture + Design*, 1–2/91, pp. 73–75; DOE, Housing Awards Publications, 1975, p. 21 and 1980, p. 51.

The Brow, Halton Brow, Runcorn New Town, WA7
1969. Runcorn Development Corporation. R. Runcorn

Halton Brow was the first scheme to receive public attention for a design based on the concept of curtailing traffic speed through the integrated design of its buildings and environment. Its long culs-de-sac took on the appearance of winding country lanes (Fig. 3.50), varying in width and set in an environment of dense tree and shrub planting. The houses were randomly arranged around small informally shaped parking courts located on either side of the culs-de-sac. A separate footpath

Figure 3.49 Black Road: pioneered community architecture.

CHAPTER THREE • THE ENGLISH REGIONS

Plan of the Estate

Figure 3.50 The Brow: a break through in residential road and footpath design.

system leading to children's play areas and open space was built into the design (Fig. 3.51).

After completion, the design was thoroughly researched and it proved to be as safe as a conventional layout. Its principles were ultimately embodied in *Design Bulletin 32* published in 1977 and numerous local authority planning and design guides thereafter.

AJ, 21/3/79, pp. 385–596; AJ, 14/10/70, pp. 889–902; AJ, 21/3/79, pp. 585–596; Colquhoun, I., and Fauset, P., *Housing Design in Practice*, pp. 63–64; DOE, Housing Awards 1969, pp. 23, 33–34; AJ, 21/3/79, pp. 585–596.

Warrington New Town
1979–1986. Warrington and Runcorn Development Corporation Architects' Department or as stated. R. Birchwood unless indicated

In the early 1980s, Warrington and Runcorn Development Corporation's Architects and

205

Figure 3.51 A country lane in the Brow.

Consultants continued to develop the concept of highly landscaped, pedestrian orientated environment (Fig. 3.52).

Admirals Road/Curlew Grove, Birchwood, WA3 (1979). The layout of this scheme of 120 houses offers views of interest and variety upon every turn. The housing is set in a mature landscaping setting and the colourful cream brickwork on the housing with red brick bandings and quoins makes it very distinctive.

Gorse Covert Road/Stanmore Close and Darnaway Close, WA3 (1984). The semi-detached houses and bungalows in this scheme, designed for first time buyers, set a good standard for private sector housing. The wide-frontage houses are grouped informally around two culs-de-sac with an open space in the centre.

Cromwell Avenue/Gregory Close and Cavendish Close, Old Hall, WA5 (1984). *R. Sankey for Penketh.* This scheme of almost 300 houses, made up of one- to three-storey housing was planned to emphasise the central tree-lined pedestrian route which focuses on a "gateway" leading to the local centre. The spine road is a tree-lined avenue with frontage housing and a flowing alignment to limit traffic speeds. It gives access to a series of pedestrian/vehicular courts of housing [1].

Old Hall Road/Nansen Close, WA5 (1986). *R. Warrington Bank Quay.* These 115 two-storey houses are grouped around two large culs-de-sac. Most are semi-detached but houses in visually key places in the culs-de-sac are grouped as L-shaped terraces to create a greater sense of enclosure [2].

CHAPTER THREE • THE ENGLISH REGIONS

Figure 3.52 Landscape dominated environment in the Birchwood/Oakwood area of Warrington New Town.

Redshank Lane, Oakwood, WA3 (1984). *MacCormac Jamieson & Prichard.* In its construction and appearance this project of 360 houses and flats reflects Cheshire's traditional half-timbered housing. The layout comprises groups between 8 and 18 dwellings built around mews courts, which are linked by a footpath system. A strong edge is given to the development by locating the flats which peak to four storeys along Redshank Lane.

Admirals Road, Oakwood, WA3 (1981). *Terry Farrell Partnership.* This scheme is located adjacent to Birchwood Brook and woodland and was planned to have three distinct areas. Separated by green spaces, these groups of 30 to 35 dwellings built along village lanes were conceived by the architects as "places". The houses were designed to be flexible with a "universal core" common to each dwelling containing the services, stairs, kitchen and bathroom. Thereafter they were flexible and capable structurally of being extended as individual residents wanted.

[1] Colquhoun, I, and Fauset, P.G., Housing Design: an International Perspective, pp. 96–97; [2] Ibid, pp. 94–95; AJ, 13/9/78, pp. 471–485; AJ, 21/1/81. pp. 94–96; AJ, 8/12/82, pp. 37–41; AR, 10/85, pp. 46–55.

Sunningdale Community Project, Chapelhill Road/Hopfield Road, Wirral, CH14
1988. Brock Carmichael Associates R. Leasowe/Birkenhead

When, in the mid-1960s, the four towers on the Sandbrook Lane Estate in Moreton were proposed, the local newspaper commented that they would bring a touch of Manhatten to the West End [1]. By the mid-1980s, the blocks had deteriorated and drastic measures were required.

The solution determined for the 15-storey Wheatfield Heights was to refurbish it. This included over-cladding to reduce energy costs and converting its 85 flats into sheltered housing for elderly people. The nearby maisonettes were demolished and replaced with 24 two-storey flats and four new shops facing the street. They were grouped to create

Figure 3.53 Sunningdale Community Project.

a large landscaped courtyard, which accommodates car parking, and pleasant well-used communal gardens and a summerhouse. First floor flats have balconies overlooking the courtyard from where intruders are instantly noticed (Fig. 3.53). There is a communal meeting hall at the entrance to the courtyard, which is controlled by a 24-hour watch.

AJ, 3/8/88, pp. 33–47; [1] Ibid., p. 34; *BB*, Spring 88, p. 14.

Cumbria

New Village, Harriston, Aspatria, Allerdale, CA7
1978. Napper Errington Collerton Partnership. R. Aspatria

Harriston was built as a mining pit village but by the 1970s it had declined so seriously that, with the exception of a small number of buildings, it needed complete renewal. The new houses built by Allerdale District Council comprised 70 three- and four-bedroom houses, 6 flats and 20 mobility standard bungalows They were designed in the from of simple cottages grouped around a large green to give the feel of a Lakeland village (Fig. 3.54). The white roughcast blockwork walls, Welsh and Westmorland slate roofs and window and door detailing are all common to the area.

AJ, 9/1/80, pp. 76–90; *AJ*, 16/1/80, pp. 129–139; RIBA Northern Regional Housing Group, *Housing North*, p. 7.

Regeneration of George Street and Queen Street, Whitehaven, CA28
1975–1984. Winskell Barnett, 1992–2002: SRB Dockland Project. R. Whitehaven

The centre of Whitehaven represents a unique piece of urban history for it survives

CHAPTER THREE • THE ENGLISH REGIONS

Figure 3.54 Harriston: regeneration of a Cumbrian village.

as England's first Renaissance planned town conceived in the seventeenth century and mainly built in the eighteenth century. Laid out by Sir John Lowther, a friend of Sir Christopher Wren, as a coaling port for his mines, Whitehaven became a fashionable town with streets of fine Georgian housing.

By 1960, the centre of the town had become a picture of decay and dereliction as the local economy declined. In the mid-1970s, the Old Town Centre was designated an outstanding conservation area which enabled Copeland District Council to seek funding from the Department of the Environment for improvement. It then made 75 per cent grants available to stimulate housing improvement and initiated the redevelopment of cleared sites. The new housing in Queen Street/George Street, completed in 1975, retained the essential architectural character of the eighteenth century housing; colour-washed rendering, stone architraves around windows and shallow-pitched slate roofs (Fig. 3.55). Further phases followed in the 1980s in George Street/Scotch Street, and in Duke Street/Queen Street.

AJ, 1/10/70, pp. 658–661; RIBA Northern Regional Housing Group, *Housing North*, p. 17.

Webster's Yard, Highgate, Kendal, LA9
1989. Hanson Walford Marston. R. Kendal

Webster's Yard shows how new sheltered housing for elderly people (in this instance for sale) can be woven into the fabric of old towns producing an exceptional living environment. Fortunately the local planning authority accepted 25 per cent car parking which enabled a dense scheme appropriate to the site to be achieved.

The scheme is entered from Highgate where existing four-storey buildings were restored and converted into shops with flats above. From here there is a central pedestrian route that passes through a series of courtyards and steps up a steep slope to the lane at the rear of the site. The first courtyard is New Inn Yard, which is a long narrow stone paved space containing 36 sheltered dwellings designed in the form of three-storey stepped-back flats and maisonettes. A conservatory (Fig. 3.56) divides New Inn Yard into two parts and gives access to communal facilities and a lift. Beyond this is the small Lower Yard around which are eight sheltered

Figure 3.55 Whitehaven: regeneration of the Georgian centre.

flats and the Upper Yard containing four houses fronting on to the rear lane and a further eight flats. The scheme included the relocation of the Dowker Arch originally built in 1833.

The materials – second-hand Welsh roofing slates and rendered blockwork which is now the substitute for stone in Cumbrian housing – reflect the Lakeland tradition.

AJ, 24/5/89, pp. 34–45.

Liverpool

Liverpool wrestled with its housing problems throughout the twentieth century and this has continued to the present day. In the 1990s, the **Liverpool Housing Action Trust (HAT)** both demolished and renovated tower blocks and developed new housing for people affected by the clearance, including extra care sheltered housing for elderly people. The current issue of large areas of unwanted pre-1919 terraced housing, particularly in the north of the city, is being addressed by the **New Heartlands Housing Market Renewal Pathfinder**. In contrast, the new housing market in the city centre is thriving as can be seen in areas around Duke Street. To cap this, the city succeeded with its bid to be European Capital of Culture 2008. A number of Liverpool's housing successes follow.

New Build Co-operative Housing, Liverpool
From 1978. Innes Wilkin Ainsley Gommon; The Wilkinson Hindle Halsall Lloyd Partnership; Brock Carmichael Associates; McDonnell Hughes; R. Liverpool Lime Street

---

The co-operative housing movement began in Liverpool during the early 1970s with tenant

Figure 3.56 Sheltered housing for elderly people at Webster's Yard, Kendal.

management buy-outs from private landlords in order to seek improvement grants. The co-ops grew in strength in the early 1980s out of opposition to the militant City Council's housing policies. A number of tenants groups were not prepared to wait to be rehoused by the City Council. Instead, they formed housing co-operatives to procure their own new housing. In June 1983, they held a protest march to the City Council and successfully secured support and building sites at no cost. The government seized the opportunity to demonstrate its own new found housing philosophy and personal support came from Michael Heseltine then the Secretary of State for the Environment.

The co-ops ranged in size from 20 to 60 family units. Supported by one of Liverpool's co-operative development agencies, they registered as a non-equity housing co-operative with limited liability. When the houses were completed the co-op members became tenants paying standard fair rents but they were also collectively the landlord, responsible for management and maintenance. Three of the most innovative co-ops were those at Weller Street, Hesketh Street and the Eldonian Village.

The **Weller Street**, **L8**. R. *Liverpool Lime Street/St Michaels*. The co-operative, established in 1977, pioneered a participative approach to design, producing simple two-storey houses grouped around small landscaped courts. The process was most significant. The co-operative organised itself into sub-committees to consider design, education, social events, etc. Design decisions evolved through a process of education involving visits to schemes, slide shows, and "planning for real" at weekly design meetings. It took 2½ years, which is a long time to maintain people's interests.

Newland Court, **Hesketh Street**, **L17**. R. *Liverpool Lime Street/St Michaels*. Development began in 1979 as a consequence of the clearance of housing in Liverpool 8 from where tenants joined with families who had once lived at Hesketh Street to form a co-operative based on Hesketh Street. The scheme comprised a range of dwelling sizes from two- to seven-bedrooms designed around landscaped courts. The co-op was anxious to avoid the "Corpy" image which included avoiding an over landscaped look (Fig. 3.57).

The Eldonian Village, **Vauxhall Road/ Eldonian Way**, **L3**. R. *Liverpool Lime Street/ Sandhills*. The Eldonians were the most well known co-operative at the time particularly because they received personal support from Michael Heseltine in securing funding for their scheme. The architecture has a traditional private sector image with a high degree of individuality (Fig. 3.58).

The Eldonians have moved on considerably beyond their initial housing objectives into the wider field of urban regeneration. They have established a commercial garden centre as an employment generation project, developed other forms of skill training to help people find work, and converted an old warehouse into a sports centre.

AJ, 8/9/82, pp. 51–58; AJ, 18/7/84, pp. 35–42; 45–50; AJ, 8/8/84, pp. 18–19; AR, 4/85, pp. 57–61; RIBA/CIOH, *Tenant Participation*, pp. 48–49; Colquhoun, I., *Urban Regeneration*, pp. 89.

Minster Court, Crown Street, Liverpool, L7
1984. Kingham Knight Associates. R. Liverpool Lime Street

Minster Court was one of the first projects to demonstrate the potential for converting unwanted inner city council flats into private housing for sale. It was built by Liverpool City Council in the 1930s and its design was very much influenced by European inner city

CHAPTER THREE • THE ENGLISH REGIONS

Figure 3.57 Hesketh Street co-operative housing.

Figure 3.58 Eldonian Village: pioneer of co-operative housing.

development of the time particularly in Amsterdam. By the 1960s, the flats had degenerated and demolition appeared to be the only solution. However, Barratt Urban Renewal (Northern) Ltd. purchased the blocks for a peppercorn amount.

They enclosed the court by blocking off the former archways and constructing new walls and railings that limited entrance to a single point where there was 24-hour security. This created an internal courtyard from which the dwellings were entered. Access to upper floor flats was by newly constructed, brightly lit, glazed staircases towers, which served a small number of dwellings on each floor. A new roof, paintwork and street lighting all added to the appearance of the scheme. It proved very popular (Fig. 3.59).

DOE, Housing Design Awards 1985, p. 58.

213

Figure 3.59 Minster Court, Liverpool: 1930s council flats converted to private sale.

3-12 Old Haymarket, Liverpool, l2
2000. Arkheion Architects (Developer: Urban Splash). R. Liverpool Lime Street

Old Haymarket was the first joint venture project undertaken by Urban Splash in partnership with the Maritime Housing Association. The scheme of three refurbished buildings and one new block is located on a triangular site in the heart of the centre of Liverpool (Fig. 3.60). It comprises 27 mixed-tenure apartments – a number of the dwellings were sold by Maritime on a shared-ownership basis to attract a variety of people to the development – and twelve retail units on the ground floor. The dwellings are entered through a courtyard, which was beautifully paved. The design took maximum benefit of existing features, especially the red brick elevations.

www.buildingforlife.org

Manchester

Manchester's housing renaissance began in the 1980s at **Castlefields** where new development and beautifully restored warehouses, converted into business and residential uses, nestle with canals and railway viaducts. The Central Manchester Urban Development Corporation was the catalyst

CHAPTER THREE • THE ENGLISH REGIONS

Figure 3.60 Urban Splash at Old Haymarket, Liverpool.

but much initiative came from creative entrepreneurs, such as **Urban Splash**, whose creative spark in the early 1990s has led to much transformation. Nearby at **Hulme** a whole new neighbourhood is nearing completion; its Urban Design Guide formed the basis for Manchester's City Development Guide.

Lately the emphasis has moved to the north-east to **Great Ancoats** and the **New East Manchester** regeneration area which is planned to realise 12,500 new homes, primary and secondary schools and 130,000 sq.m. of business and retail space, and triple the population from 27,000 to more than 90,000. Two guiding objectives are driving New East Manchester – active community participation in redevelopment, including a say in who the development partner will be, and the creation of living neighbourhoods rather than housing estates (*RIBAJ*, 10/06, pp. 38–42).

Hulme Redevelopment, M15
1991–1998. R. Manchester Deansgate Unless Otherwise Stated

The redevelopment of Hulme was seen at the time as a model for the sustainable urban neighbourhood of the future. The main housing developers were a consortium of housing associations led by Guinness Trust and North British (NBHA), and Bellway Urban Renewal.

The scheme was pump-primed in 1991 by a successful City Challenge bid of £37.5 million

215

for major infrastructure and environmental works to start an extensive programme of housing renewal, economic and social regeneration. The total capital investment drawn in by this exceeded £200 million. The plan involved the demolition of over 2,500 deck-access dwellings including the notorious "Hulme Flats" and building over 1,250 new rented dwellings and a further 2,000 houses for sale by Bellways.

The planning and design commenced with the production of an Urban Design Guide which set out the vision for the area and the major urban design principles, which were as follows:

- Development of streets which promote sociability, community and natural surveillance, all designed to limit traffic speeds to 20 mph.
- Permeability, that is, a neighbourhood that is easy to move around in with strong links to surrounding areas.
- A sufficiently high density to support a wide range of shops and services.
- Development which is sustainable environmentally, socially and economically by encouraging energy efficiency, recycling, public transport and urban ecology, and allowing the area to adapt to future change.
- A street hierarchy using three-storey housing along the principle routes and two storey on residential streets.
- Careful treatment of corners, vista and landmarks – the traditional points of reference in the city.
- Dwellings to achieve a National Housing Energy rating of 9.
- Residents to fully participate.

These principles have produced a variety of colourful social housing designs. The private housing is rather plain and the best is the three-storey town houses overlooking the new Hulme Park. Overall the development will need high-quality maintenance, particularly the external environment. Regrettably, it lacks finish as undeveloped land stands unused which works against everything that has been achieved so far.

Aquarius, Aquarius Street (1995). *Ainsley Gommon Wood for Guinness Trust, R. Oxford Road.* This development contains 68 houses and 97 flats for rent, designed in three-storey form around courtyards but closely relating to the street pattern. The glass-fronted circular staircases to the flats are distinctive.

St Wilfred's, Mary France Street (1994). *NBHA's in-house architects for NBHA.* The curved facades of the two- and three-storey terraces flow with the street grid and are punctuated at corners by a range of features such as communal entrances, balconies and special windows (Fig. 3.61). The public square at Mary France Street is a green space with railings in the manner of a London square.

Boundary Lane/Bonsall Street (1995). *OMI Architects for the Guinness Trust, R. Oxford Road.* This scheme is in the form of three- and four-storey rectangular blocks with a five-storey circular tower marking the entrance to the scheme on Boundary Lane. A second phase has 41 dwellings and 2 shops.

Mallow Street. *NBHA in-house architects for NBHA.* This scheme contains 83 dwellings. These are built in along streets with a multi-coloured brick aesthetic. The corners are strongly emphasised with three-/four-storey towers.

Chichester Road (1994). *PRP and Triangle for NBHA.* This is a development of 55 houses and 83 flats. The family housing is in two- and three-storey form whilst in the south-east corner the site, flats, with balconies form a prominent gateway to the whole of the Hulme area.

Homes for Change, Old Birley Street (1996). *Mills Beaumont Leavey Channon. R.*

CHAPTER THREE • THE ENGLISH REGIONS

Figure 3.61 St Wilfred's, Hulme: finely curving terraces following the street pattern.

Oxford Road; second phase: C. Cooper (URBED). Planning began in 1991 when the Guinness Trust was approached by Hulme residents and small businesses to develop a mixed-use scheme. The result is a most distinctive scheme (Fig. 3.62) comprising 50 flats and maisonettes and 1,500 sq.m. (16,000 sq.ft.) of managed workspace – including shops, offices, studios, a small performance area which doubles up as a meeting room and a cafe – in a four- to six-storey urban building. The workspace, built in a shell-and-core format to allow varying sizes and configurations of units, is confined to the two first floors and has its own external entrances. The dwellings above are reached through a secured courtyard via open access decks. The second phase completes the enclosure of the courtyard.

Rolls Crescent/Halston Street, **M15** (1997). *ECD Architects.* Commissioned by North British Housing Association this scheme contains 67 dwellings designed in a traditional low-rise street pattern with brightly coloured towers punctuating the corners and intersections of Rolls Crescent (Fig. 3.63). All houses have private gardens

22/6/06, p. 47; *BD*, 3/2/06, p. 13; *R&R*, 28/7/06, p. 8; www.buildingforlife.org

South at Didsbury Point (between Cavendish Road and the Princess Parkway, A5103), Didsbury Point, M20
2006. Masterplanners: EDAW Europe. Architects: Calder Peel Partnership; Manchester. R. Burnage (from Manchester Piccadilly); Metro link from Manchester

This is a good example of urban housing – "an urban village" [1] – in a suburban location designed to a density of 59 dwellings per hectare (24 dw/acre) with a car parking ratio of 1.3 per dwelling. The project, built by Countryside Properties, comprises 414 dwellings for sale in two- to four-storey development including up to five-bedroom family houses, two-storey apartments and ground floor apartments designed for people with physical disabilities. None were affordable as it was considered there was a sufficient number already in the area.

The masterplan envisaged neighbourhoods of street housing with a variety of design in each street. Manchester City Council was keen to see existing trees preserved and new ones planted – often as street trees, which, with a lively planting policy, has resulted in a very green environment. Building materials used – red brick, white render and cedar cladding – are bright and colourful and enhanced by large windows and balconies (Fig. 3.72). Local materials and the local workforce were used as much as possible in accordance with Countryside Property's policy on sustainability.

[1] www.buildingforlife.org

Figure 3.72 "Urban village", South at Didsbury Point, Manchester.

Number One Deansgate, Beetham Tower, 303 Deansgate, The Edge, M3
2002–2006. Ian Simpson Architects. Broadway Malyan R. Deansgate

Three glass residential towers in close proximity of each other at the northern end of Deansgate are new landmark buildings, which make a significant contribution to the regeneration of this part of the centre of Manchester.

Number One Deansgate (*Ian Simpson Architects*) was part of the redevelopment of the centre of Manchester after the IRA bomb explosion on 15 June 1996. It is a mixed-used scheme developed by Crosby Homes comprising two distinct elements – a retail podium above which is a glazed triangular residential tower containing 84 apartments on 14 floors. The tower is clad with a double skin façade of glass. The inner is a fully sealed, double-glazed aluminium framed window system that provides the weather resistant envelope and the necessary thermal and acoustic requirements. The outer skin to all except the top floors is an unsealed single clear glazed louver system. Each apartment has access to the semi-external terrace formed between the inner and outer skins (*AT Detail*, 1/02, p. 12).

The Edge (*Broadway Malyan*) has a similar triangular profile to Number One Deansgate, cascading from 20 to 10 storeys on a site overlooking the River Irwell. The scheme, developed by Countryside Properties, comprises 275 apartments, two external courtyards and gardens on a podium above car parking, and mixed uses at ground level.

The Beetham Tower (*Ian Simpson Architects*) (see Fig. 3.47 on page 202) is a clear reflection of Manchester's confidence in the future. It is 155 m (500 ft) tall and has 47 floors. It contains 219 residential apartments, office space and a 279-bedroom Hilton Hotel. The four-storey podium at the base of the tower contains the public rooms of the hotel. The apartments start on the 24th floor and there is a mix of one- to three-bedrooms apartments. With its simple glazed rectangular, stepped profile, the building is a unique landmark for the city (*AR*, 6/06, p. 40; *Prospect*, 10/04, p. 29).

Plymouth Grove PFI, Ardwick, M13
2007. PRP Architects. R. Piccadilly/Ardwick

The regeneration of Manchester's Plymouth Grove Estate by M. J. Gleeson, the Harvest Housing Group and the Nationwide Building Society was the first development of its kind in the UK to be funded through a (£100 million) Private Finance Initiative (PFI). The estate was built in the 1970s and comprised 1,050 local authority dwellings, most of which were two-storey flats and houses. The layout was Radburn with cars and pedestrian separated. It was notorious for crime and vandalism, guns, drugs and low demand. Its alleyways were rat runs down which the offenders could disappear even in the daytime. Furthermore the estate looked inwards which heightened the sense of social exclusion felt by residents. At the beginning of the project in 2003, 400 dwellings were unoccupied.

The remodelled estate was planned to be an urban village with a 50:50 split between private sale and social rented housing to create a social mix of people. To achieve this, a third of the estate – 450 homes – was demolished, with 650 new homes for outright sale to be built over 3–5 years. The rest have been refurbished, with many dwellings turned round to front onto roads and improve security. Rat

Figure 3.73 Estate regeneration at Plymouth Grove, Manchester.

runs have been eliminated and a new mile-long Home Zone (known as the Green Route) created where children can play in safety. This includes three parks along its length. A new village centre with shops and offices with housing above were all part of PRP Architects' masterplan which set out to create a balanced and sustainable community (Fig. 3.73).

PFI as a means for funding housing regeneration has regularly been questioned. Gleeson's response is to claim that they have a committed financial interest in ensuring the estate does not fall back into its old ways after the building work is complete: the introduction of a large number of houses for sale is an important part of their long-term strategy.

B, supplement: 2006 Regeneration Awards, p. 35; Regenerate, 3/2007, pp. 16–17.

OLDHAM

Selwyn Street Housing and Coppice Park, Oldham and Rochdale Housing Market Renewal Pathfinder, Coppice, Oldham OL8
2006. TADW Architects and Crumlin Lonsdale Landscape Architects. R. Oldham Werneth

Selwyn Street was the first new scheme by the Oldham and Rochdale Housing Market Renewal Pathfinder and was developed by the Great Places Housing Group. It is a model example of new street housing in urban areas (Fig. 3.74). The site formerly contained houses and flats built in 1986, which were very small for the large families living in the area (mainly of Asian origin) and the layout had no relationship with the original nineteenth century street pattern.

CHAPTER THREE • THE ENGLISH REGIONS

Figure 3.74 Urban street housing at Selwyn Street, Oldham.

The scheme comprises 18 family homes at a density of 53 dwellings per hectare (21 dw/acre). A variety of tenure was offered – ten were for rent, four for shared ownership, and four for market sale. The dwellings are all large with overall areas ranging from 99 sq.m. (1,064 sq.ft) for a four-bedroom house to 158 sq.m. (1,700 sq.ft) for a seven-bedroom house. The houses are L-shaped, taking their form from the earlier Islington Square development which Great Places had found successful (pp. 219–221). All dwellings have individual carports and small gardens as preferred by the residents. A huge retaining wall was built between the two rows of terraces to cope with the steeply sloping site. The housing's image is bright and modern with mono-pitched roofs, white rendered upper storeys and finely designed metal gates and railings (Fig. 3.75). The attention to detail includes the design of the entrance doors with colourful tiled surrounds adding to the doorstep appeal.

Solar panels and wind turbines were installed on the roofs but photovoltaics were rejected due to the long payback periods. Grey water is recycled. A new urban pocket park adjoins the development providing a place for children's local play.

Nearby at **Malton Street** is a further scheme of terraced family houses for Great Places by TADW Architects featuring bold red, yellow and orange coloured frontages, and top eco-rating. TADW Architects also designed an excellent scheme of urban infill housing at **4–8 Market Place** and **107 Mealhouse Brow**, **Stockport SK1** (2007. R. Stockport).

R&R, 22/9/06, p. 8; *Regenerate*, 01/07, pp. 42–43; *Inside Housing*, 26/1/07, p. 11; www.buildingforlife.org

SELWYN CLOSE/COPPICE PARK

Figure. 3.75 Selwyn Street: layout of houses and adjacent park, by courtesy of TADW Architects and Crumlin Lonsdale Landscape Architects.

Salford

Salford Quays, The Quays, M5
1985. (Masterplanners) Shepherd Epstein and Hunter. 2005. (Architects) NV Buildings, 2005: Broadway Malyan; Waterside at the Lowry, 2005: DLA Architecture Ltd. M. from the Centre of Manchester

The masterplan for Salford Quays, prepared in 1985, envisaged the regeneration area being developed on a three way split between housing, commercial uses and leisure. Considerable success came in the 1990s from securing the Lowry Centre, designed by Michael Wilford (after the death of his partner James Stirling), and Daniel Libeskind's Imperial War Museum. The Quays housing (Vancouver, Winnipeg and St Lawrence Quays), built in the 1990s, is well laid out and well-detailed externally with block-paved streets and mature planting.

In the mid-2000s, Countryside Properties developed three high quality, 17-storey towers with curved front façades (NV Buildings) along the waterfront of Huron Basin (Fig. 3.77). These contain private apartments for sale that proved very popular to purchasers.

The "Waterside at the Lowry" is an 11-storey tower accommodating 165 apartments and penthouses just across the water from the Lowry Centre. It stands on a two-storey podium of retail shopping and car parking which is finished with natural sandstone ashlar masonry. The tower is clad with panels of pre-cast concrete coloured to match the stone.

Prospect, 10/04, p. 29; *Planning*, 3/11/06, pp. 14–15.

CHAPTER THREE • THE ENGLISH REGIONS

Figure 3.76 Salford Quays: quality high-rise towers for private sale (Broadway Malyan).

Southern England

BERKSHIRE

Point Royal, The Green, Rectory Lane, Easthampstead, Bracknell, RG12
*1961–1964. Philip Dowson and Derek Sugden of Arup Associates.
R. Bracknell*

This 18-storey block of flats in Bracknell with circular partly underground parking, is one of the most distinctive architectural features in any of the English New Towns. It comprises 102 flats above ground floor entrance podium with six flats on each floor, central lift lobby and ground floor entrance. It has a striking polygonal form with one convex and one concave side, all suspended by dramatic thrusting cantilevers from the narrow ground floor podium (Fig. 3.78).

It is particularly noted for the precise and refined quality of the pre-cast external frame and its generous glazing. The car park and ground floor are constructed in board marked reinforced in situ concrete with sloping brick outer sides to a ha-ha. The detailing emphasises the modelling potential of the material, with features such as rainwater gargoyles, circular columns, slab support walls and splayed soffits treated with visual consistency. The tower is Grade II listed.

AJ, 13/5/64, pp. 1099–1112; EH, *Something Worth Keeping (New Town Housing)*, p. 7.

Figure 3.77 The Ryde, Hatfield: one of the great housing schemes of the twentieth century (p. 253).

CHAPTER THREE • THE ENGLISH REGIONS

Figure 3.78 Point Royal, Bracknell: a landmark feature in the new town.

The Liberty of Earley House, Lower Early, Reading, RG6
1996. PRP Architects.
R. Earley

This scheme is typical of the many sheltered housing developments built by local authorities and housing associations to meet the needs of the growing numbers of elderly and frail elderly people now often in their 80s and beyond. This project caters for all needs from low to high dependency where a 24-hour caring service is required. It was designed as a Category $2^1/_2$ Sheltered housing project (with Extra Care) but is run as a Registered Care Home.

It contains 30, unfurnished two-person self-contained flats and six bedsits. The provision of communal and ancillary accommodation, including assisted bathrooms, lounge (Fig. 3.79), central catering kitchen and dining room, enables special care registration to be sought on a flat-by-flat basis, or for the whole project. The attractive lounge has a high sloping ceiling and large windows looking into the central garden. Each floor has its own common areas and facilities and there is a guest bedroom for use by relatives.

Figure 3.79 Liberty of Earley sheltered housing for frail eldereople: morning coffee in the lounge.

The building is U-shaped (Fig. 3.80) and the planning of the circulation space avoids central corridors, which allows seating areas to be provided in bay windows along the corridors from which the beautifully planted central garden (Fig. 1.21) can be fully appreciated.

BUCKINGHAMSHIRE

The Turn, Middle Turn, Turn End, Haddenham, Nr Aylesbury, HP17
1968. Peter Aldington. R. Haddenham and Thame Parkway.

This small group of three houses had a profound influence in the late 1960s as architects looked for design approaches to replace the modernism of the high-rise council estate. Peter Aldington was keen that the housing should be sympathetic to, and enhance the village in which the houses were located, without resort to pastiche. The outcome was a design that was sensitive and most appropriate. The interplay of roofs, the use of clay tiles and white walls, simple stained timber openings particularly caught the imagination of architects (Fig 3.81). The houses were planned around courtyards to obtain south and west sunlight and maximum privacy. The spatial quality of the interiors is superb with high sloping ceilings, changes of level and a wealth of colour from the materials used in the building and the fabric of the house. Mud

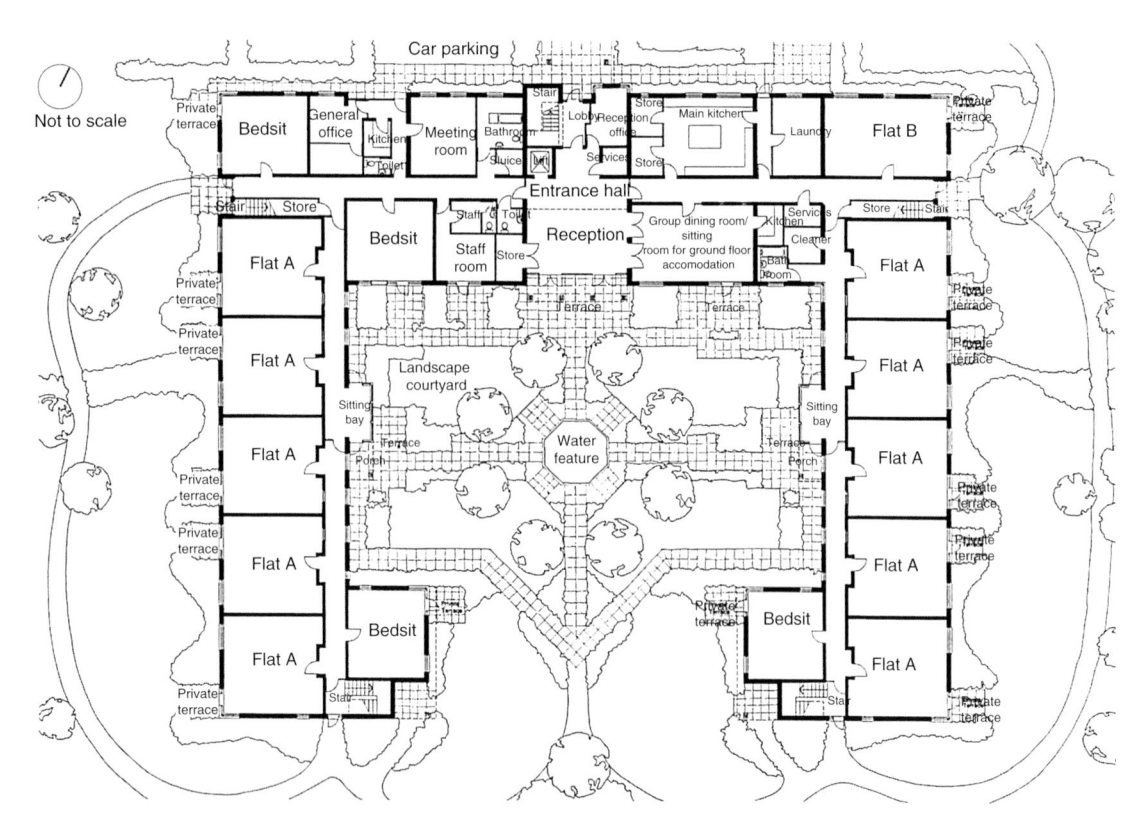

Figure 3.80 Liberty of Earley designed around a well planted courtyard garden (from PRP Architects, *Place and Home: The Search for Better Housing*, Black Dog Publishing, 2007, p. 82).

brick tile capped walls around the perimeter of the site were integrated into the design.

The garden to the Aldington's own house is a secret delight and its relationship to the house is superb (Fig. 3.82). During warm weather the glazed wall around the courtyard opens to create an extra living space. The scheme was Grade II listed in 1998 and upgraded to Grade II* in 2006. English Heritage commented on the design, "it is an exceptional and influential example of the reworking of local vernacular precedent and plan forms to create modern village housing" [1].

[1] *EH*, p. 12; *AR*, 8/68, pp. 102–105; *AR*, 9/89, pp. 71–76; *AJ*, 2/9/70, pp. 532–536; *RIBAJ*, 10/96, pp. 56–62; *Concrete Quarterly*, 7–9/68.

Lyde End, Bledlow, Nr Princes Risborough, HP27

1977. Aldington & Craig; Project Architect Paul Collinge (Private Transport Required)

The site for these five houses was owned by Lord Carrington, the former Foreign Secretary, who set the brief for the development and maintained a personal interest. He wished to provide high-quality housing to rent for village residents, which would make a contribution to and form part of the village. However, he considered it best to rely upon the architect to determine the sizes of the dwellings and how many would fit on the site. The houses are single-storey except for the two-storey house at the

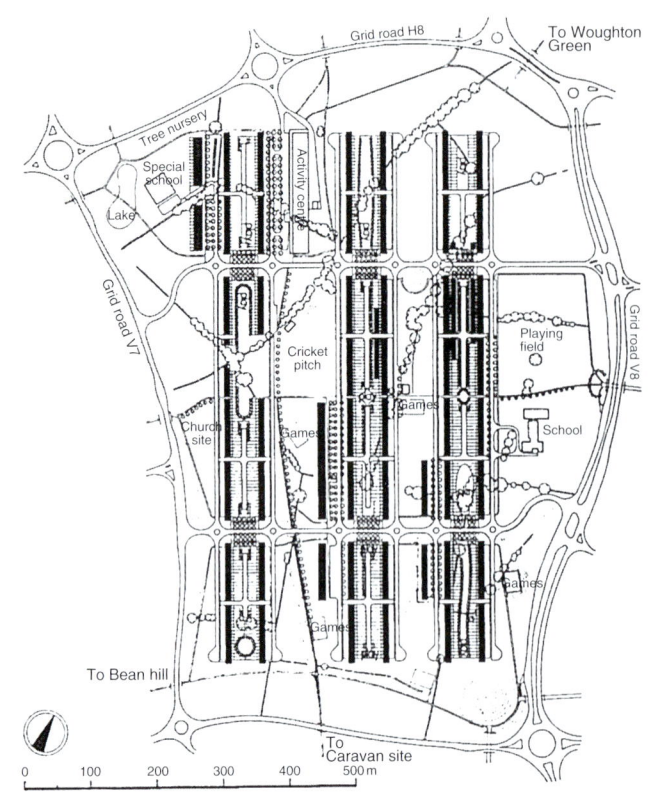

Figure 3.86 Milton Keynes: layout of Netherfield (AJ, 10/12/75, p. 1250).

Figure 3.87 Early terraced housing in its now mature landscape setting.

Figure 3.88 Waterside development at Peartree Bridge.

was created in two loose concentric rings of housing which cluster around a vehicular court in the centre where the cars are parked under tiled roof car ports (*AR*, 9/78, pp. 243–246).

MKDC Architects' designs for **Neath Hill** (1980) (Fig. 3.89) marked a great change to more traditional layouts. The main roads follow the contours in large curves, of which two- and three-storey brick dwellings with pitched roofs are grouped around short brick-paved mews courts (Fig. 3.90) (*AJ*, 4/2/76, pp. 229–233; *AJ*, 15/04/81, pp. 691–706).

France Furlong, **Great Linford** (1979). *MacCormac and Jamieson.* This development reflected Richard MacCormac's interest in suburbia as the residential convention of the twentieth century (*AR*, 10/85, pp. 53–54). It is a cozily familiar scheme built in brick and tiles with timber windows, but with a relatively structured layout. The setting back of pairs of semi-detached houses along the curving main street to create parking courts is an effective

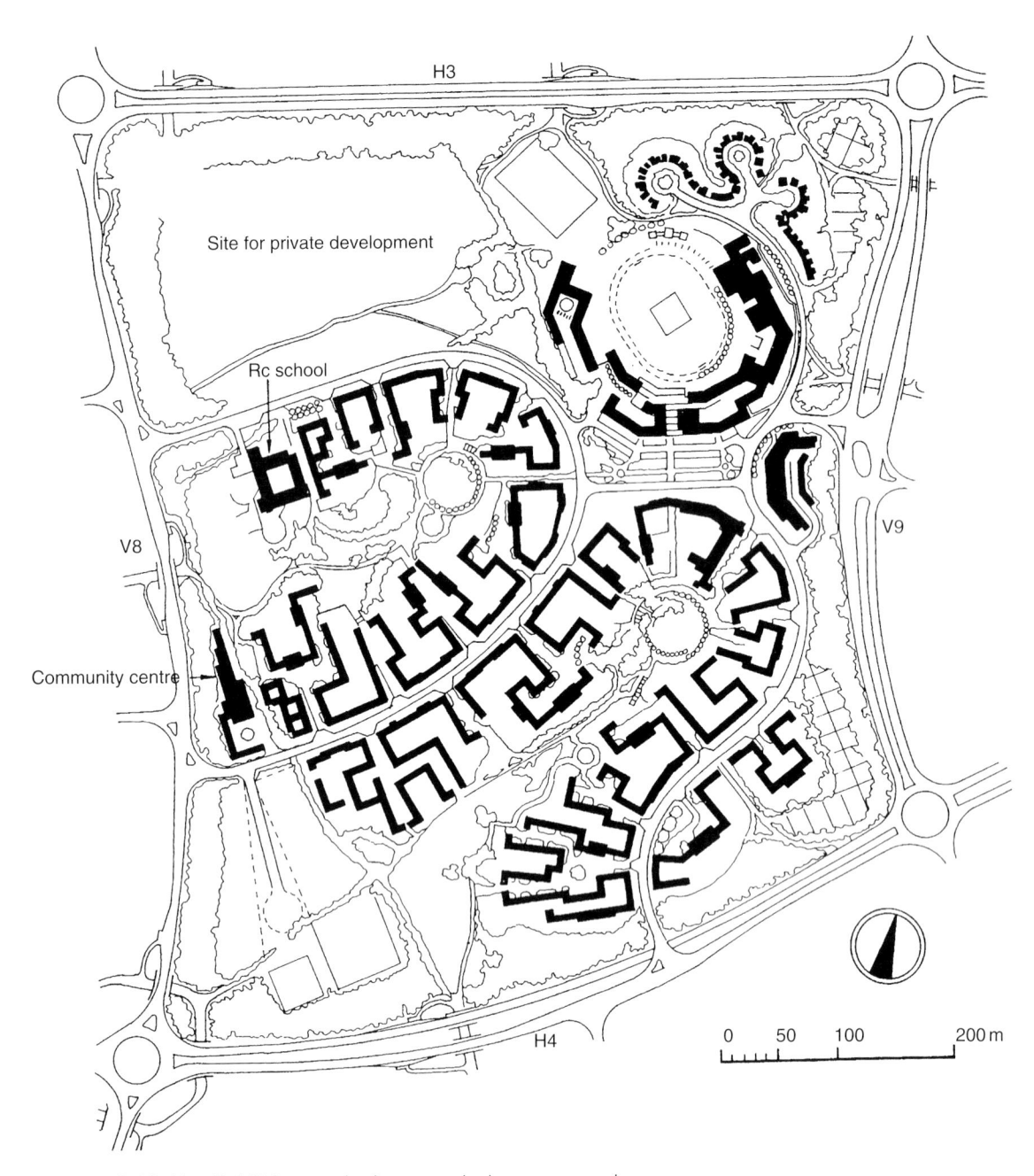

Figure 3.89 Neath Hill forecasted a new design approach.

way of minimalising the impact of parked cars on the street (AJ, 1/10/80, pp. 627–629).

Colquhoun and Miller's **Oldbrook 2** (1982) has a formal layout with the 250 dwellings grouped around well-detailed and planted block-paved courts. The "floating" roof over the bedroom loggia is a generous feature giving a useful external space at the top of the houses (Fig. 3.91) (AR, 4/83, pp. 30–35).

CHAPTER THREE • THE ENGLISH REGIONS

Figure 3.90 Mews Court at Neath Hill.

Figure 3.91 Successful high-density housing in a central neighbourhood at Oldbrook.

243

is part of the Broughton settlement being masterminded by English Partnerships as a sustainable urban extension to Milton Keynes, providing housing for more than 1,000 people. The timber-framed scheme was developed by RSL Places for People and provides 229 dwellings for private sale, affordable and intermediate rent in one-, two- and three-bedroom apartments and houses (*B*, Regenerate supplement, 9/05, pp. 50–51; *BD*, 10/8/07, p. 9).

Hampshire

Wyndham Court, Commercial Road, Southampton, SO15
1969. Lyons Israel Ellis. R. Southampton Central

This imaginative block of flats, maisonettes and shops, built on a prestigious city centre site in Southampton, has been Grade II listed. The development is predominately a concrete structure, designed to match the nearby 1930s Civic Centre – one of the most dominant buildings in the city centre. The housing was intended to be for above-average renting to professionals which meant that every detail was designed for a quality finish including the powerful, sculptured form of the building which offsets the fears normally associated with too much exposed external concrete (Fig. 3.95).

EH, p. 6.

John Darling Mall: Supported Housing for People with Physical Disabilities, Boyatt Wood, Eastleigh, SO53
1985. Hampshire County Council Architects (County Architect: Colin Stansfield-Smith, Project Architect: David White). R. Eastleigh

Hampshire County Council Architects Department was best known in the 1980s for

Figure 3.95 Wyndham Court, Southampton, designed to match the Civic Centre.

its school buildings but this project contains all the same qualities. It was built for people who require intensive care to help develop their skills sufficiently for independent living. The building is completely sheltered by a single covered translucent roof, which is particularly suitable for the residents to move around, regardless of the weather, in what appears to be an external environment (Fig. 3.96).

The accommodation includes 24 bedsitting rooms, 6 sheltered flats and shared common space with sitting areas and a large room that can be used for concerts and games (Fig. 3.97). The bedsits, which were intended for short-stay use, are grouped in fives or sixes with shared dining and sitting rooms. The sheltered flats cater for potentially permanent occupation with a generous kitchen/living room, bedroom and bathroom that

CHAPTER THREE • THE ENGLISH REGIONS

Figure 3.96 John Darling Mall, Eastleigh: a peaceful internal garden.

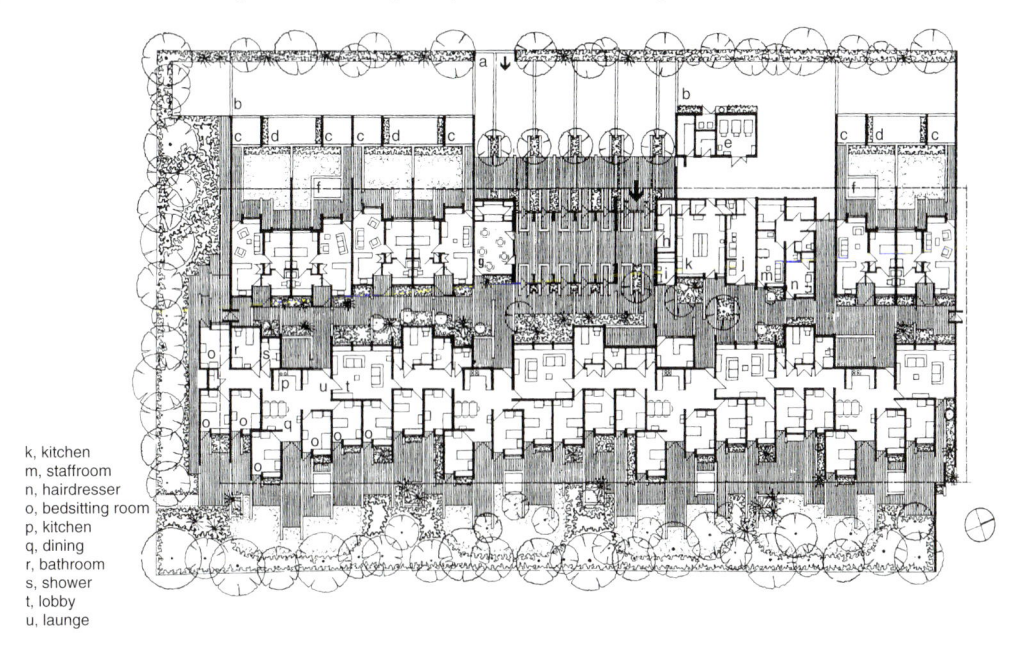

k, kitchen
m, staffroom
n, hairdresser
o, bedsitting room
p, kitchen
q, dining
r, bathroom
s, shower
t, lobby
u, launge

Figure 3.97 John Darling Mall: layout plan.

can be specifically tailored to suit the needs of the individual resident. All dwellings have their own front doors and milk and post is delivered daily. Brickwork is light coloured and the planting was chosen for its all-year quality.

AR, 6/86, pp. 58–61; *BB*, 9/92, pp. 22–23.

247

Figure 3.99 Oakridge, Basingstoke: mixed-tenure housing incorporating shops and community buildings.

housing which were pursued with idealist zeal (Fig. 1.2). Their housing at **Westholm** (1) and **Birds Hill** (2), designed in 1906, is an early example of workers cottages grouped around greens and culs-de-sac. These groups of houses, with their roughcast walls, prominent tiled roofs and picturesque dormer windows and chimneys, show the full variety of Parker and Unwin's early housing design. Other architects involved in designing housing were M.H. Baillie Scott, C.M. Crickman, and Parker's assistants, Cecil Hignett, Robert Bennett and Wilson Bidwell.

The most significant pre-1914 housing in Letchworth is **Rushby Mead** (3). The **Cheap Cottages exhibition** of 1905 attracted wide publicity. The objective was to build housing for agricultural workers at a cost of £150 per dwelling. Some designs demonstrated new techniques to speed up construction. This included building steel and reinforced concrete framed housing rendered externally. In total 114 cottages were built between the railway and **Icknield Way** (4).

Lytton Avenue contains the major part of the 1907 **Urban Cottages exhibition** entries in the section between Gernon Road and Pixmore Avenue (5). The cottages are in pairs or groups, facing a small green and pedestrian cul-de-sac to the west and east of the road.

Information and maps are available at the First Garden City Museum, 296 Norton Way South, which was formerly Barry Parker's office.

CHAPTER THREE ● THE ENGLISH REGIONS

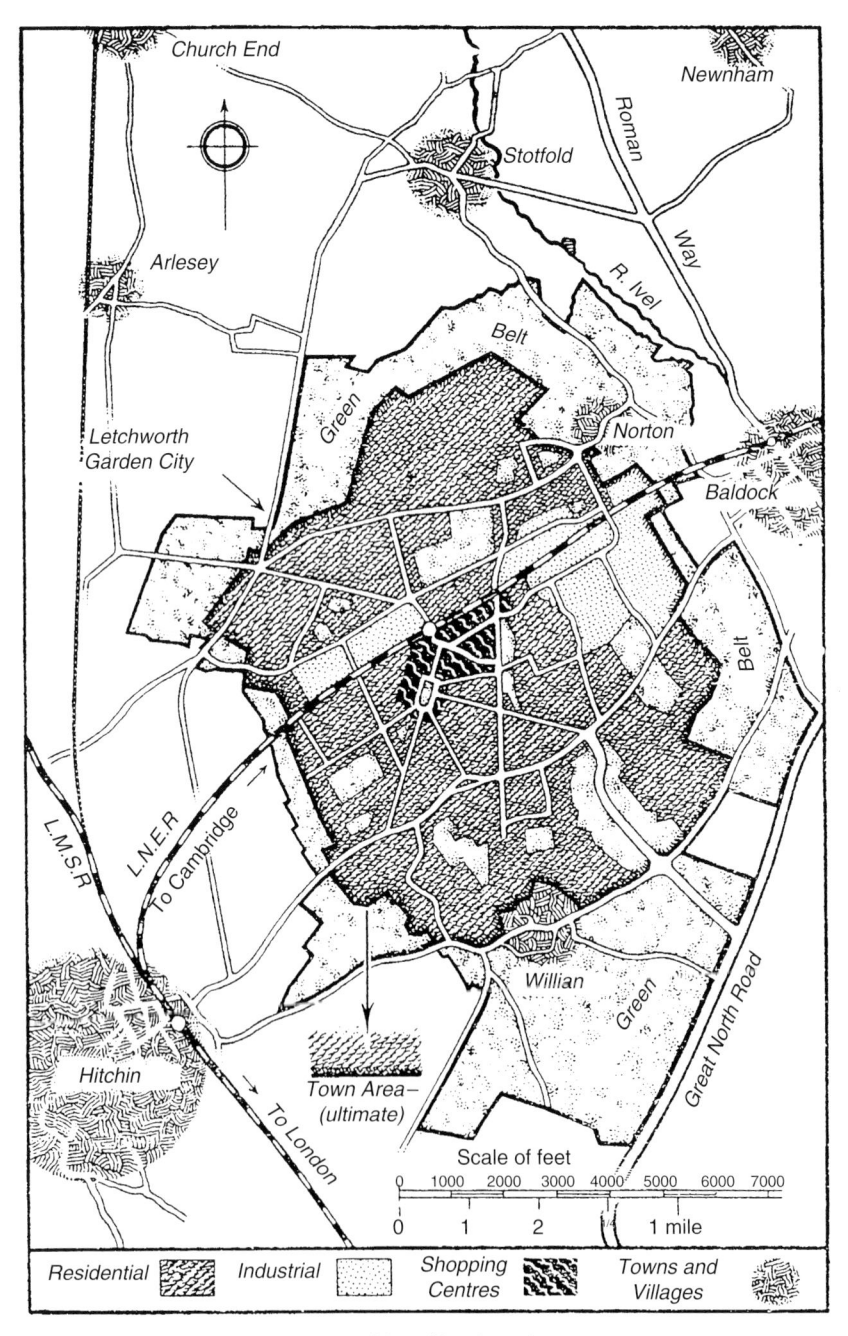

Plan of Letchworth

Figure 3.100 Letchworth Garden City (plan from Garden Cities of Tomorrow (originally Tomorrow: A Peaceful Path to Real Reform, written by Ebenezer Howard in 1898), Faber and Faber, London, 1902, 1946. Also published in Town and Country Planning Association publication, Letchworth Jubillee Edition, Vol. XXI, No. 113, September 1953. Reproduced with the assistance of Letchworth Garden City Heritage Foundation and the Town and Country Planning Association).

Figure 3.101 7–17 (odd) Lytton Avenue (C.M. Crickmer 1907).

Addresses of housing referred to above are:

(1) Westholm: numbers 1–24 and 162–176 (even) Wilbury Road.
(2) Birds Hill (South side): numbers 9–27 (odd) with numbers 2–122 (even) Ridge Road.
(3) Rushby Mead: numbers 2–42 (even), 44–58 (even) by Parker and Unwin, 60–78 (even), 86–144 (even), 103–115 (odd) by Parker and Unwin.
(4) The principal houses of the Cheap Cottages Exhibition, Icknield Way: numbers 123 (steel framed), 217, 219, 212 (listed), 241; Nevells Road: numbers 203, 205, 206, 208, 212, 216, 220; Norton Way North: numbers 7 and 7A (by Baillie Scott and listed); The Quadrant (West Side): numbers 1, 6, 8; Wilbury Road: numbers 122, 126, 248, 150–156 (even) and 160, 158 (reinforced concrete framed house developed by John Brodie, Liverpool City Engineer).
(5) Lytton Avenue: numbers 3, 5, 7–17 (odd), 19–25 (odd) (Fig. 101).

Welwyn Garden City, AL8
Started 1919. Louis de Soissons.
R. Welwyn Garden City

Ebenezer Howard was determined to secure a second Garden City site but he did not succeeded until 1919 with a site just north of Hatfield. Louis de Soisson's Masterplan (Fig. 3.102) of 1919, with its Beaux-Arts-style centre, has changed very little and it still works today. It seems remarkably at ease with the motorcar despite the absence of the road hierarchy that dominates the later new towns. The central gardens provide a strong focus and sense of place for the town as a whole.

houses at 82–124 (even) and 83–125 (odd), Knightsfield (1955–1956) have been Grade II listed. They are three-storey houses, flats and maisonettes, ingeniously designed to mask the complexity of the house types within. The neo-Regency appearance is unusual but carried out with conviction.

In 1948, following the passing of the New Towns Act, Welwyn became a new town and it has now expanded by over 100,000 people but it still remains a beautiful place in which to live.

AR, 2/27, pp. 175–182; Eserin A., *Welwyn Garden City*, The Chalford Publishing Company, 1995, pp. 8–9; Girardet H., *The Gaia Atlas of Cities*, Gaia Books Ltd., pp. 54–55; EH – New Town Housing, p. 7.

Figure 3.102 Welwyn Garden City: plan by Loius de Soisson, 1920 (from Purdom, C.M., *The Building of Satellite Towns*, Weidenfeld and Nicolson, 1925 and 1949; reproduced by courtesy of J.M. Dent, a division of The Orion Publishing Group (London); further tracing of copyright approval unsuccessful).

Louis de Soissons chose the red brick cottage neo-Georgian style of architecture – using clay dug locally as the building material. Although other architects worked on housing schemes and buildings, all designs had to be approved by de Soissons personally, thus ensuring a unique conformity and standard of excellence. The houses in **Parkway** (early 1920s), which overlook the central garden most typify the architectural approach (Fig. 3.103). Much of Welwyn Garden City's housing is grouped around culs-de-sac (e.g. **Handside Close**, early 1920s) to promote the sense of community that Howard wished to achieve. Louis de Soissons's town

The Ryde, Hatfield, AL10
1966. Phippen Randall and Parkes (now PRP Architects). R. Hatfield

Established in 1962 by Michael Bailey, the Cockaigne Housing Group built 28 single-storey courtyard houses with landscaped gardens (see Fig. 3.77 on page 232), a tennis court and a common room for a day nursery and evening activities in what was then fields adjacent to the railway in Hatfield New Town. Cockaine was, and still is a co-operative housing society and most of the members of the group were gathered through a front-page classified advertisement in *The Times*.

The first tasks of the group were to find a site and funding. Michael Bailey wrote of the difficulties of this in *The Listener*: "We tried the Building Societies. They were polite too – but we must understand that in the event of their financing us there must be no new-fangled ideas. The houses must be good traditional semi-detached, of tile and brick" [1]. The scheme was eventually supported by a small number of officials in the Hatfield

Figure 3.106 The Ryde: large windows link the inside with garden and courtyard.

pp. 38–41; Housing Design Awards 2006 publication, pp. 46–49; PRP Architects, *Place and Home: The Search for Better Housing*, Black Dog Publishing, 2007, pp. 132–133 + other pages.

Kent

Span Housing, New Ash Green, DA3
1967-1969. Eric Lyons and Partners. R. Longfield

New Ash Green was the apotheosis of Span's vision, a complete village for between 5,000 and 6,000 people in the rural countryside of Kent, complete with appropriate services and community facilities. The plan approved in 1967 envisaged a mixture of private housing and housing for rent built by the GLC. Span proceeded to develop the housing for sale and the shopping centre but in 1969 when the GLC pulled out Span was left in financial difficulties.

The development was divided into a number of small neighbourhoods of around 100 houses. The Span developments were laid out in typical Lyons manner with short terraces around landscaped pedestrian spaces with grouped car parking (Fig. 3.107). The mono-pitched houses with timber and tiled panels between the party walls remain today almost untouched by time. The benefits of communal maintenance (pp. 22–24) of houses and environment are clearly evident. The landscaping has matured to create a splendid setting. The two-level shopping centre clusters around a linear square and its car parking nestles within a forest of trees and plants.

After the collapse of Span Developments, the rest of the village was completed by Bovis and Architect/Planners, Barton Wilmore Associates.

AJ, 15/5/68, pp. 1109–1114; *AJ*, 23/7/69, pp. 138–140; *AJ*, 8/12/71, pp. 1265–1268.

Ingress Park, Ingress Park Avenue, off London Road (A226) Greenhithe, Dartford, DA9
2001. Architects: Gardner Stewart Architects. R. Rotherhithe

Ingress Park comprises 950 new dwellings, live-work units, shops and a new school on a

CHAPTER THREE • THE ENGLISH REGIONS

Figure 3.107 Unchanged Span housing at New Ash Green.

Figure 3.108 Ingress Park, Kent set a standard for the Thames Gateway.

29 hectare (10.6 acre) site within the Thames Gateway growth area on the south side of the River Thames, about 1 mile east of the Dartford Crossing. It is set in the grounds of the Grade II listed Ingress Abbey that were landscaped by Capability Brown. The brownfield site was formerly used as a marine training college and industrial paper mill. The developer, Crest Nicholson, restored the Abbey, its follies and parts of the grounds at a cost of £6 million which helped offset the amount of affordable housing required to 10 per cent. A key landscape feature of the site is a countryside walk, which integrates Tudor mounds, numerous follies, a tree-lined boulevard, and a grassed amphitheatre (Fig. 3.108) superbly framed by new housing designed to match the Abbey building.

The dwellings range from four-bedroom houses to one-bedroom apartments over garages. A 24 m fall from the top of the site down to the river gives extensive views over the roofs of houses below. The main access road gradually winds down to the river and, off it are eight areas of houses each with its own individual architectural character and materials. Many groups are in crescent form but one was designed to resemble the character of a fishing village. The highest-density housing is at the bottom of the hill fronting formally onto the new riverside walk. The aim of this variety was to give the development an organic feel and break down its overall scale.

AJ, NHBDA Awards Report, 7/06, pp. 42–43; *Green Places*, 6/06, pp. 18–21; *Countryside Voice*, Summer 2006, pp. 84–85; www.buildingforlife.org

---

"Fishing Village", Dunlin Drive, off Pier Road (A289)/Maritime Way, St Mary's Island, Chatham Maritime, ME4
2003. PCKO Architects. R. Gillingham

The Royal Navy pulled all its operations out of Chatham 20 years ago, leaving a vacant 140 hectare (57 acre) riverside site, Chatham Maritime, which is now one of the largest regeneration schemes in the Thames Gateway. By 2015, it will accommodate some 3,000 houses.

St Mary's Island is superbly located with good views over the River Medway. The scheme was developed by Countryside Maritime Limited and provides 53 three- and four-bedroom houses and 100 two- and three-bedroom apartments. No affordable housing was required as there is housing association development nearby. The design draws on traditional Kent seaside village architecture with timber cladding, bold colours and steeply pitched roofs (Fig. 3.109). The layout is organic in form with dwellings mostly grouped around culs-de-sac. The three largest apartments blocks are in a horseshoe shape that wraps along the river frontage. Car parking is at a ratio of 1.5 per dwelling but the design minimises it's impact through parking within courtyards, away from the streets and riverside walkways, or partly hidden away in undercrofts. Elsewhere the houses have small front gardens with on plot car parking and integral garages.

The construction was prefabricated timber-framed because of the skilled labour shortages in the South-East of England. It was the first time the system had been used for

Figure 3.109 St Mary's Island, Chatham: prefabricated timber construction fundamental to the project's success.

volume house building. All timber was from sustainable sources certified by the Forestry Commission. The scheme earned top SAP and "Good" eco ratings from the BRE.

R&R, 9/3/07, p. 23; www.buildingforlife.org

Lacuna, Kings Hill, West Malling, Kent, ME19
2003. Clague Architects. R. West Malling

Lacuna is the central part of the redevelopment of a former Battle of Britain airbase that was owned jointly by Kent County Council and Rouse Kent Ltd. (developers: Sunley). The masterplan proposed 1,850 dwellings, commercial development, a school, community hall, doctor's surgery, nursery, golf course and a hotel.

The scheme contains 180 dwellings with a further 80 by Berkeley Homes. Clague Architects produced a tight village masterplan at an average density of 58.5 dwellings per hectare (23.7 dw/acre) with car parking at a ratio of 2 spaces per dwelling and 1.5 for apartments. The hierarchy of spaces – High Street, squares, back lanes and small intimate areas in front of small groups of houses – reflects Kent vernacular architecture and follows the principles of the *Kent Design Guide* (Fig. 3.110). Eleven basic house types were used in detached, semi-detached and terraced form. These ranged in size from two- and three-bedroom flats to three-, four- and five-bedroom houses The first houses to be built were in brick masonry construction but, due to the high-quality finish required and the shortage of labour, prefabricated timber-framed Super E Homes were imported from

Figure 3.110 Canadian timber-framed housing at Lacuna, Kingshill village centre, Kent.

Figure 3.111 The Cresent, The Village, Caterham-on-the-Hill, Surrey.

Canada. This reduced construction time from 28 to 12 weeks, which had cash flow benefits for the developer. The houses are very energy efficient and have a timber aesthetic that is bright and modern.

Birkbeck, D., and Scoones, A., Prefabulous Homes: The New Housebuilding Agenda (2005), Constructing Excellence, pp. 36–38; www.buildingforlife.org

SURREY

The Village, Caterham-on-the-Hill, Guards Avenue, Caterham-on-the-Hill, CR3
2005. John Thompson and Partners and Barlow Henley Architects. R. Caterham

"The Village" was developed by Linden Homes in the grounds of Caterham Barracks, which was no longer required for military purposes. The scheme was a mixture of new housing and conversion of the existing buildings to accommodate a variety of residential tenures. In total 348 new dwellings were built. Ninety-six of these were affordable and mostly for rent from the Guinness Trust. The entrance to the site is by the restored cricket pitch, which is surrounded by new housing and large mature trees. From here the roads are designed to promote "place" over the car with measures such as changes in surface and speed reducing corners that slow down the motorist. Places have been created in varied urban forms including streets, squares, a boulevard and a crescent (Figs 3.111 and 3.112).

Before the development started, local people expressed concern about the quality of development but this was overcome by involving them in the design including staging community planning weekends. Linden Homes took seriously the need to create a sustainable community by providing playgrounds, a half hourly bus service into Caterham and contributing over £3 million in the Section 106 agreement including the gift of a number of existing buildings to the community. The Caterham Barracks Community Trust set up in 2000 now has facilities for recreational activity, a nursery, further education and training for children and adults. It is also helping to preserve and enhance the natural and built environment, including the site's former chapel. In 2005, the Trust had an asset base of £3 million.

Figure 3.112 The Village: site layout plan demonstrates skilful urban place-making (John Thompson & Partners LLP).

B, Awards supplement 2006, p. 59; B, 14/10/05, pp. 14; B, Housing and Regeneration Supplement, 11/05, p. 58; www.buildingforlife.org

SUSSEX

Self-build Co-operative Housing, Diggers, Golf Drive, Hollingby, Brighton, BN1 and Sea-Saw, Vines Cross Road off Wilson Avenue, Whitehawk, Brighton, BN2
1995. Architype. R. Brighton

The Diggers. This tenant self-build co-operative scheme on a steeply sloping site comprises nine detached and semi-detached houses for rent. Housing Association funding came through the South London Family Housing Association (SLFHA) and CHISEL (Co-operative Housing in South-east London). The co-operative built the scheme as contractors to SLFHA. They earned "sweat equity" from their labour, which could be cashed in if they left, or traded in for additional features in their homes. They chose the Segal method of post-and-frame construction because of its straightforward design and construction methodology. The breathing walls and the grass roofs in the scheme were developments of the method by Architype.

The houses are grouped around a central green with car parking at the edge of the site. The design exploits the slope with a split-level section that opens out on to south-facing conservatories and balconies (Fig. 3.114).

Figure 3.113 Urban regeneration in Calne (p. 280).

Figure 3.114 The Diggers: Segal self-build in Brighton.

The houses are extremely well insulated and energy bills are very low.

Sea-Saw is located at Kemptown on a site alongside Brighton's racecourse. It comprises 24 dwellings, which face south across a hill towards the sea. The use of a single type of house was a requirement of housing association funding but despite this the conservatories and verandahs offer the tenants ample scope for personalising their home.

AT, 2/75, pp. 26–33; AJ, 8/6/95, pp. 37–38; AJ, 7/11/96, pp. 48–50; AJ, 17/7/97, p. 51; AT, 2/97, pp. 26–28.

South-west England

BRISTOL

Bristol waterside development
R. Bristol Temple Meads

Since the early 1980s, Bristol has made a significant mark in regenerating its waterside heritage through the conversion of former warehouses and other buildings into housing and the construction of new development on vacant sites. There are interesting groups selling for upwards of £150,000. The local Asley Vale Action Group which initiated the scheme and identified potential self-builders originally intended similar house designs but the eventual plot owners preferred individual solutions (Fig. 3.119) whilst agreeing to use a common set of materials and eco objectives which included:

- House construction of timber frame and, with few exceptions, materials from category A – the most environmentally sustainable category – of the BRE's Green Guide.
- Thermal insulation standards generally of 250 mm in walls – 100 mm more than the building regulations at the time. Most have gone for insulation based on recycled paper.
- Use of photovoltaic solar collectors, providing up to 23 kwh of electricity for the whole site.

The original scheme also included a site for six sheltered housing units and the conversion of the former office block on the site into community workshops. Regrettably, neither had come to fruition by 2007. Nevertheless, despite set backs, on the original ideal the scheme is a great achievement and a significant lesson to other groups of people intending to go down the same route.

R&R, 25/3/05, pp. 20–21. *The Guardian* (G2 supplement), 12/4/07, pp. 18–19.

DEVON

Waters Edge, Bridge Road, Shaldon, TQ14
2004. Harrison Sutton Partership. R. Teignmouth.

Waters Edge is an excellent example of regeneration in a small town and design that respects the local architectural character in a simple and tasteful way. The scheme comprises 43 houses for sale and 7 affordable houses and apartments. The density achieved was reasonably high at 42.4 dwellings per hectare (17 dw/acre) with a car parking ratio of 1.5 spaces per dwelling. Key spaces are a riverside walk with a row of houses overlooking the estuary (Fig. 3.120) and a small green within the scheme which relates perfectly in scale to the houses around it). The dwellings were designed specifically for the

Figure 3.119 St Werburgs self-build housing, Bristol.

CHAPTER THREE • THE ENGLISH REGIONS

Figure 3.120 Waters Edge, Shaldon, Devon: design reflects local urban form and materials.

site. Their walls are rendered in white and pastel shades of colour found locally. The use of Devonian sandstone and red ochre rendered walls, particularly in the parking courts, greatly enhanced the scheme. Further interest comes from lifting the height of some of the ridges and the variety of chimneys.

The first design for the development was refused by the local planning committee, which was upheld at an inquiry. The developer, Midas Homes Ltd. responded by engaging the local community in the next stages of design and giving a number of Section 106 benefits to the local area such as the affordable dwellings and financial contributions to education and open space. Midas Homes has grown in stature considerably since this experience. Its schemes at Gun Wharf, Plymouth (pp. 277–279) and Broadclose Farm, Bude, Cornwall EX23 (Fig. 3.121) (Architects: Trewin Design Partnership) were both winners in the 2007 Housing Design Awards.

Housing Design Awards 2007 publication, pp. 20–23, 28–31; B, 20/7/07, p. 49; www.buildingforlife.org

---

Oak Meadow, Livarot Walk, South Molton, nr Barnstaple, EX36
2005. Gale & Snowden. R. Private Transport Necessary

This is a most interesting scheme of 35 houses and flats on the edge of a village

269

Figure 3.121 Broadclose Farm, Bude, Cornwall (photo: Midas Homes).

in South Devon. Built by the Devon and Cornwall Housing Association the affordable housing incorporates a host of environmentally friendly features in addition to the use of a large amount of timber from green sources for the construction. Most significant is the twin frame system. This enables very thick layers of insulation to be used which reduces heat loss and cold bridging. The houses are in terraced form to minimise the amount of external walling and heat loss. They are naturally ventilated and windows are triple glazed. Some houses even have larders, which are naturally cooled, to the temperature of the surrounding earth to cut down on the size of refrigerators needed by individual households.

The layout ensures the best orientation for the dwellings. High-quality timber fencing, which matches the timber houses, and turf screening (Fig. 3.122) provide privacy in rear gardens. The simple treatment of the roads and footpaths with simple standard curbs and timber bollards and fencing helps the scheme fit into its rural setting.

Inside Housing, 23/6/06, p. 47; *B*, Supplement: *Sustainability Awards 2005*, p. 47.

Dorset

Rural Housing: Abbotsbury Glebe, DT3; Redlands Farm, Broadwindsor DT8; Bryanston Hills, Blandford St Mary, DT11
1997, 1992/1993 and 2005. All schemes by Carey Morgan Architects Ltd. (formerly Ken Morgan Architects). (Private Transport Necessary)

A number of recent housing developments in Dorset villages illustrate a good understanding of how to achieve high-quality design in rural areas.

Abbotsbury Glebe, on the eastern edge of the village was commissioned by the Raglan

Figure 3.122 Oak Meadow, South Molton, Devon: sustainable rural housing.

Housing Association and the Diocesan of Salisbury. It comprises 22 two- and three-bedroom rented and shared equity houses and 8 four-bedroom houses for sale. They were built in a mixture of local stone and render, with a combination of thatch and slate roofs. All have chimneys (Fig. 3.123). At the entrance to the scheme, a terrace built at an angle fronts on to the main village road. Behind this terrace the other houses are grouped along a new street and around a village square. The design and detailing of the roads and footpaths reflect the typical village wall-to-wall hard surfaced space (Fig. 3.124). Cross-subsidy was essential to secure affordable rents – the builder/developer produced the social elements of the scheme for a price specified by the Housing Association and the Diocese and, in return, the land for the freehold element was sold to the developer for a price at the bottom of the local market. An overriding condition was that the houses should only be occupied by local people (*Building Homes*, 14/6/91, pp. 20–22).

Broadwindsor also reflects the local village vernacular of stone, rendering, thatch and slate and benefited from cross-subsidy (Fig. 1.28). It contains 14 two- and three-bedroom houses for rent, 26 two-, three- and four-bedroom houses for sale and one house for the vendor. The scheme links two existing roads in the village with a new street, contrary to the highway engineer's preference for culs-de-sac.

Bryanston Hills, Blandford St Mary is laid out along village lanes with buildings defining the spaces. The housing is simple in design and finished in a variety of coloured rendering and brickwork with emphasis on creating individual or small numbers of dwellings

Figure 3.123 Rural housing at Abbotsbury Glebe, Dorset.

(Fig. 3.125). The planners insisted on two landmark "folly" buildings, one as a gateway to the development and the other as a "signpost" to the scheme for drivers skirting past on the bypass. The latter has a cupola to twin with the nearby church of St Peter and St Paul in Blandford St Mary. The lanes have tight corners to slow traffic down. Parking is within the curtilage and in rear mews parking courts, which contain a number of houses to ensure natural surveillance of parked vehicles. Every front garden was planted as part of the scheme to make the lanes appear leafy. The scheme was commended in the 2005 Housing Design Awards (Housing Design Awards 2005 Publication, pp. 46–47).

Poundbury by Dorchester, DT1
Started 1993. Developer: Duchy of Cornwall. Masterplanner: Leon Krier. Coordinating Architect: Percy Thomas Partnership, Bristol. R. Dorchester

The new Poundbury development on the western edge of Dorchester has been the focus of much debate due to the involvement of HRH, the Prince of Wales. Leon Krier's

CHAPTER THREE • THE ENGLISH REGIONS

Figure 3.124 Abbotsbury Glebe: axonometric drawing of site layout.

Figure 3.125 Rural housing at Bryanston Hills, Blandford St Mary, Dorset.

273

masterplan is based on a Continental urban grid of boulevards laid out in a classical manner. The total development is envisaged to contain some 3,000 dwellings with neighbourhoods centred on a formal square surrounded by civic buildings designed in the manner of Greek temples and Italian Renaissance towers. It will be mixed use with housing, workshops, employment and shopping within which all the housing will be in walking distance of communal facilities. The village will take 25 years to build which its promoters consider will enable it to grow organically.

The first phase contains 250 dwellings, 50 percent of which are owned by the Guinness Trust (Fig. 3.126). Fifteen or more architects have been involved, each being responsible for a small area only to avoid an estate image. The layout reflects urban-villages principles and despite criticism of the architecture being pastiche, is most innovative. An important feature is how the road system "engages" traffic. Instead of excluding or calming traffic, it is "civilised" within a permeable layout of urban spaces of human scale, which avoid long vistas that allow drivers to accelerate. The streets have been designed as coherent spaces from house wall to house wall in the style of the traditional village (Fig. 3.127). Residents contribute communally to the quality of this space by designing and maintaining plants and flowers in a narrow strip of garden in front of their house. Junctions have tight radii to reduce speeds and limited sight lines to make drivers slow down or stop. Car parking and garages for a provision of two spaces per dwelling plus visitor parking is catered for in street parking on wider roads and in garage/parking courtyards at the rear of the houses. Some of the larger courtyards include housing to provide natural surveillance and reduce the possibility of burglary from what would normally be a highly vulnerable location. Where houses abut open space they are designed to overlook it, or a substantial wall provides privacy to rear gardens.

RIBAJ, 11/95, pp. 6–11; *B*, 15/9/89, p. 60.

Walpole Court, Puddletown, nr. Dorchester, DT2: sheltered housing for elderly people
1985. Sidell Gibson Partnership. R. Dorchester

The inspiration for the English Courtyard Association came from Noel Shuttleworth in the mid-1970s when searching for accommodation for his widowed mother. He could not find a place of reasonable size situated in pleasant surroundings, near to shops and amenities, where she could remain independent, feel secure and receive emergency help – and she could pay for it out of a modest fixed income. His solution was for himself to build sheltered housing of which Walpole Court is a fine example.

The scheme contains 23 two- and three-bedroom cottages and flats grouped in the form of the traditional alms-house courtyard (Fig. 3.128). The first phase of development centred on the conversion of a beautiful nineteenth century mellow brick and stone cottages and stables, with bell tower and spire. This forms one side of the courtyard. The second phase and main part of the project is grouped around two other sides of the courtyard (Fig. 3.129). The architecture blends with the traditional local vernacular and materials. The grounds are landscaped to create the atmosphere of a country house garden or College courtyard. These are maintained by a couple employed as warden and caretaker who live in a flat near the entrance to the scheme.

Each of the cottages offers a high degree of flexibility of use dependent upon the extent of physical disability of the occupant(s). Ground floors have shower/w.c. and stairs

CHAPTER THREE • THE ENGLISH REGIONS

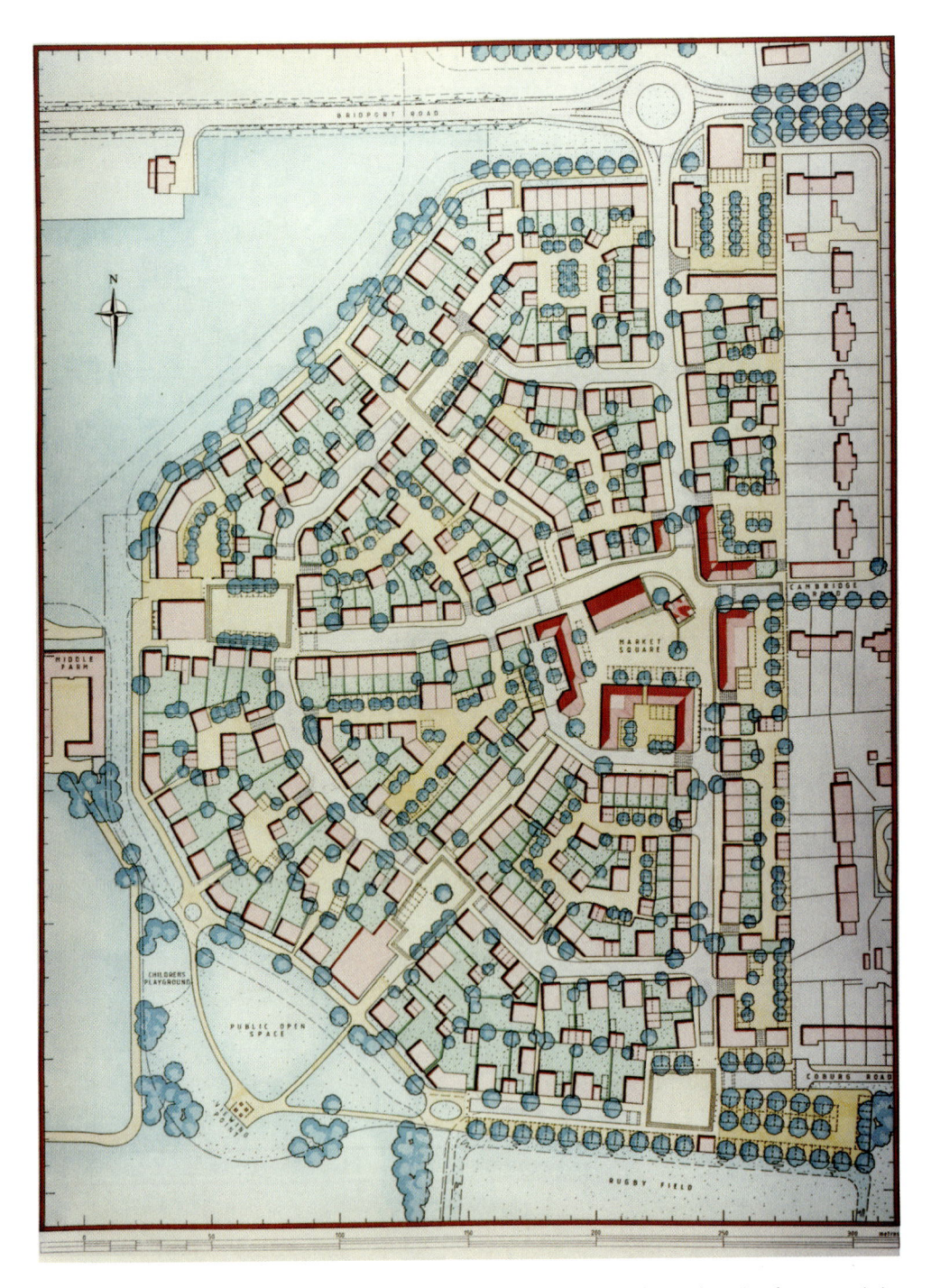

Figure 3.126 Poundbury: layout of the first phase, laid out around a network of spaces into which vehicles have almost full access (plan by Alan Baxter & Associates and published in DETR, Places Streets and Movement. 1998, p. 30, Crown Copyright).

275

Figure 3.127 Poundbury by Dorchester: vision of HRH Prince Charles and Leon Krier.

Figure 3.128 Walpole Court, Puddletown: modern lifestyle for elderly people in a traditional almshouse setting.

CHAPTER THREE • THE ENGLISH REGIONS

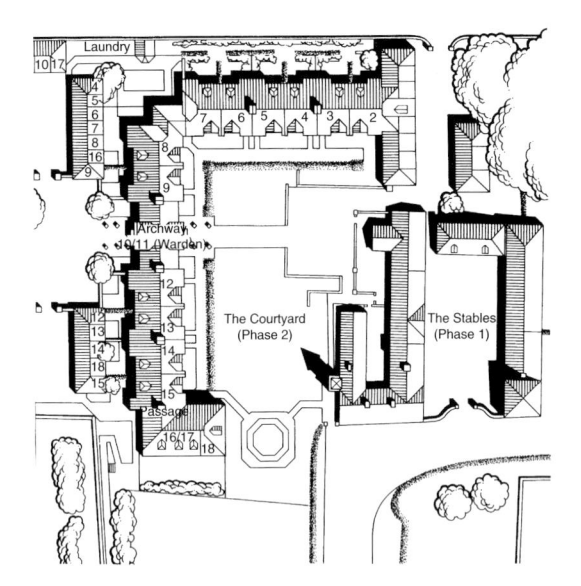

Figure 3.129 Walpole Court: site layout.

which accommodate stairlifts giving residents several choices of living arrangements as they become more frail. The extra bedrooms allow for couples to sleep separately if necessary and to accommodate live-in help when needed. All windows are set to lower level to allow a good view out when sitting down.

AR, 10/85, pp. 56–61; B, 30/10/87, pp. 30–35.

GLOUCESTERSHIRE

Rural Housing, Ebrington, nr Chipping Campden, CV36
2005. Percy Thomas Partnership. Private Transport Necessary

This small infill development of 17 houses, built by Westbury Homes in a North Cotswold village, demonstrates how new housing can be successfully integrated into the fabric of an old village. The site was the yard to Home Farm, which was the only building on the site to be retained. Five of the new houses face on to the village street, eight onto a new lane that runs through to the bottom of the site (Fig. 3.130) where a further four form an edge to the development. Four of the houses are affordable: two front onto the village street and two are within the courtyard behind.

The scheme was designed in accordance with the Cotswold Design Guide and the character and proportions of the existing village. There is a mixture of storey heights from one-and-a-half to maintain the scale of Home Farm Cottage to two with low eaves. Four houses are two-and-a-half-storeys to provide a change of scale. A variety of building materials was used for the construction of the houses including ashlar stone, rough-cast render, natural slates, brown clay tiles and pantiles. The timber windows are either casement or sash. Dormer windows have gabled, hipped roofs or flat leaded roofs. All the houses have chimneys constructed to local details. The new lane was designed as a shared access way. This and other groundworks have a natural feel as if they had been there forever. All dwellings have grass verges at the front and some have trees in front gardens. Rear gardens are screened by high natural Cotswold stone walls and garages are skillfully integrated into the layout to relate directly to house plots.

AT, 5/05, pp. 50–55.

PLYMOUTH

Gun Wharf, Cannon and Cornwall Street, Devonport, PL1
2006. Lacie Hickie Caley Architects. R. Devonport.

Gun Wharf is a mixed-tenure scheme on the site of a former 1950s housing estate in one of the country's 39 most deprived neighbourhoods. It was developed by a partnership

277

Figure 3.130 Rural housing at Ebrington, Gloucestershire.

between Devon and Cornwall Housing Association, the South West Regional Development Agency and Midas Homes. The scheme comprises 99 dwellings: 35 for private sale, 46 for rent and 18 for shared ownership affordable housing. The dwellings range from one- and two-bedroom apartments and two-bedroom maisonettes to two- to four-bedroom houses. The density of development was 43 dwellings per hectare (17/acre).

The scheme considerably lifts the area. "It has a sense of character – it is a genuine place, not an estate" [1]. The site layout aimed at reviving the historic character of the area, lost during the Second World War, by creating a Georgian circus (Fig. 3.131). Streets were designed as homezones to ensure a pedestrian friendly environment. The main street in the development drops gently down the site framing the views of the River Tamar below (Fig. 3.132). Much of the success of the scheme comes from the modern use of trad-itional materials – slate roofs, stone and timber cladding, white render and large windows – and the way the modelling of the houses and the distinctive rooflines reflect changes of level. The floor design uses cobbles from the site and skillfully accommodates 93 car parking spaces on street and in bays.

Local residents were greatly involved in the design process, and participation included "planning for real" and the selection of the architects, all of which helped bring the community together. The scheme was the Medium

CHAPTER THREE • THE ENGLISH REGIONS

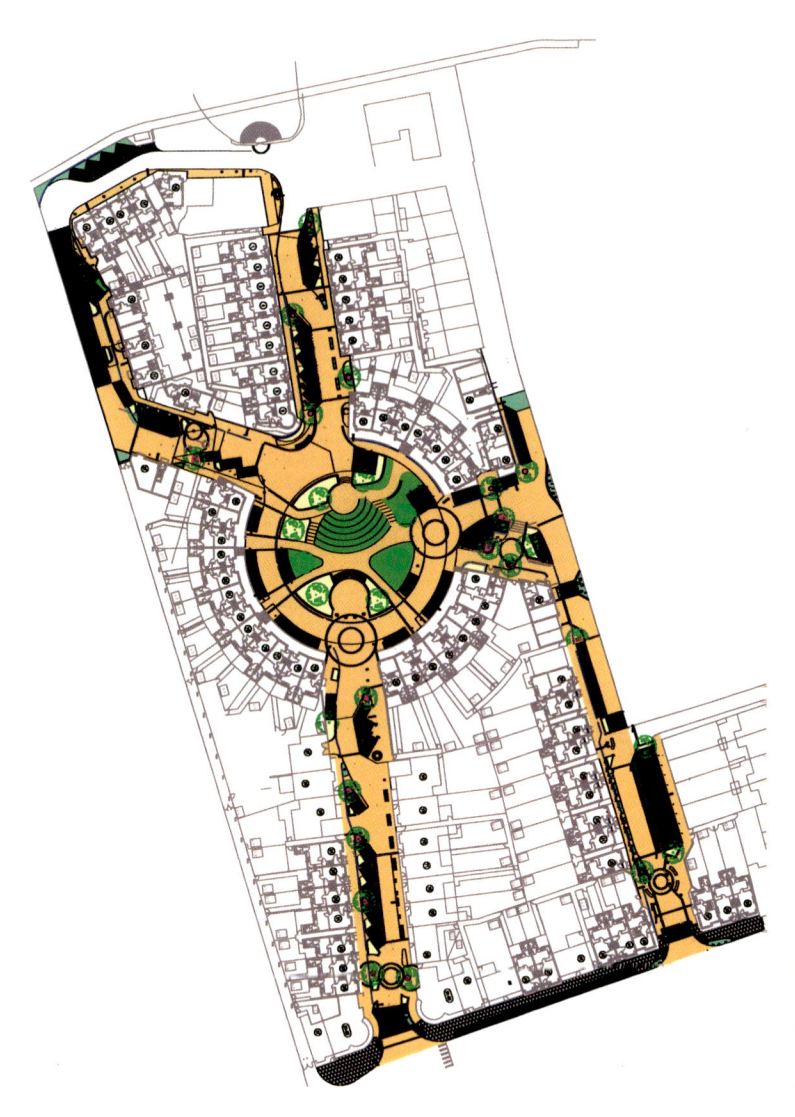

Figure 3.131 Gun Wharf: site layout plan (plan by Lacie Hickey Caley Architects reproduced by courtesy of Midas Homes).

Housebuilder winner in the 2007 Housing Design Awards.

[1] Michael Manser, *AJ*, NHBDA Report 7/06, pp. 38–39, 50–51; *BD*, 28/4/06, p. 11; *B*, 12/5/06, p. 22; B, supplement: 2006 Regeneration Awards, p. 35; Housing Design Awards 2007 publication, pp. 20–23; *B*, 20/7/07, p. 48; www.buildingforlife.org

SOMERSET

Bridge Care, sheltered housing for elderly people, St John's Road, Bath BA1

1991. Fielden Clegg Architects. R. Bath

Bridge Care is a residential home for 32 frail elderly people built on a site overlooking the River Avon. The design uses the slope of the

Figure 3.134 Crown Street Buildings against the Grade 1 listed Corn Exchange, Leeds (p. 290).

Figure 3.135 Bridge Care: lunch-time in the communal hall/dining room.

in their own homes. Secondly, the gardens are immaculately cared for by the warden's husband, which has proved preferable to contract maintenance. Finally, the presence of a 24-hour resident warden on site is vital to the scheme's success – residents are looked after until they can no longer do so themselves when alternative living arrangements are made by relatives or by the Association.

B, Housing Design Awards 1993, 11/93, p. 17.

Yorkshire and Humberside

BEVERLEY

Market town housing, Beverley, HU17
R. Beverley

The central area of the small market town of Beverley possesses a number of extremely well-designed private and housing association developments that contrast markedly with the speculative housebuilders estates on the periphery.

Globe Mews, **Dog** and **Duck Lane** (1982). *David Ruffle Associates*. Built by Tallishire Limited, this scheme demonstrates that there is sound commercial potential in developing urban sites with compact high-density housing for sale (Fig. 3.137). The layout followed a design brief drawn up by the local planning department. The houses are a mixture of two- and three-storeys grouped around a tight mews court of Essex Design Guide proportions. Each has its own small walled garden at the rear. The massing of the buildings and the varied roofline combined with the screen walls and garages are very much in scale and character with its location. The use of integral garages has enabled a high density of 29 dwellings per acre (72 dw/ha) to

Figure 3.139 New rural settlement, Scalebor Park, Burley-in-Wharfdale.

16 stone clad larger properties and three blocks of housing in converted former hospital buildings. The parking ratio is 0.6 spaces per dwelling located in groups or on street with some garages integral with the housing – very low for such a rural location. The density of the square is 35 dwellings per hectare (14.5/acre). The communal spaces and planting is managed on behalf of the residents at an annual charge of around £200 per year. The project shows the popularity of a formal historical set-piece. The selling price for the dwellings in mid-2004 was between £266,000 and £410,000, which placed the development far beyond the reach of most of the existing rural community.

www.buildingforlife.org

Kingston upon Hull

In comparison with other cities in the north of England, Hull has been slow in developing its extensive waterfront, yet it was one of the first to convert warehouses into housing in the early 1980s along its mediaeval High Street. The Deep "submarium" by Terry Farrell, which stands at the entrance to the River Hull from the Humber, is a focus for what could be achieved. There are now plans to build 3000 new dwellings in the city centre and tackle its severe housing problems through the Gateway Housing Market Renewal Pathfinder.

During the 1980s and 1990s, Hull developed three highly innovative housing projects for the time. The creation of a new

CHAPTER THREE • THE ENGLISH REGIONS

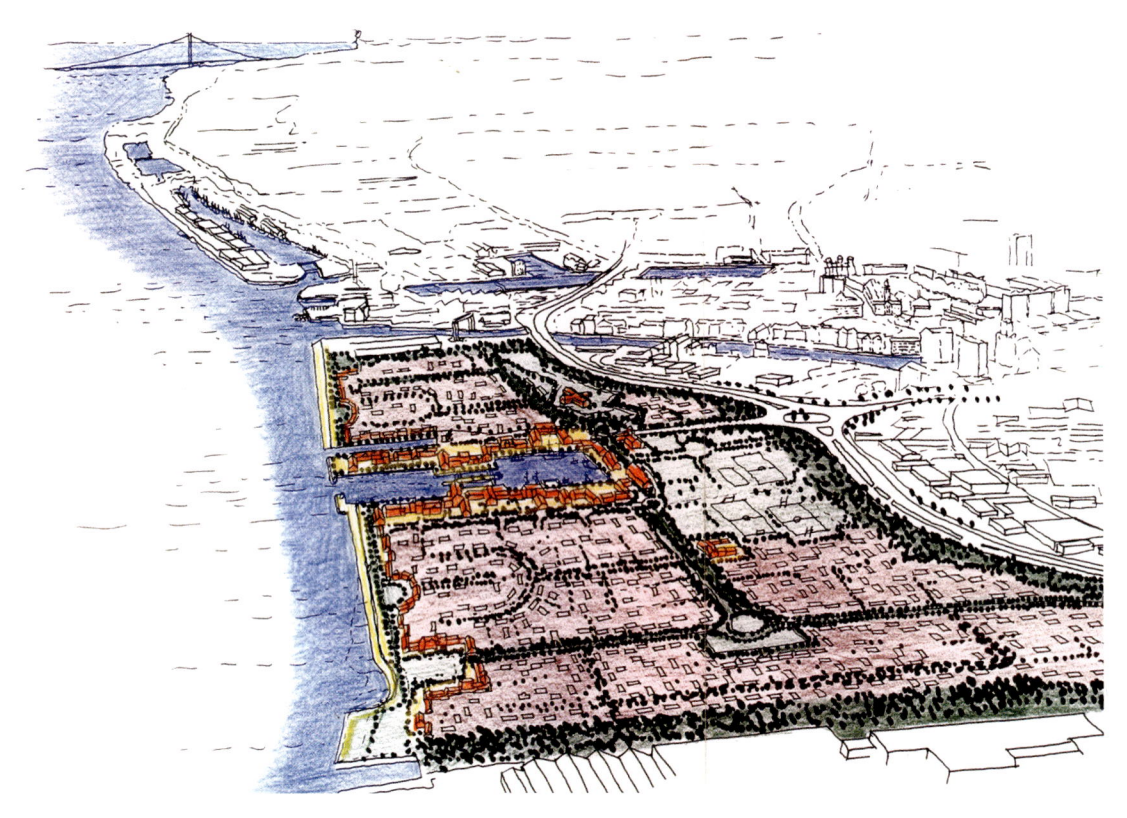

Figure 3.140 Victoria Dock, 1986 concept drawing (Hull City Architect's Department).

1,200 dwelling village at **Victoria Dock**, South Bridge Road, HU9 by Bellway Urban Renewal (Architects: Hull City Council Technical Services Department and Brown Smith Baker) included the reconstruction of 2 miles of river promenade and a new park (Fig. 3.140). The joint venture project at **Gipsyville** (Askew Avenue, HU4) with Keepmoat Ltd. (Masterplanners: Hull City Council Technical Services Department) regenerated an inter-war council estate, retaining and improving half the existing housing whilst clearing the rest and redeveloping the sites with private housing. Half of Keepmoat's profits from the sale of new private houses were ploughed into improving the Council housing. Both schemes have been successful in raising quality of life and encouraging people to continue to live in the city (B, Regenerate (supplement), 4/06, pp. 26–33).

North Hull Housing Action Trust, Greenwood Avenue, HU6
1999. Brown Smith Baker and Partners (Hull); Hull City Council Technical Services Department; Gammond Evans Crichton Ltd; Hurd Rollands Partnership; The Wilkinson Hindle Halsall and Lloyd Partnership. R. Hull Paragon

---

The third achievement for Hull in the 1990s was the designation of the North Hull Estate, in 1992, as the first of six, Housing Action Trusts (HAT) in Britain. Its task was

287

Figure 3.141 North Hull HAT: transformation of an inter-war cottage estate.

to improve 2000 inter-war, cottage-style houses and develop approaches to social and economic regeneration. Tenants participated extensively in the design process, and the refurbishment of the houses and environment has been implemented to a very high standard (Fig. 3.141). In addition to the mandatory improvements – re-roofing, new doors and windows, damp proof courses, dry-lining internally, etc. – most tenants were offered the opportunity to select their own additional improvements from a menu of choices ranging from rear porches, to French windows, wall lights, higher-quality kitchen units, and many more. Each item was valued on a points system and the choice could be made up to an agreed level. A small number of new houses were built to accommodate young people and families who were living with their parents and needed their own accommodation.

The physical improvements were supported by social and economic initiatives to raise the level of personal awareness, health and self-esteem, particularly on the part of women. Training and education to enable people to acquire employment skills and education opportunities were made available. Some local people worked for the contractors or for the HAT itself. The "exit strategy" included the establishment of a Community Development Trust to continue the social/economic development and ensure the sustainability of the investment.

LEEDS

Chapel Allerton Town Street redevelopment, Leeds LS7
1970. Leeds City Architects. R. Leeds.

This small scheme in an old village that was encompassed long ago by the city of Leeds contrasted greatly with much of the other local authority housing built in the early 1970s. The houses now appear somewhat dated but at the time the scheme was much admired, particularly the layout (Fig. 3.142). The previous houses were cleared as part of the city's slum clearance programme but several fine buildings remained on the periphery the site including the Weslyan Sunday School, the Nags Head Hotel, Leak Cottage and The Old House.

The mix for the 38 houses was typical of the time – 25 per cent one bedroom, 45 per cent two bedroom and 30 per cent three bedroom. The housing cost yardstick then allowed garages to be provided on a one for one basis. The key feature of the scheme was the use of the former Town Street for pedestrians only leading to an existing shopping centre to the west and to the local primary school. This was made possible by the construction of three new roads around the site. The informal layout of dark brick clad houses follows the line of the curved pedestrian route and opens out into well-proportioned squares echoing the quiet atmosphere of the former village.

AJ, 1/12/71, pp. 1245–1247.

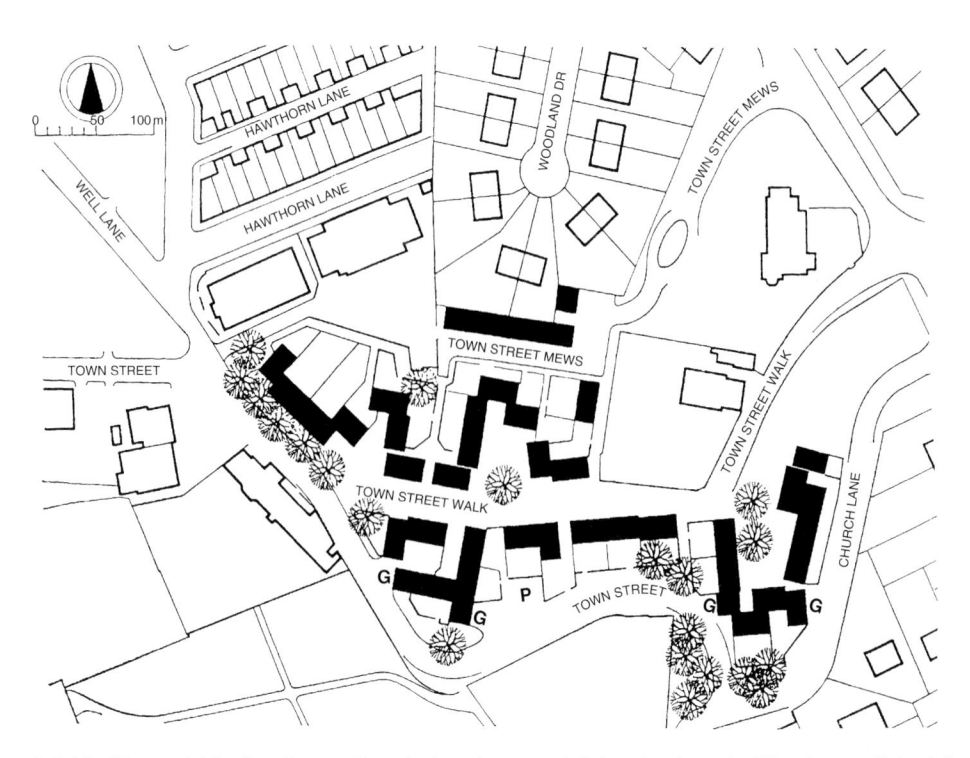

Figure 3.142 Chapel Allerton Town Street development (plan by Leeds City Council Architects from *AJ*, 1/12/71, pp. 1245–1247).

The Calls/Leeds City Centre, LS2 and LS10
From the mid-1980s. Architects as mentioned. R. Leeds

The regeneration of the Calls below the railway was initiated by the Leeds Urban Development Corporation during the mid-1990s (Fig. 3.143). This has been followed in recent years by a massive building of high rise development in the Calls and the city centre generally. (*AJ*, 22/5/97, p. 33).

One of the largest developments is at the refurbished **Clarence Dock** on the River Aire beside the Armouries Museum where there will eventually be 1,100 dwellings in six apartment buildings (*2004 onwards. Masterplanners and Architects, Carey Jones Architects*). Other schemes include the **Fearn's Island Mills** scheme – a mixture of conversion of Grade II listed mills and new seven-storey building (*2005, Cartwright Pickard*) (*BD*, housing supplement, 30/6/06), **North Street** – 80 apartments including twelve affordable homes (*2006, Carey Jones Architects*) (*R&R*, 7/7/06, p. 10), and Crown Street buildings.

Crown Street Buildings, Leeds LS2 (2004)
Allford Hall Monaghan Morris. R. Leeds

This is a mixed-use development in a triangular block adjacent to the Grade I listed Corn Exchange by Cuthbert Broderick (see Fig. 134 on page 282). It contains 55 flats on three levels including penthouses on a setback fifth floor above a two level base of commercial

Figure 3.143 The Calls, Leeds riverside regeneration from the Centenary Bridge with (right) housing by DLA Architecture Ltd and (left) office development by Allen Tod Architects.

space in the ground floor and basement. The external elevation to the city is a robust and lively combination of pressed Victorian bricks and coloured faience infill panels which graduate in colour from a cobalt blue from the elevation on Calls Lane through to acid green to bright yellow on the third elevation. Amongst the other achievements of the scheme was the incorporation of an existing terrace, now refurbished as shops and apartments. On the direction of Leeds City Council no parking was provided.

The housing is entered through a new private landscaped courtyard at first floor level. Access to the three levels above is by decks suspended from the building line with private gangways leading to individual doorways. This makes apartments more private than they would otherwise have been. The project received a Housing Design Award in 2006.

Housing Design Awards 2006 publication, pp. 16–19; *AJ*, NHBDA Report, 7/06, pp. 34–35, 58–59; *BD*, 4/11/05, pp. 14–15.

Second Millennium Village, Allerton Bywater, nr Castleford, WF10 (Phase 1)
2006. Philip Rickinson Architects
R. Castleford

Allerton Bywater, situated 10 km south of Leeds city centre, was a former coal mining village. The concept of creating a Millennium Village was launched in 1998 by Deputy Prime Minister, John Prescott, as a follow on from the Greenwich Millennium Village in London – "It would be equally as good as its predecessor" [1]. It is also one of seven sites for development as part of the government's Sustainable Communities Plan.

The village is being developed by English Partnerships. The masterplan proposes 520 homes, 25,000 sq.m. of commercial and community space for 4,000 residents. An essential part of the management of the project was the establishment of the Allerton Bywater Community Partnership as a limited company with residents as directors to find and maintain funding for the shared facilities. Further involvement created opportunity for training in construction with the developers and the renovation of the former miners' centre at the village green.

The first phase of development by Miller Homes contains 43 dwellings ranging from two-bedroom apartments to four-bedroom houses. A fifth of the dwellings are affordable. A stringent benchmark was set to reduce home energy consumption by 20 per cent, domestic waste by 50 per cent, increase plot and dwelling size and to provide adaptable IT cabling to each home. The houses also had to gain an EcoHomes top score of "excellent". The scheme includes home zone areas to create an environmentally friendly environment. The architectural approach looks conventional (Fig. 3.144) in comparison to the multi-coloured housing at Greenwich but English Partnerships accepted that Allerton Bywater "is not London" and that innovation requirements would mean that the build cost would exceed the sales value [2].

[1] *B*, Regenerate supplement, 4/05, p. 7; [2] *B*, Regenerate supplement, 9/06, pp. 46–47; *R&R*, 22/9/06, p. 9; *B*, 2/3/07, p. 45.

Sheffield

Park Hill/Hyde Park, Duke Street, Sheffield, S2
1961. Sheffield City Architects,
J.L. Womersley (City Architect),
J. Lynn, I. Smith, A.V. Smith; Park Hill
Regeneration. Hawkins Brown.
R. Sheffield Midland

Park Hill. The site overlooking the railway station was considered suitable for high-density,

Figure 3.144 Allerton Bywater: Yorkshire's millennium village.

housing by Sheffield City Council in the 1950s because it was close to the city centre and was on the windward side of the industrial area of the Don Valley. There was open space nearby and the topography of the site allowed scope for planning high flats with ample light, air and magnificent views (pp. 13–15 and Fig. 1.8). The scheme comprised 495 flats and 500 maisonettes built at an average density (net for housing) of approximately 56 dwellings per acre (138 dw/ha) The terraces of dwellings were arranged to create a series of large inter-locking courtyards containing children's play spaces, kick-about areas, seating places, etc. (Fig. 3.145). The scheme included a primary school, shopping centre originally containing 31 shops, 4 public houses, a social centre, laundry, boiler house, Garchey refuse station and garages.

The structure was a reinforced concrete frame, partly board marked, with concrete balcony fronts and brick infill in four shades – a progression of purple, terracotta, light red and cream. The steeply sloping site made possible a continuous flat roof of even height and for the access decks at every third floor to come out at ground level. The width of these "streets in the sky" was an essential part of the social concept for recreating the spirit of the former terraced streets and enabling direct access for milk floats and other services to all front doors. Whole streets

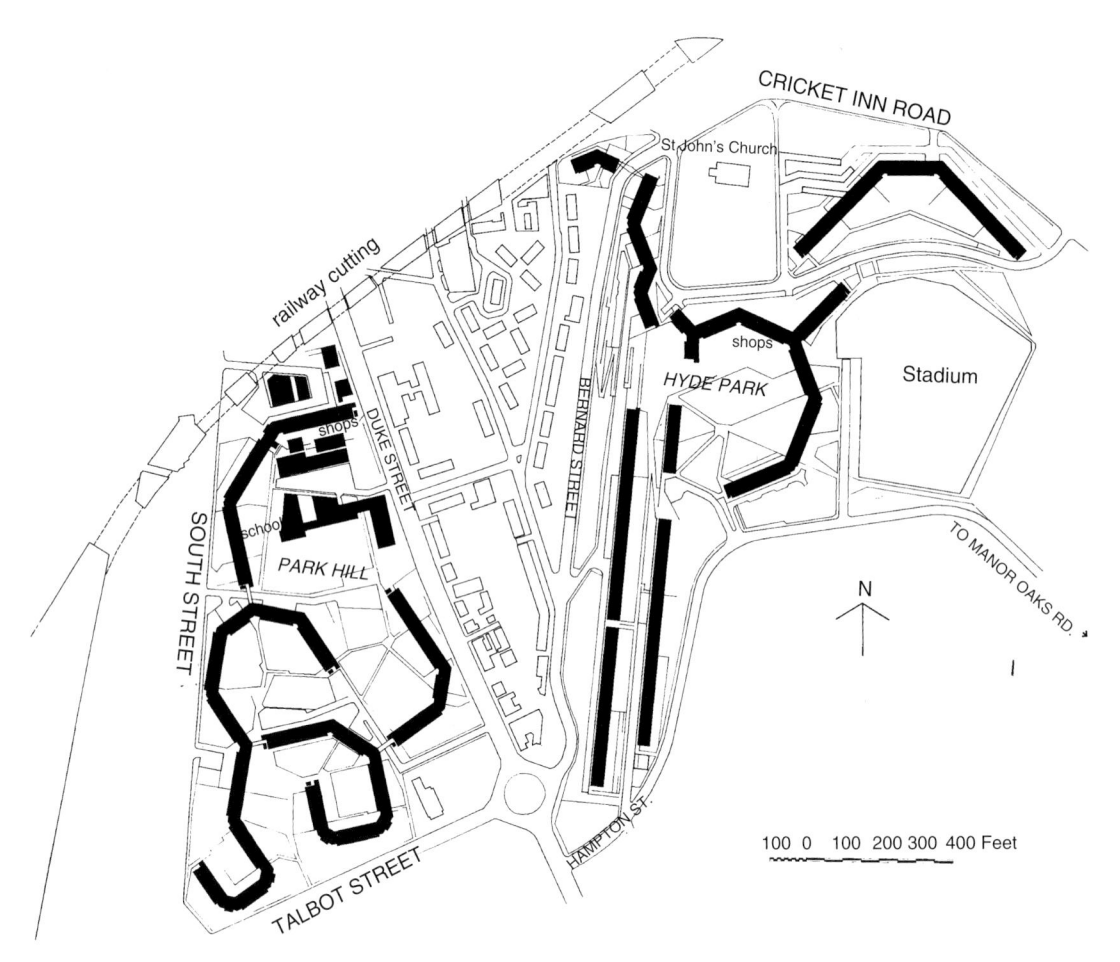

Figure 3.145 Park Hill and Hyde Park (from Sheffield City Council, Ten Years of Housing, p. 39).

of people were transferred from the old to the new housing, which meant that everyone knew their neighbours. People were positively helped to settle in and social groups were set up. During its early years, Park Hill was a showpiece of social housing.

Park Hill is now Grade II* listed and cannot be enveloped. This has been taken on board by developers, Urban Splash, who with architects, Hawkins Brown, have planned with English Partnerships, the Housing Corporation and Sheffield City Council to carry out regeneration proposals which will include new dwellings for sale, and for rent through the Manchester Methodist Housing Association and housing for shared ownership. Whilst the proposals require huge sums of money for repairing the concrete structure and the flats themselves, and attracting mixed tenure, much emphasis has been placed in the proposals on raising the image of the estate through extensive landscaping of the external spaces, including providing allotments and a bowling green. Also important is the provision of shopping, offices, industrial space, health and community buildings, and a large car park (Fig. 3.146) (DBS Architects, Sheffield, 1993).

Figure 3.146 Regeneration proposals for Park Hill (drawing reproduced by courtesy of Hawkins Brown, Urban Splash, Studio Egret West and Binary Heart).

Hyde Park. A second scheme followed in the mid-1960s, built on the higher ground above Park Hill. This contained 1,313 flats and maisonettes at a density of 46 dwellings per acre (114 dw/ha). The development was in two distinct parts, two long terraces of four-person flats with six-person maisonettes above which follow the contours, and a deck access scheme up to 18 storeys. It was likened to an Italian hill town but was never as successful as Park Hill. During the early 1990s, most of Hyde Park was demolished except Castle Court, which was enveloped and improved for the World Student games and as accommodation for young people thereafter (Fig. 3.147). The two long terraces were also over-clad in colourful brickwork and rain screen cladding.

Sheffield City Council, *Ten Years of Housing in Sheffield*, 4/62, pp. 38–55; *B*, 22/4/55, pp. 669; *AJ*, 23/8/61, pp. 271–286; *AR*, 12/61, pp. 405; *RIBAJ*, 12/62, pp. 447–471; *AJ*, 21/7/65, pp. 157–170; *AJ*, 20/8/69, pp. 465; *RIBAJ*, 10/95, pp. 52–60; *B*, Housing Design Awards, 11/93, p. 13; *AJ*, 6/10/05, pp. 16–17; Park Hill Regeneration: *AR*, 3/07, pp. 74–77.

Gleadless Valley, Blackstock Road, S8/S14

Early 1960s. Sheffield City Architects. R. Sheffield Midland

Gleadless Valley is a complete example of a 1950s/early 1960s mixed-development scheme (see p. 9). Started in 1955, the estate was planned to accommodate some 17,000 people in 4,451 dwellings. The site was divided naturally into three neighbourhoods by a large area of woodland but linked by a footpath system. Each neighbourhood was provided with its own junior and infant school, shopping centre and other communal facilities (Fig. 3.148).

The general pattern of development included two-storey houses, three-storey block of flats, and four- and six-storey maisonettes. Three 13-storey tower blocks crowned the hilltop at Herdings and formed the architectural climax of the development. The layout was a model for hillside housing demonstrating many ways of building on steep slopes. The form of housing was determined by the extent and direction of the slope. On

Figure 3.147 Castle Court: Over-cladding and new life for part of the Hyde Park flats.

very steep slopes, for example, Fleury Road, completed in 1962, "upside-down" houses were built with the living room on the first floor and the bedrooms below. Six-storey maisonettes had bridge access to an intermediate level entrance. On less severe slopes "mezzanine" entrance houses were developed which enabled living rooms to be close to the ground without steps down to the garden. Where houses were arranged down the contours, the houses were generally narrow fronted to reduce the extent of stepping between dwellings. Where the site was very steep, the terraces were staggered to allow footpaths to run diagonal with the contours.

AJ, 20/8/69, pp. 466; Sheffield City Council, *Ten Years of Housing*, 4/62, pp. 14–27.

Figure 3.148 Hillside housing at Gleadless Valley, Sheffield.

YORK

New Earswick, YO31
1901. Parker and Unwin. 1966. Refurbishment: The Louis de Soissons Partnership. R. York + local transport

New Earswick began 1901 when Joseph Rowntree purchased an estate of 150 acres (60 ha) near his cocoa factory, some 3 miles north of York. Here he and his architects, Barry Parker and Raymond Unwin built the first stages of an urban village that has continued to be developed up to the present day.

Although the site was flat, the planning of the village took full advantage of the natural features on the site. Trees and hedgerows were preserved but the sensitivity of the design is best seen in the south-east of the site where the houses follow the line of the brook (cover). Unwin believed that the layout of the houses should be free from the constraints of the street pattern. Consequently pedestrian paths weave their way through the housing to the village green around which are arranged the shops, school, church and the Village Institute (the Folk Hall). The first cottages were full of picturesque interest with long, low, red pantiled roofs overhanging walls finished with roughcast render. After 1918, the need for severe economies resulted in much simplified designs but despite this the village has a strong sense of identity due in no small part to Parker and Unwin's plan and

Figure 3.149 New Earswick: successful conversion to a Radburn layout.

landscaping treatment which ties the whole village together.

In the late 1960s major refurbishment took place, which included bringing the houses up to Parker Morris standards, more easily accommodating the motorcar and landscaping the open spaces between the houses. The road and footpath pattern separated pedestrians from vehicles along Radburn lines in order to increase accommodation for motorcars. This considerably enhanced the quality of the village (Fig. 3.149) except that many of the original chimneystacks were removed. Development has continued in recent years with the completion of new lifetime homes and a village for elderly people – Hartrigg Oaks.

AR, 60/78, pp. 327–332.

Lifetime Homes: Alderway, Conifer Close, Spruce Close, Jasmine & Acuba Close, New Earswick, YO31
1996. Jane Darbyshire & David Kendall Ltd. R. York + Local Transport.

Jane Darbyshire's extension to New Earswick was based on a thorough study of both the principles behind the original designs of Parker and Unwin and the improvements made in the late 1960s. The proposals comprised 89 dwellings in a mixture of two-storey houses and flats and bungalows. These are clustered around

Figure 3.150 Lifetime homes at New Earswick.

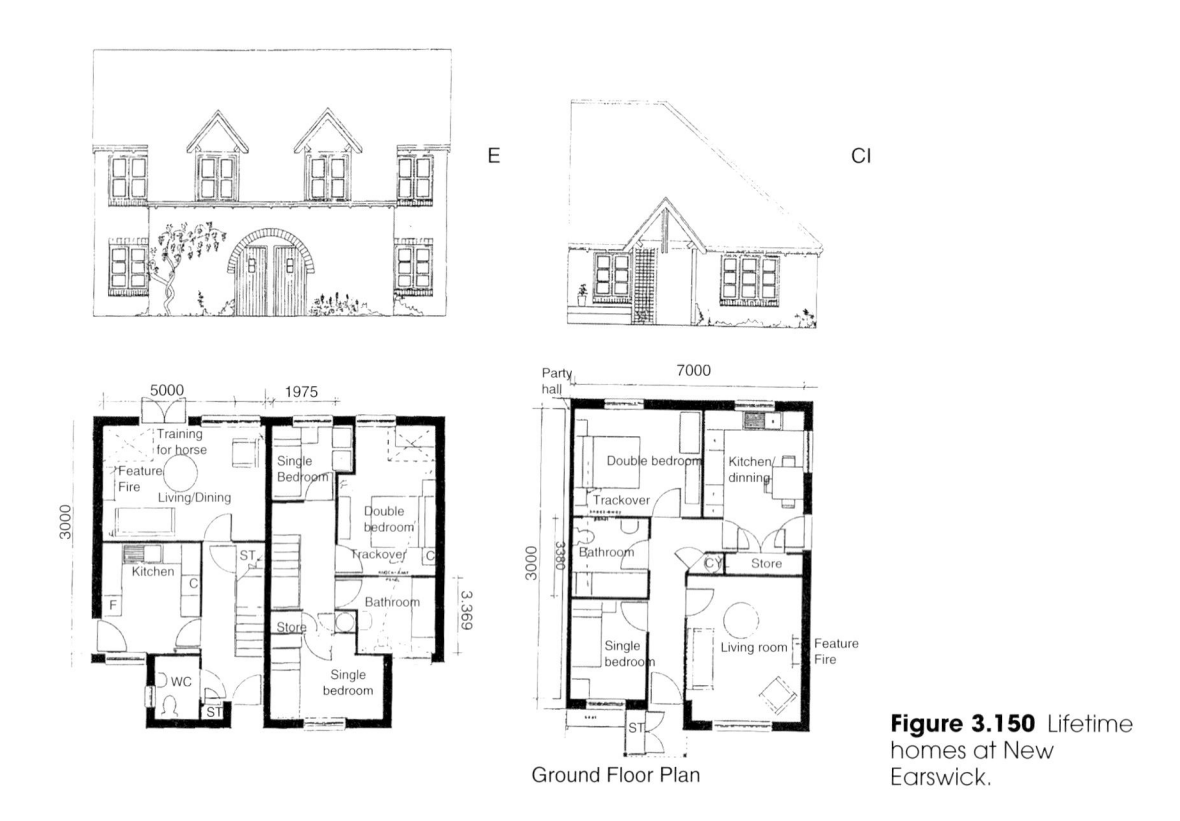

carefully landscaped shared open spaces and a linear Village Green, which creates a focus for the development. The layout reflects the Radburn principles adopted for the environmental improvements in the 1960s, which had proved successful. This resulted in some housing fronting on to pedestrian routes but clustered at the back around small, secluded culs-de-sac. The new houses were generally semi-detached with a gated private outdoor link from front to rear. This together with the careful location of visitor parking avoided any misunderstanding of front and back.

All dwellings were designed to "Lifetime Homes" standards (pp. 31–33). They would be accessible and adaptable, to the needs of the occupiers, throughout their lifetimes (Fig. 3.150). The houses were built of traditional materials – clay pantiles and Yorkshire slop mould bricks – and given an intimate scale with low eaves lines and sheltering porches.

Bretgate/Walmgate, infill housing, YO1
1982. York University Design Unit. R. York.

The City of York possesses many fine examples of new infill housing which makes a modern contribution to the quality of the historic scene. Bretgate was one of the earliest examples and, as such, it set the standard that has rarely been surpassed. Commissioned by the York Housing Association Ltd., the 53 flats replaced an area of slum housing within the city walls.

The housing was built on the street boundaries of the site, which enabled a large internal block-paved courtyard to be created. This provides space for car parking, but the surface treatment of block paving, which matches the brickwork of the housing, gives the space a very pedestrian feel. The now mature trees were very carefully located to avoid overshadowing in the courtyard. These, together with the simple railings around front gardens and other items of street furniture, create a simple environment appropriate to a site in the centreof York.

The design of the housing made use of the roof space by incorporating inset balconies overlooking the courtyard below, which take full advantage of their sunny orientation. This adds to the sense of friendliness in the courtyard and has been a great success (Fig. 3.151).

A second scheme of great note in the centre of York by the Design Unit is Margaret Philipson Court, Aldwark.

DOE/RIBA/NHBC Housing Design Awards 1983 publication, p. 44.

Figure 3.151 Bretgate, York: compact housing within the city walls.

Supported housing unit and apartments, Moss Street, York, YO23
2006. Bramhall Blenkharn, R. York

The site, bounded by Moss Street and Scarcroft Lane, is on the North-west corner of Scarcroft Green, and is close to York's city walls. Yorkshire Housing's brief was to create a supported unit (a refuge for women and their children suffering abuse) and a range of 22 apartments for market sale to fund the refuge.

The design makes maximum use of the site with apartment buildings close up to the back edge of the footpaths to Moss Street and Scarcroft Lane to make space for a green environment within the site. Along Moss Street, the apartment buildings are brick with largely slate roofs. Set against this are two-storey rendered bays set parallel with the road edge. At the corner of Moss Street and Scarcroft Lane the apartments were designed to visually turn the corner. The supported unit is at the back of the site. Its design was deliberately bold to be non-institutional. It is constructed with timber clad flank walls

Figure 3.152 Supported housing at Moss Street, York.

which surround a more open building with windows sited to maximise daylight whilst respecting the privacy of the occupants and avoiding overlooking of surrounding properties. The rest of the building is clad in blue render and patinated copper. The result has been well received by the occupants and the local community (Fig. 3.152).

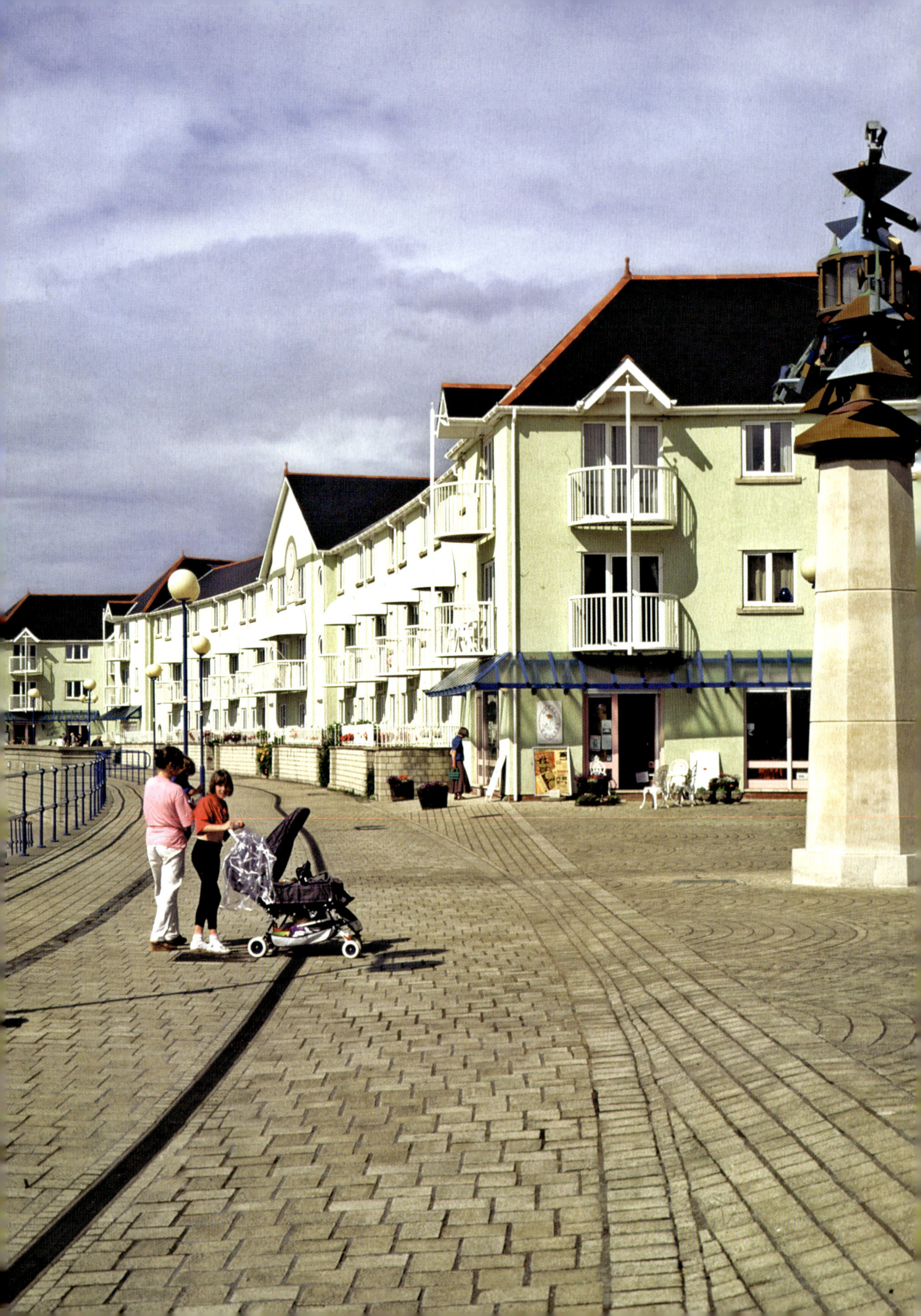

Wales

Figure 4.2 Wales: location of schemes.

1. Cardiff
2. Gwynedd (formerly Caernarfonshire and Merionethshire)
3. Swansea

CARDIFF

Cardiff Bay Regeneration, CF99
1987. Regeneration strategy: (Masterplanners) Llewelyn-Davies Planning; architects as mentioned. R. Cardiff Central/Cardiff Bay/Penarth

Designated in 1987, the Cardiff Bay Development Corporation commissioned Llewelyn-Davies Planning to produce an overall "Regeneration Strategy" for 1,100 hectares (2700 acres) of old derelict docklands of Cardiff and Penarth. The key to the urban design concept was the construction of a barrage across the entrance to the bay to create a 200 hectare (500 acre) freshwater lake. This proved highly controversial as many people wished to preserve the natural habitat that existed on the mud banks. The Development Corporation ceased to exist

Figure 4.1 The Promenade, Swansea Maritime Village (p. 307).

in 2000 by which time it had created a mix of 4,800 new dwellings, 79 hectares of open space (195 acres), and, in addition, substantial amounts of commercial, leisure and industrial development. This includes Richard Rogers's Senedd – the home of the National Assembly for Wales – and the Wales Millennium Centre.

Amongst the first residential developments to be completed was **Atlantic Wharf**, where in the mid-1990s the very fine nineteenth century Spillers and Bakers warehouse was refurbished and converted into housing (Fig. 4.3). Most of the housing in Atlantic Wharf (Schooner Way) is traditional but this is much tempered by the mature landscape structure provided in association with a canalside walk. The edge of the development is framed by three- and four-storey terraced housing lining the long, newly constructed Lloyd George Avenue, which links Cardiff Bay to the

Figure 4.3 Cardiff Bay: conversion into housing of the 1893 Spillers & Bakers Ltd Warehouse at Atlantic Wharf.

city centre (Fig. 4.4). Other developments of note are:

Adventurers Quay (*design: Richard Reid; second stage: Osborne V. Webb and Partners*), located close to the National Assembly building, is a mixture of town houses and flats located on a prominent point at Roath Basin (Pierhead Street) (Fig. 4.5). **Sovereign Quay** (Fig. 4.6) at Havannah Street overlooks the Graving Docks and is part of a complex of buildings including the landmark St David's Hotel.

Penarth Haven (*Halliday Meecham*), across the bay, is a pleasant waterfront scheme of two- and three-storey town houses and flats designed around the former dock system (Fig. 4.7).

GWYNEDD (FORMERLY CAERNARFONSHIRE AND MERIONETHSHIRE)

Holiday housing, Porthmadog, LL48
1974. Philips/Cutler/Philips/Troy (now PCPT Architects Ltd). R. Porthmadog

Whilst this scheme mainly provides second homes, its design was highly admired at the time of its construction because of the dense grouping of buildings in a wild natural landscape (Fig. 4.8). It is best seen from high up on the walls of Harlech Castle from where the houses seem to rest with some uncertainty on the flat estuary below. Its sharpness contrasts

Figure 4.4 Lloyd George Avenue.

Figure 4.5 Adventurers Quay, viewed from across the Cardiff Bay waterfront.

significantly with its landscape setting. Initially the design caused controversy from both the public and the local planning authority, but when built it became accepted and admired. Clough Williams-Ellis, whose Portmerion is just round the corner, commented that these little harbour houses are "special" in design ... the sawtooth skyline of their roofs, alternatively pitched this way and that in a single span, is fidgety, yes, but becomes interesting and then acceptable as one recovers from the initial shock.

AJ, 18/9/74, pp. 650–653.

SWANSEA

Maritime Village, Swansea, SA1
1975+. R. Swansea

Swansea was the first industrial seaport in the UK to set about its problems of dockland and industrial blight in a comprehensive way. It did so without an Urban Development Corporation or any other form of direct government intervention. However, maximum benefit was taken of South Wales's special economic status with respect to government aid, but its success came entirely from public initiative as the City Council, during the 1980s, managed to exploit every form of public finance and seek effective partnership arrangements with the private sector. The scheme also benefited from the City Council ownership of most of the land, which simplified the planning process and the phasing of the infrastructure works.

One of the first buildings to be completed in 1975 was a new leisure centre and 54 local authority houses. The Marina opened in 1982 and private sector developments quickly followed. Today the Village has a conference hotel, a food store, offices, shops, restaurants, an art gallery, a hostel, a boat club and

CHAPTER FOUR • WALES

Figure 4.6 New housing at Sovereign Quays overlooking the Graving Docks.

Figure 4.7 Penarth Haven.

Figure 4.13 The atrium in the Swansea Foyer.

Foyer (p. 34). The brief was to provide a building that created a suitable environment in which integrated work, training and independent living could be offered to the young people. The building envisaged for the project was the former Swansea Working Men's Club, constructed in 1885 with listed elevations but eventually only the front facade was preserved as the building was too dilapidated.

The interior is most striking with a splendid glazed atrium, mosaics and an internal colour scheme intended to create an optimistic and fun environment, which the young people could enjoy (Fig. 4.13). The atrium forms a street from where staircases lead to individual "houses" occupied by four or five young people. Within their house each young person has their own bed-sit with a WC/shower, and there is a shared kitchen/living space. There are 33 bedsits in total, two of which are suitable for full wheelchair use, and one guestroom plus rooms for training and leisure and a residents coffee area with space for a small café (Fig. 4.14).

AJ, 19/6/97, pp. 33–40.

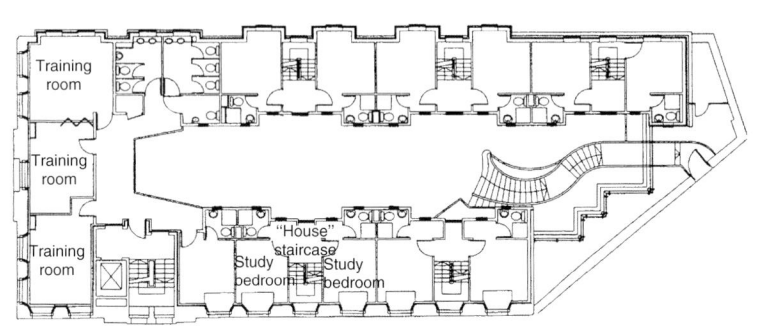

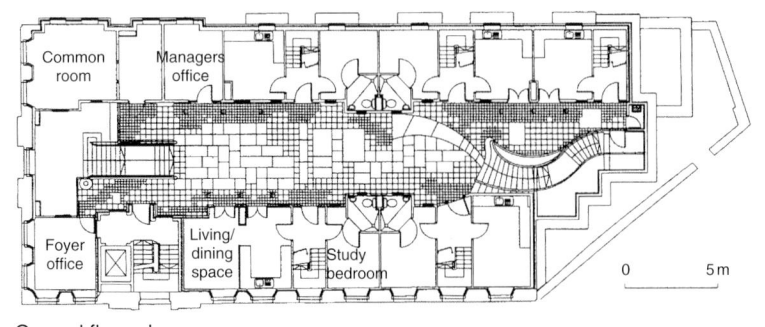

Figure 4.14 The Swansea Foyer floor plans.

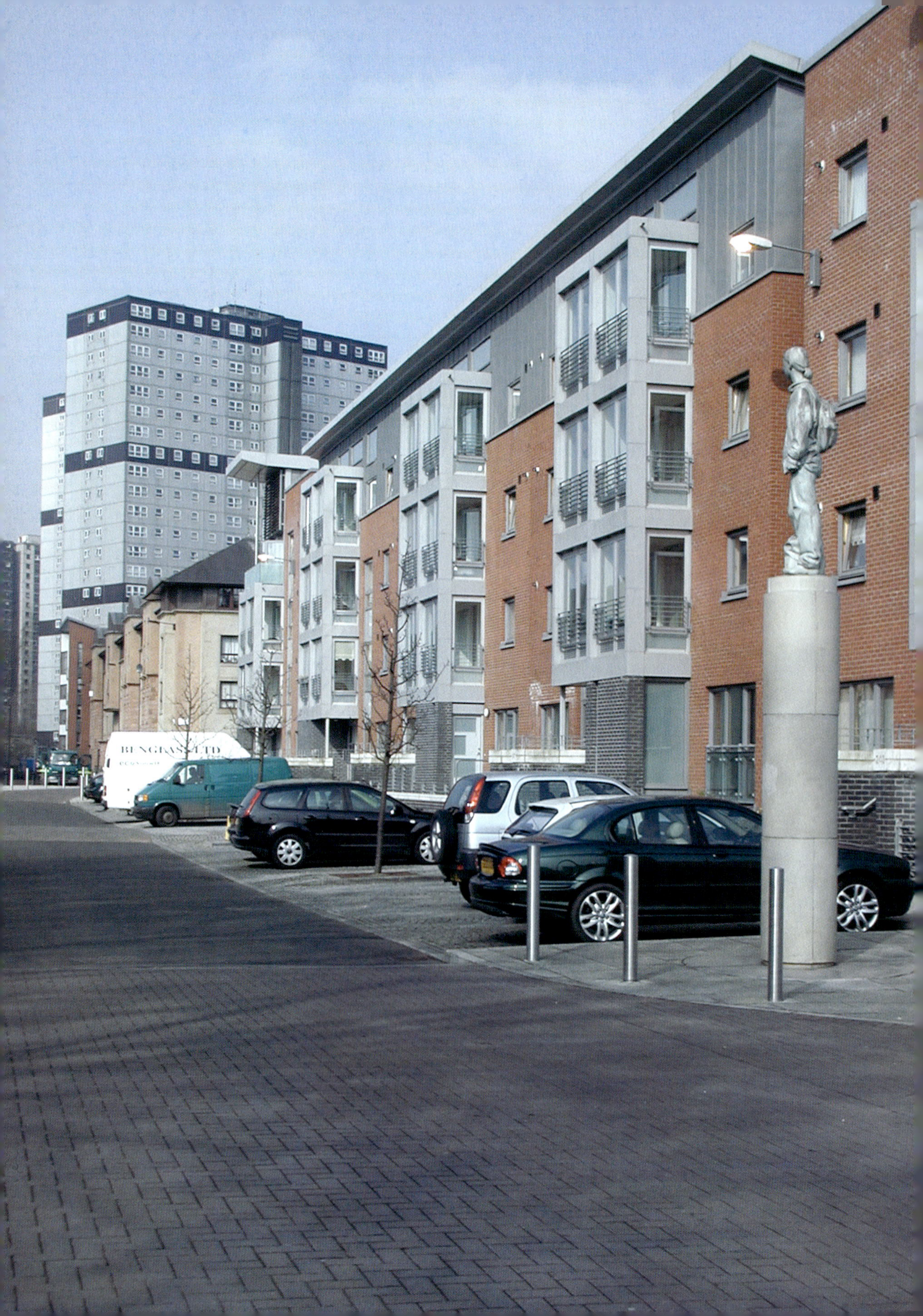

Scotland

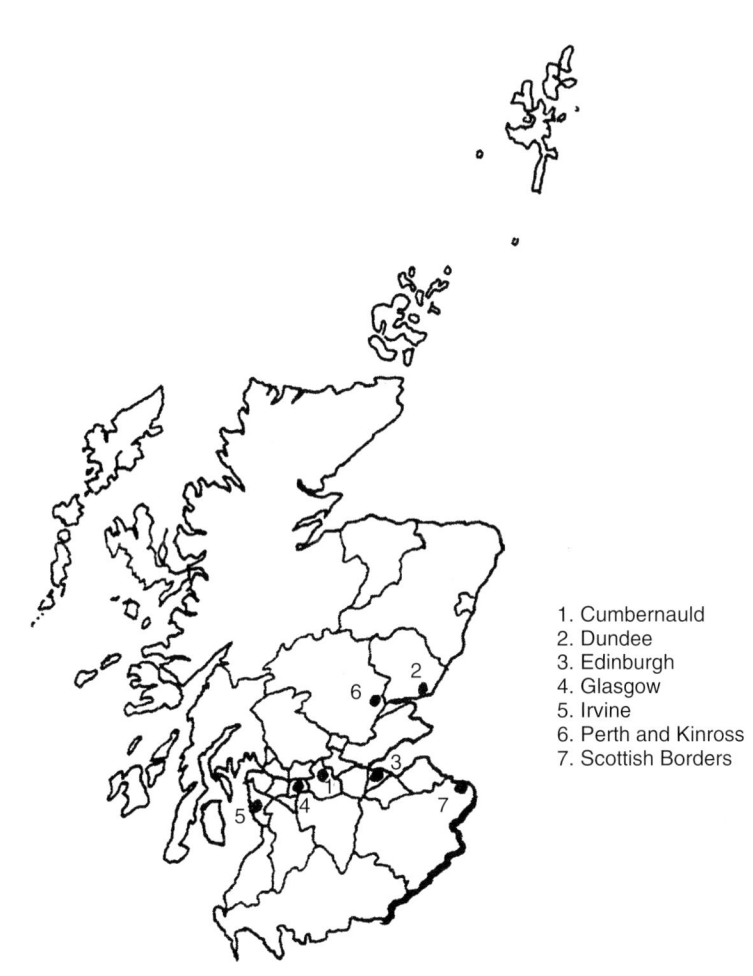

5

1. Cumbernauld
2. Dundee
3. Edinburgh
4. Glasgow
5. Irvine
6. Perth and Kinross
7. Scottish Borders

Figure 5.2 Scotland: location of schemes.

Figure 5.1 The New Gorbals, Glasgow (p. 336).

Introduction

Scottish housing merits separate consideration for a number of reasons. Whilst in recent years there has been a merger of design approach with the rest of Britain, the traditional harled and painted walls, crow foot gables, small pained sash windows (often with wide surrounds), steep slate roofs and bold chimneys gave Scottish housing a national identity. Sir Basil Spence's sketch of proposed fishermen's housing at Dunbar (Fig. 5.3), drawn in 1950, perfectly captured the spirit which has remained a strong influence even on the most modern designs [1]. There is also the spirit of Charles Rennie Mackintosh, which is evident in some of the designs.

Generally there is also a wider historical acceptance of tenement living in Scottish towns and cities. By the sixteenth century, flats were well established in market centres in Scotland as the preferred building form for merchants and tradesmen. This closely resembled the experience of continental Europe where urban settlements were often separately administered from their rural hinterlands. Later town expansions in Scotland followed this principle and housebuilding was mainly in the form of flats, whilst in England most housing was based on variations of the terraced house. The Scottish Victorian and Edwardian working class tenement are therefore the logical development of the sixteenth century merchants' flats but in England the minimum subdivision of the terraced house was the "back to back" [2]. The practice of living in flats continued into the 1950s and 1960s when it was translated by local authorities into tenement housing in the peripheral estates and high rise. Between 1955 and 1975 no other local authority in Britain matched the scale of Glasgow's ambitious programme of public sector housebuilding.

Since 1980 there have been remarkable changes with housing policy in Scotland aimed at stimulating social and economic regeneration of the large council estates. Much of this has been achieved through tenant empowerment as exemplified in the emergence of the tenant co-operative movement. The influence of this on housing design has been significant.

Figure 5.3 Fishermen's housing, Dunbar, East Lothian: sketch by Sir Basil Spence, 1950 (from Willis, P., *New Architecture in Scotland*, Lund Humphries, London, p. 8).

Inter-war years policies

By the end of the First World War Scottish towns and cities, particularly Glasgow, had an overwhelming legacy of poor housing and overcrowding left by the Industrial Revolution. By 1919, 700,000 people were packed into the centre of the city in tightly knit housing built in the backlands behind the street buildings with access limited to narrow lanes and closes. Between 1919 and 1939 a third of a million new dwellings were built in Scotland, of which public authorities built 67 per cent. However, little of this building relieved the slums, as the new housing was let to higher wage earners. To overcome this dilemma, the specific task of building "working class homes" [3] was eventually handed to the Scottish Special Housing Association (SSHA) founded in 1937, but little was achieved until after 1945.

Low rents policy

This policy emerged from the industrial unrest in Glasgow in 1915 and the rent freeze imposed by central government. Thereafter, rents in both the public and private sectors continued to be at such a low level that they seldom reached a sufficient level to support an adequate programme of management and maintenance. Subsidy from the general rates gave some assistance to council housing, but the culture of low rents through custom and practice has remained a feature of Scottish housing.

Cottages or flats

During this period there was considerable tension between the advocates of the garden city ideas from England and the Scottish tenement tradition. Essentially the urgency of its housing problems was so great that Glasgow's housing committee was resorting to forms of "modern" flats familiar in Europe. Its opponents considered these were unsuitable for Scotland in terms of climate and sunshine [4]. Both types of housing were built but the issues were to become even more vital after the Second World War.

Non-traditional housing

New construction methods were actively pursued to build housing more quickly. This appeared to have the benefit of overcoming shortages of skilled craftsmen whilst offering alternative employment to the workers in the declining steelworks, shipbuilding and coal-mining industries. From 1925, steel framed houses were built in Glasgow, Edinburgh, Dundee and other locations. These were two storeys in form and traditional in appearance. Timber housing also appeared and at the same time the no-fines poured concrete construction technique was introduced from the Netherlands.

Years of ambition 1945–1979

Just under half of Scotland's present housing was constructed between 1951 and 1979, mostly by local authorities. In Glasgow, where housing had become a great political issue the City Council built the greatest number. Until the early 1950s most of the new housing built was of the cottage type, with many local authorities using factory made steel, timber and concrete systems.

Peripheral estates

The peripheral estates resulted from the concern of the major cities about the flight of their population to the new towns. The housing consisted mainly of three- and four-storey tenements (Fig. 5.4). The largest of

Figure 5.4 Typical peripheral estate tenement (photo by Glasgow City Council).

these estates – Castlemilk, Easterhouse, Drumchapel and Pollock – contained over 10,000 dwellings each with large populations of over 50,000 at Easterhouses and 34,000 at Castlemilk. The estates were a long way from the city centre and the tenants' natural roots, added to which there was an acute lack of local shops and community facilities. It resulted in a concentration of poor people on the estates with low standards of living and poor health.

Non-traditional housing

To build quickly, industrialised systems and standard plans were extensively adopted. Requiring only semi-skilled and unskilled labour, the Scottish Office positively encouraged system building as a way of reducing the impact of manual job losses from the declining heavy industries and unemployment. Some systems employed, such as timber houses from Sweden (Fig. 5.5), produced high-quality housing, but the result generally from using concrete systems for peripheral estate development was a drabness of appearance that did little to enhance the lives of the people.

High-rise housing

Although the development of the peripheral estates continued after 1955, attention moved towards the replacement of the slums in the centre of Glasgow. The size of the problem called for a new development approach and Roehampton in London was seen as the model to follow. For the politicians in Glasgow, high-rise housing also had the virtue of avoiding the loss of the city's population (Fig. 5.6). Slum clearance and redevelopment was concentrated in comprehensive development areas (CDAs). A number of Britain's most distinguished architects were involved in the new developments including Sir Basil Spence who designed blocks of 20 storeys in the Gorbals. In total, 320 tower blocks were built in the city using a variety of systems of prefabrication; no-fines was, however, limited to 12 storeys. Between 1961 and 1969, approximately one-third of a million new dwellings were constructed throughout Scotland of which three-quarters were high-rise flats. The scale of the development was enormous. Right from the start there were serious management problems and by the late 1970s every sizeable town or city had its "problem" and "difficult to let" estates.

Figure 5.5 Swedish timber houses for Forestry Commission workers (photo by Tom Begg).

SLASH

The Scottish Local Authorities Special Housing Group (SLASH) was established in 1963 by Glasgow City Council in order to circumvent high costs and shortages of materials through bulk purchasing. It soon included Edinburgh and some 40 other local housing authorities responsible for four-fifths of the national output of new houses. The immediate aim was for the member authorities to use jointly ordered prefabricated high-rise flats to raise the national output by 10 per cent. To facilitate this SLASH prepared standard house plans and details with a view of reducing construction cost and time. The Scottish Development Department and the SSHA were prime movers in SLASH as was the Scottish National Building Agency. As it developed SLASH eventually produced some excellent work in promoting good standards. It gained considerable respect throughout Britain for its design and technical publications. It was finally wound up in the 1980s.

The Scottish Special Housing Association

During the 1960s and 1970s the SSHA developed its own high-rise housing and extensively used system building including no fines. Local authorities were frequently suspicious of the role of SSHA, which they saw as the Scottish Office's building agency. Regardless of this, SSHA played an important role in this period, particularly in the refurbishment of Glasgow tenements. They were also active in the Glasgow Eastern Area Renewal (GEAR) area and Maryhill Road projects where they helped to pioneer tenant participation in the design process.

The Scottish New Towns

Despite initial opposition from Glasgow District Council, the dispersal of people from the city's slums was an important part of the Scottish national housing strategy from 1951. Subsidies were available after 1957 from the Scottish Office to support the

Figure 5.6 High-rise/high-density housing adjacent the Gorbals area of Glasgow.

policy. The first of the Scottish new towns, East Kilbride, had been designated in 1947 and Glenrothes in 1948. This was followed by **Cumbernauld** in 1956, Livingston in 1962 and **Irvine** in 1966. The outflow of people from Glasgow was so enormous that its population fell from over 1 million in 1961, to just over 700,000 in 1980. The loss was mainly amongst the middle classes, the skilled and higher waged workers, leaving parts of the city with a concentration of poor people who had the least opportunity to progress.

The Scottish new towns made a significant mark in terms of their planning and design, especially Cumbernauld, where a unique masterplan and innovative housing design brought it international acclaim.

GEAR (The Glasgow East End Project)

Established in 1976, GEAR was concerned with the regeneration of a huge area to the east of Glasgow City Centre including Bridgeton, Dalmarnock and Shettleston which had suffered intense urban decay and destruction. The area contained seven designated Comprehensive Development Areas (CDAs) and had lost two-thirds of its former population. The Scottish Development Agency was given the task of coordinating a multi-agency approach to its regeneration which involved Strathclyde Regional Council, Glasgow District Council, the SSHA, the Health Board, Manpower Services and the local communities. The project significantly lifted the morale of the remaining people in the area. The quality of the refurbishment (2,049 dwellings in total) and the new housing (1,209) built by the SSHA and the housing associations, combined with large amounts of landscaping, transformed the area. Confidence in the future of the area was demonstrated by the construction of a small amount of private housing (e.g. 134 houses at Dalveen Street, 1979). Less successful were the accompanying social and economic initiatives. Housing investment was not linked to employment and much of the economic benefit was gained at the expense of other areas. However, the experience was invaluable for the urban regeneration schemes that followed [5].

Post 1979: a new culture

The culture of Scottish housing changed significantly after 1979. Stringent government expenditure cuts caused Glasgow City Council in the winter of 1983/1984 to search for ways of attracting alternative funding for the improvement of its estates. From this deliberation, the concept of Community Ownership emerged. Progressively the City Council realised it had to reduce its direct role and transfer some of its stock to co-operatives, housing associations and private sector firms to produce a healthier social mix and to open the way for some genuine choices [6]. In 1986, Glasgow City Council commissioned Professor Sir Robert Grieve to undertake an enquiry which recommended transferring to alternative landlords 25 per cent of the council's housing stock, particularly in the peripheral estates. In 1987, the first Community Renewal Partnership programme was implemented using funds raised through a covenant scheme with private investors.

The White Paper "New Life for Urban Scotland" published in 1988 set out the government's requirements for regeneration in the peripheral and other large estates. Based on the experience of GEAR, a multi-agency, co-operative approach was required which would encourage a variety of forms of tenure including home ownership. New methods of management and tenant empowerment were important to the process. Consequently, formal Partnerships were established for four of the most problematic estates – **Castlemilk** in Glasgow (Fig. 5.7), Ferguslie Park, Paisley, Whitfield in Dundee and **Wester Hailes** in Edinburgh. The Partnerships recognised the need to integrate physical, economic and social programmes to establish more sustainable communities. Amongst the major objectives were the following priorities: arresting the population decline and stabilising the community; providing a range of types of housing and tenure with a mixture of refurbishment and new housing, including homesteading and housing for sale; improving the environment; increasing local economic activity; developing better standards of health, education and community care; empowering the people to achieve these aims through participation.

Change also came from private developers working in partnership with public bodies and housing and estate regeneration agencies with a great degree of success. Most dramatic of all was the regeneration of **The Gorbals** in Glasgow, in which social/economic development, including a high percentage of home ownership, was seen as an essential part of the overall strategy.

Private sector housing

The 1980s saw the expansion of speculative housing for sale. Many developers introduced the English private housebuilding vernacular including the use of brick, which was not an indigenous material for Scotland. They sold half-timbered and other English style houses that were small and built to minimum standards with little attention to energy and other environmental issues – the main reference to Scottish vernacular was "baronial". The sale of council housing proved popular and in Scotland local authorities could, until the mid-1990s, use the whole of their capital receipts from sales for development purposes. This helped avoid some of the bitter central/local relationships that existed elsewhere in Britain.

Tenement refurbishment

The rehabilitation of the pre-1919 tenements in the late 1970s and 1980s encouraged the growth of the community-based housing associations that became key participants in urban housing regeneration. Part of the credit for this can be attributed directly to ASSIST. Formed in 1970 by Raymond Young

Figure 5.7 Castlemilk: successful regeneration of one of Glasgow's peripheral estates.

and Jim Johnston, ASSIST Architects was part of Strathclyde University before separating in 1983 to become the first architectural co-operative in Scotland. The bulk of its early work was community-based refurbishment projects. It specialised in advising the community groups on rehabilitation and renewal and did much to encourage them to campaign to save areas of the city that the planners wanted to demolish. From the mid-1980s most of ASSIST's work was new housing, which it designed with considerable success (Fig. 5.8).

Scottish Homes

From 1979, the SSHA continued its programme of new housing development with a high level of tenant participation in the design process, for example, Kirkland Street, 1981–1985, and Dalmarnock Road/Summerfield Street, 1985–1986 (AJ, 3/12/86, pp. 37–43). It was merged with the Scottish Housing Corporation in 1989 to form Scottish Homes. This created a single housing development agency with a wide range of powers to tackle Scotlands housing problems in a holistic manner.

Communities Scotland

The Scottish Assembly abolished Scottish Homes in 2001 and transferred its responsibilities to Communities Scotland (CS), which is an agency of the Scottish Executive responsible to Ministers. The fundamental aim of CS is "to make Scotland a country where everyone has the opportunity to enjoy a decent quality of life through affordable housing in strong and confident communities, having access to learning and employment opportunities, and living free from poverty, inequality and discrimination" [7]. A major task is regeneration, which includes social and economic investment in support of housing and environmental improvement. It is also concerned to deal on an equal footing with rural housing issues. In December 2004, it established a £318 million Community Regeneration Fund to run for 3 years together with 32 community planning partnerships with local authorities to tackle the problems of the most disadvantaged neighbourhoods. It is actively encouraging housing associations to follow the Egan and Latham agendas to gain efficiencies from partnering, including using modern methods of construction and bulk procurement through regional groups of housing associations. Its support for the publication *Sustainable Housing*

Figure 5.8 Community-based housing association development at West End Park Street/Woodland Road.

Design Guide for Scotland [8] is valuable in giving recommendations for both new development and the refurbishment of existing housing. The publication contains many useful case studies.

[1] Willis, P., *New Architecture in Scotland*, Lund Humphries, London, 1997, p. 50.
[2] Based on information from Dr Peter Robinson, Construction and Building Control Group, The Scottish Office.
[3] Begg, T., *Housing Policy in Scotland*, John Donald Publishers Ltd, Edinburgh, 1996, p. 43.

Figure 5.14 Westburn Avenue: glazed towers provide a focal point in the layout.

refurbishment of tenement housing and demolition of many of the unpopular high-rise blocks, replacing them with new housing. Some of the best new development is at Westburn Avenue where refurbishment was considered non-viable.

The new housing reflects community participation in the design, which involved an enormous number of drawings, computer models and slides, as well as visits to other areas. The use of terraced housing and flats achieved a density of 28 dwellings per acre (70 dw/ha), which was necessary for the scheme to be financially viable. The architecture has a strong sense of local identity with cultural precedents reflected in a distinctively modern way. This includes the use of render, Fyfestone and circular glass block stair towers which resemble Scottish baronial architecture (Fig. 5.14). A sense of enclosure has been achieved with the three-storey housing forming a focal point and centre at the lowest part of the site. A conventional pattern of streets and courts was adopted and the buildings were sited by the architects in a "pragmatic" manner [1] each responding to its own needs. Windows were positioned primarily to take best advantage of sunlight and to provide surveillance over adjacent spaces rather than produce an organised composition. The design is likened by the residents to a traditional village and has therefore retained the name Westburn Village.

AT, 2/96, No. 65, pp. 16–19; [1] Ibid., p. 17.

Figure 5.15 Craigwell Brewery, Edinburgh: successful reuse of redundant buildings.

Craigwell Mews, Calton Road, EH8
1988. Nicholas Groves-Raines.
R. Edinburgh Waverley.

Craigwell Mews was created through converting some beautiful seventeenth century brewery buildings into housing by Abbey Housing. The scheme comprised 84 four-storey town houses with three bedrooms, 3 three-storey houses with two bedrooms and 8 one- and two-bedroom flats (Fig. 5.15). The roughly U-shaped development curves round one end of a linear courtyard paved with nineteenth century setts. The houses are at the rear of the courtyard in the brick-built brewery and most of the flats are in the red sandstone former brewery offices buildings fronting Calton Road. Access to the courtyard is through the original pend.

The architects have carefully restored the buildings and preserved the proportions of the window and door openings, and have added a small number of new details. The hoist housings on upper floors had perished but were reflected in the design of the new green-stained timber balconies that project from the two upper floors of the four-storey houses. These are matched by timber features around the courtyard.

Slateford Green: car-free urban village, Gorgie Park Close, Slateford Road, EH14
2000. Hackland & Dore. R. Slateford

Edinburgh's millennium housing project was the subject of an architectural competition in 1997 commissioned by the Canmore Housing Association, the Royal Incorporation of Architects in Scotland and Scottish Homes. The brief looked for architects to explore ways in which people could live in cities with limited natural resources. The winning scheme

327

provided 121 flats and a kindergarten in a two- to four-storey form reflecting the traditional Edinburgh tenement block. Twenty-six of these were for sale, twenty-five for shared ownership and sixty-nine for social rent including seventeen for the Deaf Society and four for wheelchair use.

Its sheltering horseshoe courtyard form followed the boundaries of the site, which was previously the Gorgie railway sidings off Slateford Road. It encloses communal and private gardens that can only be accessed by residents (Fig. 5.16). The building is surrounded by natural landscape and allotments and a pedestrian scale street/cycle route, graded to provide service, drop-off and emergency access throughout. No vehicles can enter the internal courtyard and minimal parking is located for disabled flats and essential visitors. Under a Section 75 Agreement in the Town and Country Planning (Scotland) Act 1997, Canmore has to impose obligations on residents to agree, as part of their tenancy, not to park a car within the scheme or in the streets around. Complementary to the development is the City Car Club, which is a joint venture between Edinburgh City Council and Budget Car Rental. For an annual fee, members of the club have access to a fleet of cars that can be hired locally by the hour [1].

Flats are arranged in traditional Scottish tenement stair clusters and closes. Each staircase was designed to include a furniture hoist and may be retrofitted with a disabled lift. Flats for disabled people were arranged around specifically designed gardens. All areas are barrier free and routes ramped to provide access to public areas.

The timber frame design incorporated many low-energy features including breathing walls,

Figure 5.16 The Gorgie Millennium housing, Edinburgh: car-free environment.

sunspaces or winter gardens, reed-bed ponds to treat surface and storm water, natural passive ventilation systems to reduce the risk of condensation, stair lighting powered by photovoltaic cells, community heating potentially using waste industrial heat from a nearby whisky distillery to provide cheaper and more efficient heating and hot water. It has a low maintenance aluminium roof that can be recycled at the end of its life.

[1] *Sustainable Housing Design Guide for Scotland*, pp. 267–269; *AJ*, 10/10/96, p. 14; *AT*, 5/2000, pp. 38–44.

Edinburgh Old Town urban renewal, EH8
2004. (Masterplanners) Development Services Partnership – John C. Hope and Frank Spratt; (Architects) various including Richard Murphy Architects, E + F MacLachlan, Campbell + Arnott, Malcolm Fraser Architects, Ungless + Latimer. R. Edinburgh Waverley

---

The Royal Mile area of Edinburgh's old town has in recent years received a number of skillfully designed infill housing developments. These have frequently combined new development with the refurbishment and conversion to new uses of appropriate buildings. Designs reflect the mediaeval street pattern and historic character whilst ensuring the buildings are compatible with the needs of contemporary living.

Morgan Court (*Ungless + Latimer*) is new housing providing student accommodation with a supermarket on the ground floor. The south façade facing Holyrood Road was treated as a city wall and provides a definite boundary to the old town (Fig. 5.17).

Canongate Housing (*Richard Murphy Architects*) sits on the site of the former archway building to the Holyrood Brewery on the south side of Canongate. The new development consists of a shop at street level with nine flats above. Its elevation treatment attempted to make explicit references to historic buildings in the old town, many of which have disappeared (Fig. 5.18). This includes colonnades at ground floor level, external staircases, and horizontal windows in mono-pitched roof forms that suggest roof rooms once typical of the Edinburgh skyline.

Old Fishmarket Close (*Richard Murphy Architects*) reflects the architectural heritage in the same way. It received a Saltire (housing design) Award in 2004 and the judges commented "it fits comfortably into a difficult historic site and, at the same time, animates the pend in which it sits" (Fig. 5.19 and cover).

Prospect, 12/04, pp. 21–27; *Prospect*, 5/05, pp. 21–27.

Figure 5.17 Morgan Court forms an edge to the Edinburgh Old Town.

Community-based housing association development
1980s+. ASSIST Architects

The success of the various schemes built in the 1990s comes from the way they sit comfortably in their location. ASSIST Architects set out with the avowed intention not to build something that dominated the site, but rather to create a new building that would be at home. This was achieved by the use of the tenement housing form that contributes to the townscape quality of the street scenes. The use of familiar local references such as corner towers, bow and oriel windows, building materials that relate to traditional stone, has proved very popular with both the tenants and the housing associations.

West End Park Street/Woodlands Road, G3 (R. *Charing Cross*). A four-storey development for the Charing Cross Housing Association with a corner tower/conical roof (Fig. 5.8).

Carnarvon Street/St George's Road, Charing Cross, G3. 1993. (R. *Charing Cross/ St George's Cross*). Seventy-three flats and three shops for the Charing Cross Housing Association situated in a conservation area in East Woodlands. The development is four storeys in height with bay windows, traditional detailing and sculptured features to mirror the adjacent nineteenth century tenements.

Achamore Road/Katewell Avenue, Drumchapel, G15. 1994. (R. *Drumchapel*). This is a low-rise scheme in one of Glasgow's peripheral estates for the Cernach Housing Cooperative. The street elevation to Achamore Road is a mixture of two- and three-storey dwellings within which corners and the central part of the terrace were given special emphasis.

Tollcross Road/Sorby Street, G31. 1994. (R. *Carntyne*). This is a four-storey development for the Parkhead Housing Association containing seventy-one flats and two shops. Its red brick and cast stone with high-level pediments, oriel windows and glazed staircase screens harmonise well with the surrounding buildings.

James Nisbet Street, Roystonhill, G21. 1994. (R. *High Street*). Built in the 1960s by Glasgow City Council, these 200 four-storey tenement flats were taken over in 1989 by the James Nisbet Street Co-operative in 1989. The refurbishment included glazing in south- and west-facing balconies to create very cost effective sunspaces (Fig. 5.22). The scheme is well described and illustrated in *Sustaintable Housing Design Guide for Scotland*, pp. 257–259.

Prospect, Summer 1994, p. 25; *AJ*, 30/5/90, pp. 36–37.

Castlemilk Estate Regeneration, G45
1988+. City of Glasgow Department of Architecture and Related Services + others. R. Kings Park/Croftfoot

The peripheral Castlemilk Estate is located some 4 miles from the city centre. Its 9,700 dwellings, mostly four- and five-storey tenements, represented all that was paternalistic and monolithic about council house design in the city since the Second World War. After the publication of the government's "New life for Scotland" report in 1988, the Castlemilk Partnership was established between Glasgow City Council, Strathclyde Regional Council, the Glasgow Development Agency, Scottish Housing, the Training Agency, the Employment Service, housing associations, representatives of the local community and Glasgow Opportunities which spoke for the private sector.

The key strategy was to diversify tenure, taking some two-thirds of the housing out of council ownership and passing it in roughly equal proportions to housing associations and

Figure 5.22 Post-war tenements transformed at James Nisbet Street.

private tenure. The most unpopular housing was demolished and the remainder has been progressively improved. This has included topping a storey off the height of buildings, converting flats into houses, re-rendering and cavity filling external walls, renewing roof tiles and gutters, upgrading security and insulation and part enclosing balconies with glass blocks and curved metal roofs and reshaping the environment to create more defensible space and a higher standard generally (Figs. 5.7 and 5.23).

The aim of the partnership was to transform the physical condition of the estate and the economic and social life of the area. To achieve this, the Castlemilk Economic Development Agency (CEDA) was established. CEDA's task was to ensure that the economic regeneration moved in parallel with the physical development. Its work included training and job search. By supporting people wishing to set up in business through counselling and offering financial packages, it encouraged the private sector to become involved in the economic regeneration. It focused on the 16–18 school leavers aiming through training and the establishment of local "youth job clubs" to prevent long-term unemployment among the young of the area and recurrence of existing problems. The involvement of the tenants in the process of regeneration has clearly made an impact physically and has particularly helped change their attitudes, perceptions and personal awareness.

Figure 5.23 Castlemilk: physical plus social and economic regeneration at its best.

AT, 9/93, No. 42, p. 43; *Prospect*, Spring 1995, pp. 12–15.

The regeneration of the Gorbals, G5
1990+. (Masterplanners and Architects) CZWG, (Architects) Cooper Cromar Associates, The Holmes Partnership, Elder & Cannon Architects, Hypostyle Architects, Page & Park Architects, Simister Monaghan Architects, Wylie & Court, Young & Gault. U. Bridge Street

---

The Gorbals is one of the largest and most significant regeneration projects in Britain (Fig. 5.1). The overall plan for around 100 acres (40 ha) defined eight separate Regeneration Areas and envisaged an eventual population of approximately 16,000. A full range of local shops, public services and community facilities was proposed, complemented by significant opportunities for local employment. The eight areas were managed by a number of community-based agencies including the Crown Street Regeneration Project, the Gorbals Initiative, the New Gorbals Housing Association and the voluntary sector. The Greater Glasgow Health Board and the Strathclyde Police were active partners. Glasgow City Council, the Glasgow Development Agency, Scottish Homes and private housing developers were all involved in the overall co-ordination. Community involvement was seen as essential to the long-term success of the development but it proved difficult to involve people widely in other than a formal and reactive manner.

It was recognised from the outset that a narrowly based housing-led development would not deal with the inherent problems of social and economic deprivation. The poor local economy was tackled in the short term by the use of local contractors and the assessment of developers on the basis of their local employment and training proposals. In the long term the "Gorbals Initiative", a public/private partnership, was established as a local enterprise company. This stimulated employment through counselling, and supporting individuals as a means of personal development. It directly provided business, office and workspace in the area. Social regeneration included upgrading the Gorbals Health Centre, establishing a food co-operative, and a community/learning/arts centre in the listed St Francis Church. A drop-in-café offered training on video production, computing, aerobics, dancing, golf, five aside football, etc. and also provided information on training for work, welfare rights, housing, health issues and education.

Crown Street Regeneration Area

The 16 hectare (40 acre) Crown Street Regeneration Area was set up in 1990 following the demolition in 1987 of Basil Spence's Hutchinsontown "E" which consisted of 12 linked deck-access blocks known locally as the "Dampies". The overall redevelopment proposals came from a nationwide urban design competition won by CZWG. The plan proposed mixed development including almost 1000 new dwellings (75 per cent for sale, 25 per cent for rent), a new business centre, a new local centre, a budget hotel, some small office accommodation, student housing, light industrial units and a new local park (Fig. 5.24). The site was divided up into manageable packages, which were subject to a Developer/Architect Competition based on an Urban Development brief and a fixed land price so that submissions could be judged on their design merits. Each development package had strict conditions regarding management and maintenance of the development that ensured the long-term sustainability of the project.

The concept of the masterplan

CZWG's concept was to create a traditional Victorian street pattern with tree-lined boulevards and street parking forming city blocks where the front is clearly public and the back fully private. The building block was the tenement, which the plan considered to be "Scotland's, especially Glasgow's, traditional building form". Its design would meet modern living requirements with the ground and first floors of a four-storey block comprising three-bedroom maisonettes with their own front and back door and a private rear garden. Above these the two upper floors would contain one-, two- and three-bedroom flats accessed by a separate communal staircase.

These principles were the basis of the design of the early development phases. Completed in 1995, **Ballater Gardens** (Architects: Holmes Partnership) involved two private housebuilders and the New Gorbals Housing Association. It consists of three sides of a city block and provides a total of 117 flats or maisonettes and three shops. The scheme forms the "gateway" into the Crown Street Regeneration Project area and the sweeping curves of the terrace, and the corner turrets, are most distinctive. **Errol Gardens** and **Pine Place** (Architects: Cooper Cromar

Figure 5.24 Crown Street regeneration: CZWG's masterplan as built in 1998 (photo by Guthrie Aerial Photography).

Associates) consists of a four-storey development of 92 flats and maisonettes and 5 new shop units built around a private landscaped courtyard with the elevations designed in the modern image of a tenement block (Fig. 5.25). The same approach was adopted by Hypostyle Architects for the mixed rental/sale scheme at **Cumberland Street**, completed in 1997.

Gorbals East renewal area

Most interesting in this area is **Moffat Gardens** (completed 1998) on the corner of Moffat Street and Hayfield Street. This comprises a number of small housing projects grouped around a small urban square/garden.

In a deliberate attempt to introduce diversity, the New Gorbals Housing Association appointed different architects for each site. Simister Monaghan's four-storey pivotal corner block and family dwellings contrasts with Elder & Cannon Architects' "cube and ellipse" (Fig. 5.26). The designs for these schemes were based on an imaginative client's brief for "villa blocks" to form "landmarks" within the development.

Queen Elizabeth Square

The recent completion of the Queen Elizabeth Square development (Old Rutherglen Road) has made a significant mark in the area.

CHAPTER FIVE • SCOTLAND

Figure 5.25 Errol Gardens: new tenements in the Gorbals regeneration project.

Working to a masterplan produced by Hypostyle Architects, CZWG, Page and Park, and Elder and Cannon have produced three very distinct schemes that relate to each other through a common use of materials. Page and Park's **Priory Court** was designed as a crescent around St Francis Church, providing 71 one- and two-bedroom flats and maisonettes for private sale (Fig. 5.27). Elder and Cannon's scheme comprises two blocks of different heights – a horizontal block and a freestanding zinc-clad tower (Fig. 5.28). For CZWG their scheme was their first project in the Gorbals since producing the Crown Street masterplan and they rose to the challenge by placing a mixture of dwellings from family housing to

339

THE RIBA BOOK OF BRITISH HOUSING: 1900 TO THE PRESENT DAY

Figure 5.26 Cube and Ellipse: Moffat Gardens, New East Gorbals.

Figure 5.27 Queen Elizabeth Square: Priory Court wraps round St Francis Church.

Figure 5.28 Queen Elizabeth Square: two blocks of different heights by Elder and Cannon.

apartments around the perimeter of a city block, enclosing a private communal garden. On the south side is a mews of three-storey houses with curtilage parking (Fig. 5.29) whilst on the north is an L-shaped higher block containing two-storey family apartments with flats above: the family apartments are marked out by undulating elevations that snake their way around the block. Most dramatic are the ends of the blocks with cantilevered balconies (Fig 5.30).

The Gorbals has been transformed from one of Glasgow's least liked areas to one of the most popular. It demonstrates an important lesson for regeneration, which is that, "given the right market conditions, public investment in high-quality social housing can generate the conditions to increase land values and attract private developers" [1].

[1] *AT*, 5/06, p. 31; *Prospect*, Spring/95, pp. 18–21; *Prospect*, 10/97, p. 13; *AJ*, 5/12/96, p. 32; *Housing and Planning Review*, 10–11/95, p. 16; *AJ*, 4/5/94, p. 18; *BD*, 5/5/06, p. 4; *AT*, 5/06, pp. 30–35; *B*, 11/11/05, p. 22; *Planning*, 20/1/06, pp. 16; *Sustainable Housing Design Guide for Scotland* (updated 2007), pp. 233–235.

Riverside housing, Clyde Street, G15
1991. Davis Duncan Partnership. 1991. R & U Central Station/Argyle Street

This landmark project, which overlooks the River Clyde, was one of the first new housing schemes to regenerate the banks of the River Clyde. The development included 90 one-, two- and three-bedroom flats and penthouses with spectacular views over the river and beyond. Car parking is mainly located in the basement. The facade is not typical of Glasgow, but its red brick walls and wide black metal balconies are still most distinctive when viewed from across the river (Fig. 5.31).

Figure 5.29 CZWG's town houses and apartment block next to the Priory Court development.

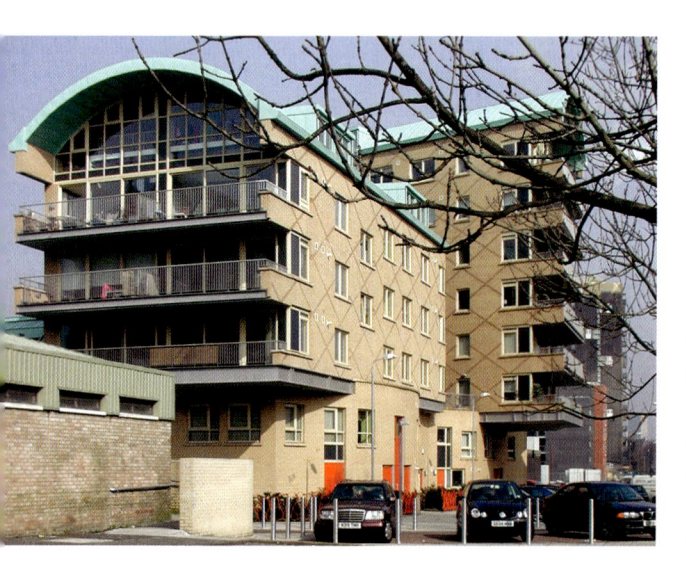

Figure 5.30 Queen Elizabeth Square with cantilevered balconies.

Graham Square, Gallowgate, G31
2000. McKeown Alexander, Page and Park, Richard Murphy Architects. R. Bellgrove.

The Graham Square housing development combines a contemporary design for new housing with the preservation of Grade B listed stone arched gateways, walling and hotel from the former Glasgow meat market (Fig. 5.32). The sites, located around a cul-de-sac off Gallowgate, were purchased by the Molendinar Park Housing Association who commissioned a masterplan from McGurn Logan Duncan and Opfer, which, although not implemented, gave an indication of the development potential.

CHAPTER FIVE ● SCOTLAND

Figure 5.31 Clyde Street apartments: early Glasgow riverside regeneration.

The McKeown Alexander housing scheme, on the left side of the square looking from Gallowgate contains 20 flats (6 for shared-ownership and 14 for rent) with a mix of one- and two-bedroom dwellings. The design retained two arches and walling, which are linked to the new housing by a structure of steel supports. The front elevations of the new housing have a variety of colours – bluish grey, ebony, silver and honey, and materials – full height glazing, zinc cladding, render, aluminium panels and cedar boarding.

The Molendinar Housing Association wanted the housing on the right side of the square to be more than normal social housing, to which Page and Park responded by designing housing with seven curved walls on the front elevation. Behind this façade the design of the two- and three-bedroom flats was based on the traditional tenement with three closes (access stairs) and eight flats per close on four floors.

Richard Murphy Architects converted the derelict Grade B Market Hotel into 17 one- and two-bedroom flats. The hotel consisted of three linked buildings. The central block was replaced with a new three-storey structure set back from the original building line. The wings on either side were rebuilt to create a private courtyard with the new centre building in which there is a glazed canopy over external staircases to the upper floor flats. Next to the arched gateway leading to the hotel is a bronze calf on a stone plinth by sculptor, Kenny Hunter.

AT, 10/2000, pp. 24–33; The Observer Review, 4/7/99, p. 8.

Homes for the Future, Glasgow Green, Greendyke Street, G15
1999. Masterplan: Park and Page with Ove Arup. Architects: Ushida Findlay, Ian Ritchie, Wren and Rutherford/Austin-Smith Lord, RMJM (Scotland), McKeown Alexander, Elder and Cannon, Rick Mather. R. Argyle Street

This scheme of 100 dwellings on a 0.6 hectare (1.5 acre) site overlooking Glasgow Green was designed by seven teams of architects,

343

Figure 5.34 Homes for the Future: a touch of Charles Rennie Mackintosh in Wren and Rutherford's design.

Glasgow's Victorian centre, close to the Theatre Royal, at an important road junction that marks a gateway into the city centre (Fig. 5.36). The triangular site therefore required a landmark building and a design competition was organised by Glasgow City Council. The scheme contains 73 apartments in blocks up to seven storeys high arranged around a courtyard garden. The accommodation includes 11 one-bedroom and 62 two-bedroom apartments with space for offices and a café bar on the ground floor of the Cowcadden block. The design drew much of its inspiration from Le Corbusier's Unité d'Habitation in Marseilles – in particular the internal streets and double volume living spaces with mezzanine first floors and fully glazed windows designed to enjoy the view [1].

[1] *AT*, 5/05, pp. 56–62; *B*, 11/11/05, pp. 4–5.

The Icon, Clyde Street, G1
2004. Elder and Cannon. R. Argyll Street

This sleek 13-storey tower adjacent St Andrew's cathedral and close to Kirkland's

CHAPTER FIVE • SCOTLAND

Figure 5.35 Homes for the Future: view of the front of the development from Glasgow Green.

historic suspension footbridge is a decisive landmark along the River Clyde skyline. It has an inventive long narrow shape tapering to a narrow façade fronting the river that enables many of the 48 flats and 4 two-storey penthouse apartments to enjoy the view. The apartments at the back of the block cleverly benefit from a large recess on the west elevation and a projection on the east, which provided the opportunities for corner windows to be provided in living rooms to optimise the view of the river. The proximity of the cathedral was carefully taken into account in choosing the finely jointed zinc cladding to the tower to create a building of exceptional quality. To add to the sculptural quality, windows on the sides were projected out from the façades (Fig. 3.37).

AT, 4/05, pp. 20–26; *Prospect*, 12/04, pp. 21–27.

IRVINE

Irvine New Town, North Ayrshire, KA12 and KA13
1966–1996. Irvine Development Corporation Architects: George Wren in Succession to Ian Downs, John Billingham and David Gosling (Roan Rutherford, Principal Architect). R. Irvine/Kilwinning

Despite the Conservative Government's dislike of new towns, Irvine Development

Figure 5.36 "The Matrix": landmark building on the edge of the Glasgow city centre.

Corporation remained in existence well into the 1990s and continued to construct housing for rent at a time when authorities were prevented from building. Amongst the early schemes, the daring use of colour at Bourtree Hill (early 1970s), and the careful attention to traditional detailing at **Braehead** (1978) received considerable acclaim.

However, of greatest interest is the outstanding work of the Corporation's architects and consultants in the 1990s who refurbished old housing and built new on small infill sites. This included the **Cochrane Street redevelopment** (Fig. 5.38), the Harbourside, Peter Street and Gottries Crescent, and Abbeygate at Kilwinning, all completed in 1995/1996. The schemes delightfully reflect influences of Charles Rennie Mackintosh. The white painted harled blockwork walls and gateposts, cast stone cills and plinth blocks, redwood joinery, natural slates, stained glass windows and decorative ironwork are wonderfully worked together to create compositions of great delight enjoyed by the local people.

CHAPTER FIVE • SCOTLAND

Figure 5.37 "The Icon" overlooking, the River Clyde: inspired by the Unite d'Habitation.

Hawthorne Place, Nethermains, Kilwinning (1988). The Development Corporation also built a number of Category 2 sheltered housing schemes with warden supervision. Hawthorne Place provides 17 two-person/one-bedroom flats and a number of two-person/one-bedroom and three-person/two-bedroom flats capable of adaption for wheelchair use. These are all accessed from three corridors which overlook well-planted gardens. The corridors radiate from a central top-lit atrium that forms the hub of the plan. Single-storey development with "single banked" corridors and this quality of internal finish is a remarkable achievement within the cost yardsticks (Fig. 5.39). The same quality of internal space was repeated at **Bryce Knox Court** (1992). Here the atrium is subdivided into different activity areas including a small library. The planting in the centre of the space creates the atmosphere of an indoor garden (Fig. 5.40).

PERTH AND KINROSS

Commercial Street, Bridgend, Perth, PH1
1978. SMC Parr Architects. R. Perth

This design sought to emulate in a modern way the scale and atmosphere of the buildings that had existed previously on the site. It also endeavoured to ensure that all living rooms had a view of the river.

349

Figure 5.38 Irvine new town: Charles Rennie Mackintosh influences at Cochrane Street.

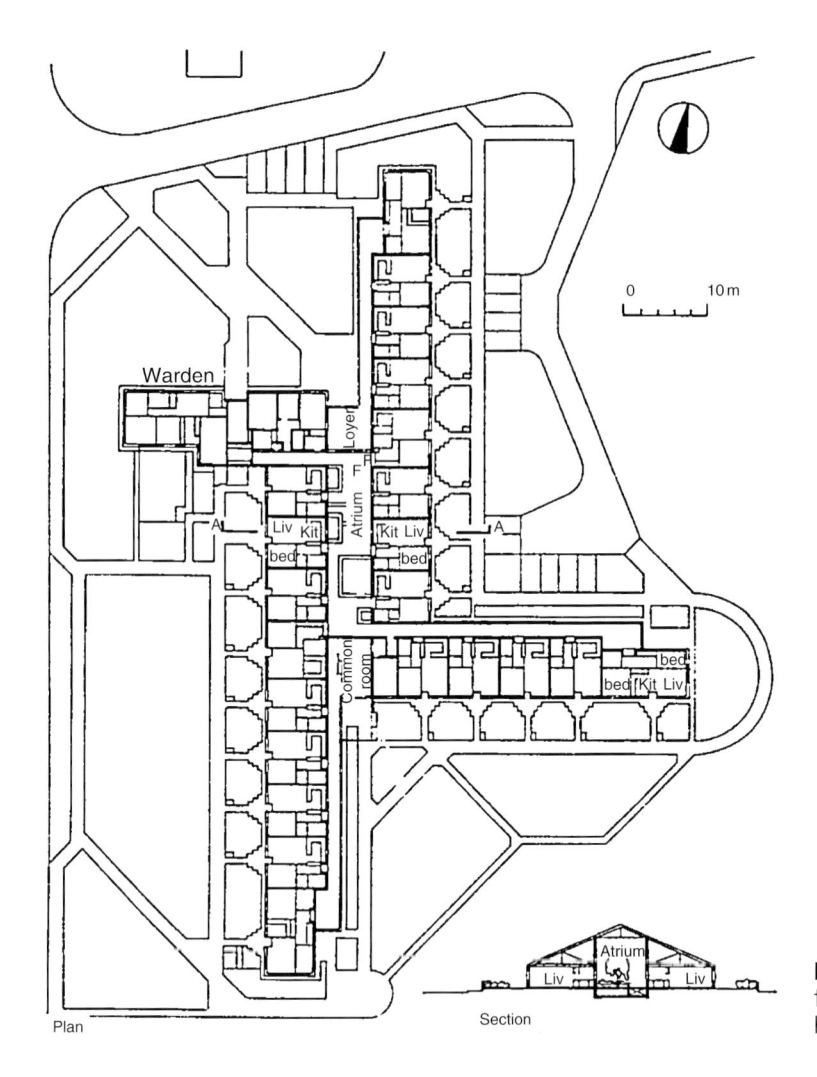

Figure 5.39 Irvine now town: sheltered housing at Hawthorn Place, Kilwinning.

The accommodation consists of 12 five-person houses, 22 three- and four-person flats and 8 four-person maisonettes, clustered in one- to four-storey blocks to create a varied roofline. Particularly well handled is the modelling of the housing on the steep slope of the site down to the river. The walls of the houses and the site works are of sandblasted blockwork relating to local stone and the windows are of dark-stained timber. The roofs are covered mostly with the second-hand grey Scottish slates that came from the demolished buildings (Fig. 5.41).

AJ, 13/12/78, pp. 1137–1149; RIBAJ, 8/83, p. 61.

Scrimgeours Corner, Comrie Street and West High Street, Crieff, Perth and Kinross, PH7
1992. Nicholl Russell Studios, Dundee. R. Perth

Scrimgeours Corner is a five-storey development built by the Servite Housing Association (Scotland) Ltd. The site was situated within the Crieff High Street Conservation area and the planning brief required the design to create

351

Figure 5.40 Bryce Knox Court, Kilwinning: sheltered housing atrium divided into different activity areas.

a focal point on the corner of Comrie Street and West High Street.

The scheme comprises 21 two-person flats, 1 single-person flat, a communal laundry room and a shop. The dwelling plans are shaped in accordance with their position on the site but living rooms and kitchens are placed to have good views (Figs 5.42 and 5.43). Externally the building takes its shape, materials and colour from the neighbouring buildings. By slicing it into two apparently separate blocks, each aligned and grafted onto its neighbouring building, the corner was opened up to create a small semi-public space which forms the entrance to the development. This also gives the impression of the development growing out of its surroundings that was a major aim of the design. Towers complete each wing at the corner in a manner wholly in keeping with Crieff's traditional architecture.

Prospect, Winter/95, pp. 14–15.

CHAPTER FIVE • SCOTLAND

Figure 5.41 Commercial Street Perth (photo by Alex Couper, SPANPHOTO of Dundee).

SCOTTISH BORDERS

Marine Square, Eyemouth, TD14
*1994. Swan Architects.
R. Berwick-upon-Tweed +
public transport*

This development of 29 mainly single-person flats is located in the heart of Eyemouth Old Town Conservation Area overlooking the sea (Fig. 5.44). Formerly occupied by a network of old industrial buildings the site had become derelict.

The design was influenced by a concern to reflect the townscape qualities of the area. It consists of five distinct buildings arranged around an open space and along the Marine Parade frontage, with flats positioned to allow frequent expression of tall narrow gables, sometimes end on to the sea. This creates an impression of height, which is further emphasised by vertically proportioned windows, steep

353

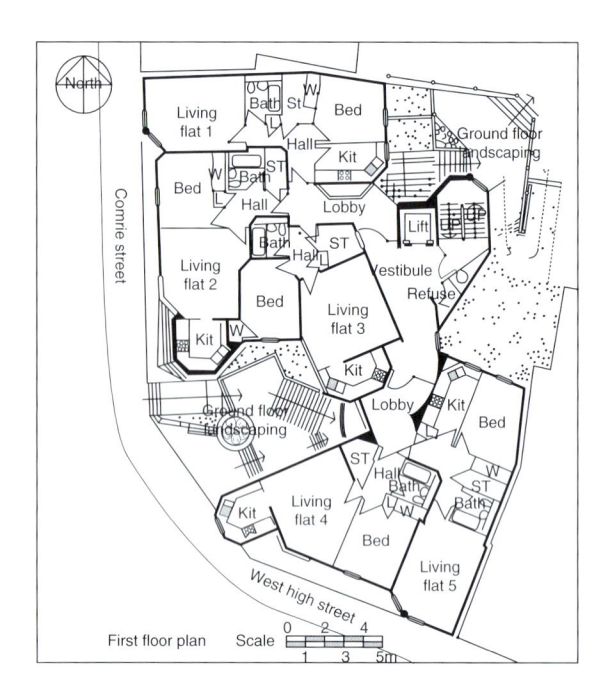

Figure 5.42 Scrimgeours Corner, Crieff: ground floor plan.

Figure 5.43 Scrimgeours Corner, Crieff (photo by Architects).

CHAPTER FIVE • SCOTLAND

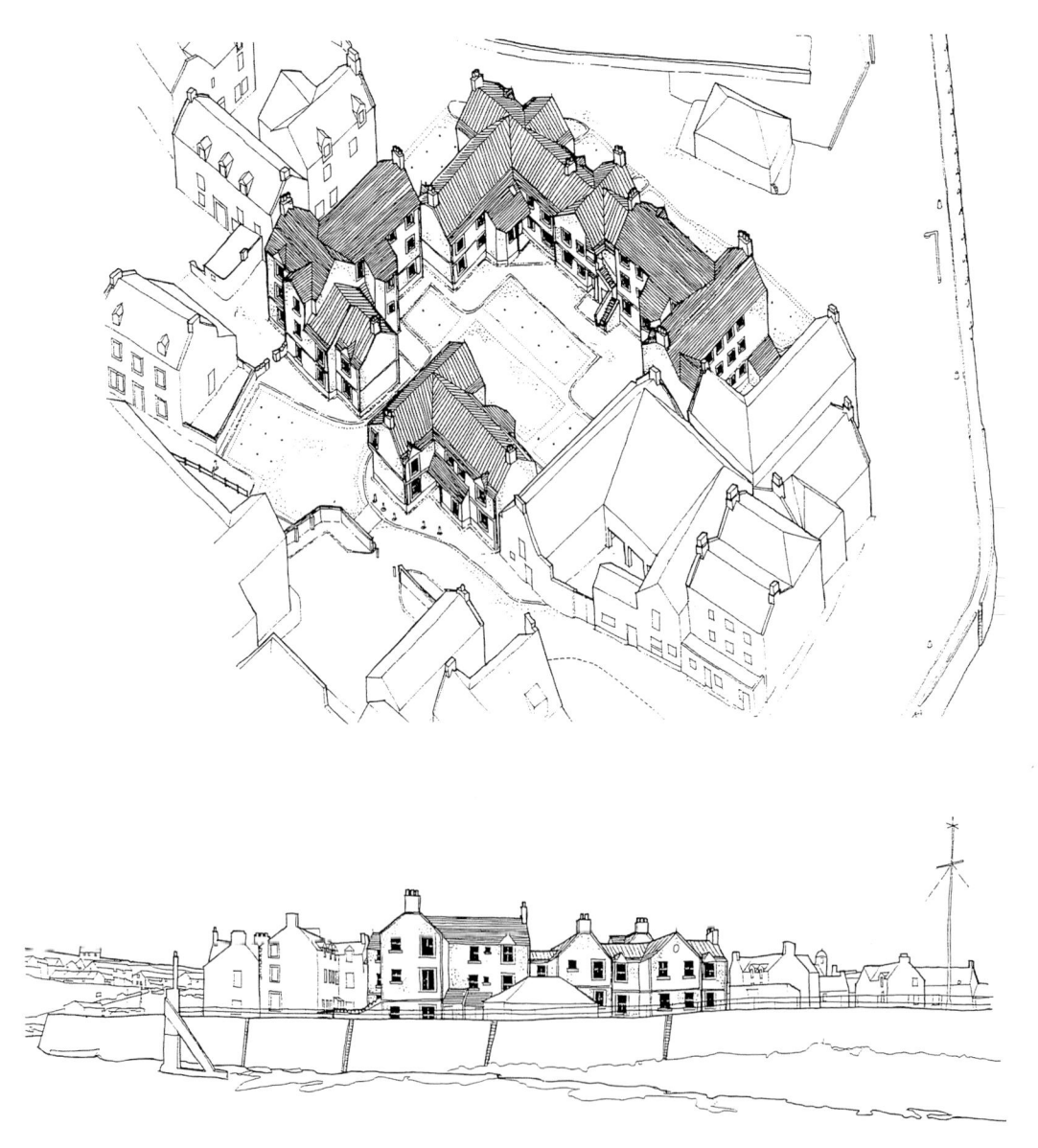

Figure 5.44 Marine Square, Eyemouth: clustering of houses around a small square and harbourfront.

slated pantiled roofs and tall chimneys. External wall finishes are dry dash, the colours of which recall those of Gunsgreen House across the harbour.

Illustrative stained glass by Joanna Scott enhances the entrances to the buildings and designs by Eyemouth High School Art Department have been incorporated into ceramic medallions made for the dormer peaks by Peter Thomas.

Prospect, Autumn/94, p. 23.

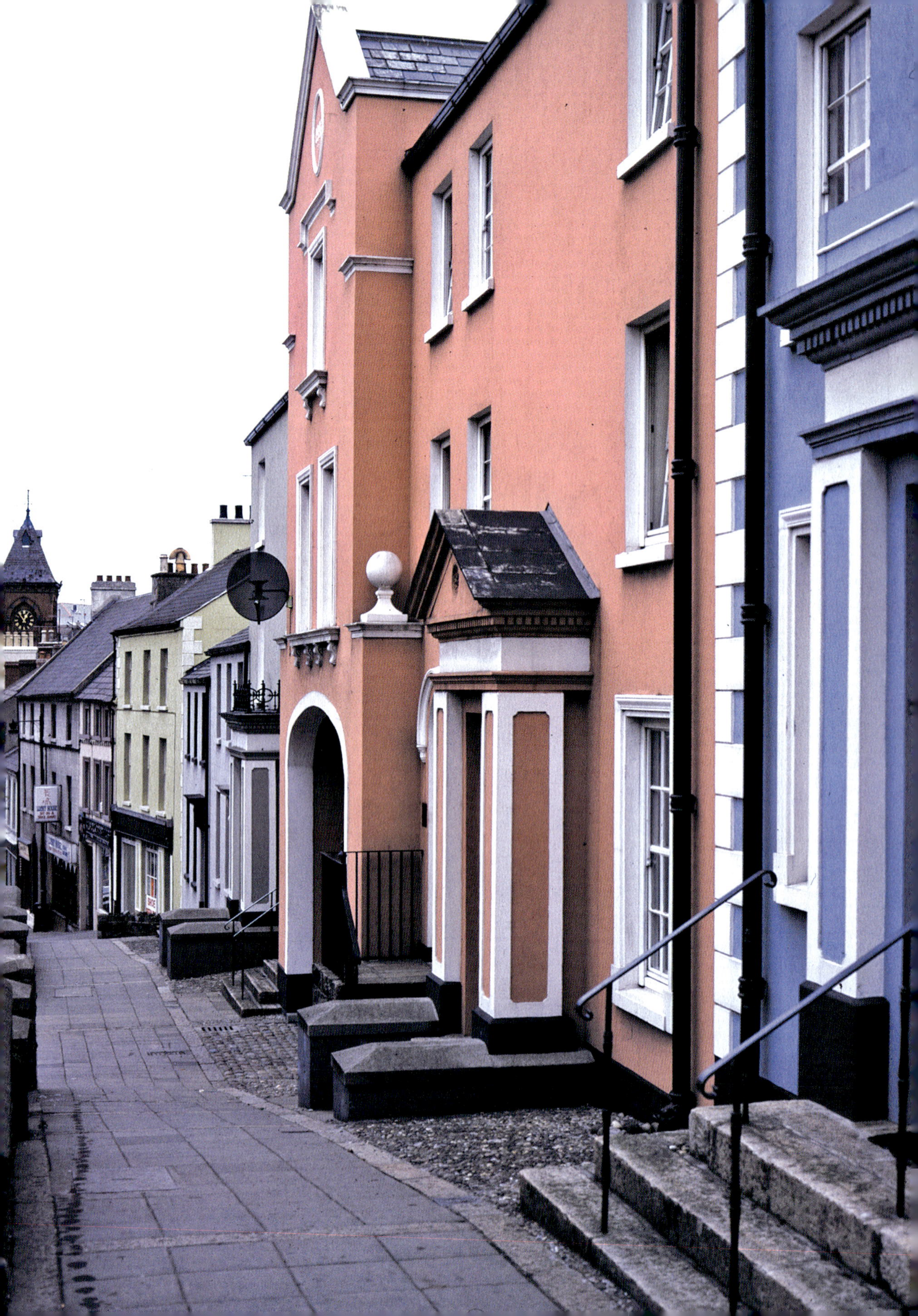

Northern Ireland

Figure 6.2 Northern Ireland: counties, towns and cities where the schemes are located.

1. Co. Armagh
2. Belfast
3. Co. Down

Introduction

Housing proved to be a highly contentious issue in Northern Ireland throughout most of the twentieth century. Between the First and Second World Wars very little was done by government nationally and locally to tackle the poor housing conditions in Belfast and Northern Ireland in general. It was a prominent part of the Civil Rights campaign of the late 1960s as public demonstrations pointed to poor housing conditions and a growing dissatisfaction with housing administration. Between 1969 and 1973 some 60,000 people were forced by the "troubles" to leave their homes, and territorialism became important as each community sought refuge in their historic districts. This added to the housing pressures, which by the early 1970s had become an overwhelming issue.

High-density housing

Change came in the late 1960s when the Belfast Urban Plan of 1969 estimated that 75,000 new dwellings should be built in the city. The need existed due to the clearance of unfit housing, the consequence of motorway

Figure 6.1 Irish Street, Downpatrick: modern interpretation of Georgian street housing. (p. 370)

clearance programmes and new household formation. Even with population dispersal to growth areas like Craigavon New Town, designated in 1965, it was estimated that new development built in the "Urban Area" would need to be above four or five storeys. As a consequence, the pattern of development followed the mainland British model with similar disastrous consequences, but aggravated by the political unrest. Over 40 high-rise blocks were built in Northern Ireland. In Belfast the largest and most notable was the twenty-storey point block built amongst the eight-storey deck-access Divis flats in the Falls Road area, providing more than 800 flats in one estate. The medium rise Lower Shankhill (known locally as the "Weetabix boxes") and Unity were also built between 1966 and 1972. In Derry City, the Rossville flats were fortunately the only high-rise development to be built in the city.

The Northern Ireland Housing Executive

In 1971 the government undertook a radical reform of housing administration involving its transfer from local authority control to an entirely new single-purpose body, the Northern Ireland Housing Executive (NIHE). This was given six key tasks:

1. Building new homes of a consistent standard across Northern Ireland.
2. Managing and maintaining existing housing estates.
3. Helping the private sector through grant aid.
4. Measuring housing conditions throughout Northern Ireland.
5. Undertaking housing research programmes.
6. Providing housing advice and information.

One of its main cultural aims has been and still remains the carrying out of its duties with fairness and equity between communities.

Progress "brick by brick" (1)

Its first house condition survey of 1974 painted a bleak picture of large areas of derelict and unfit housing with massive overcrowding. Northern Ireland was found to have the worst housing conditions in Britain if not Europe and comparisons were made between Belfast and Naples. One in four houses in Belfast were classified as unfit with a ratio of one in five for Northern Ireland as a whole. This enormous task required the support of a sophisticated research and development facility. The crisis was of such a scale that a comprehensive approach was necessary. By establishing architectural groups drawn from former public housing bodies, an excellence in design was developed. This recognised regional differences yet utilised standard house types and details.

Until the mid-1970s most development was on greenfield sites. Planned in 1973, the controversial Poleglass development was built on a former greenfield site in south-west Belfast. This development was required to alleviate pressure for housing in greater West Belfast and today it contains over 2050 homes. It initially met with hostile opposition from representatives of the majority community who feared an expansion of the minority community in West Belfast.

From 1979 onwards there was a radical shift of emphasis to inner city regeneration, which remains the major focus today.

Innovation and quality

The incoming Conservative government of 1979 halted new housing development in Northern Ireland but by 1981 it had been persuaded to identify housing as the Province's first social priority. Poor housing conditions and long waiting lists demanded immediate and sustained treatment – an intensive programme directed at the core of the problem – which was rooted in Belfast. In 1982 the Belfast Housing Renewal Strategy paved the way for a huge programme of development in the city. It identified over 40 small areas for redevelopment and a further 15 as Housing Action Areas where the emphasis would be on refurbishment. A third dimension of the strategy related to areas of private housing where the Executive was eager to encourage the uptake of renovation grants and the injection of private finance to stimulate home improvements.

Low-rise housing

During the peak years of the strategy's implementation in the 1980s and 1990s around 1,500 homes were built annually in Belfast with a further 1,500 in the rest of Northern Ireland. The policy of involving in-house and consultant architects to produce individual low-rise design solutions, within the Executive's standard range of house types, was successful. Most schemes were small in scale and used bright, colourful brickwork and rendering and a wealth of imaginative detailing (Fig. 6.3). The general pattern was for the housing to be designed around pedestrian/vehicular mews courts using a variety of

Figure 6.3 St George's Gardens, Sandy Row, Belfast, 1987, recapturing the best social features of traditional urban terraces.

Figure 6.5 Castle Street, Armagh, respecting strong architectural traditions (photo by NIHE).

Built on a city centre site, it contains 43 houses and 28 flats grouped around two well-planted block paved courts (Fig. 6.6). These have a strong sense of enclosure and are safe places for children to play in. Car parking is located directly outside the dwellings where vehicles are overlooked. The architecture is essentially urban reflecting the character of Belfast's traditional terraced housing. Multi-coloured brickwork detailing of the house elevations creates interest and the overall affect is of calmness and tranquility.

B, Housing Design Awards 1989, pp. 30–31.

Carrick Hill, Upper Library Street
1994. NIHE Design Services

Carrick Hill, which replaced the Unity Flats, illustrates the NIHE's design approach to replacing the former deck-access housing. Community participation influenced the decision to provide predominately two-storey housing around pedestrian/vehicular courts which was considered by the tenants to be the most effective means of cutting out through traffic (Fig. 6.7). Car parking in small open bays close to the dwellings was also

CHAPTER SIX • NORTHERN IRELAND

Figure 6.6 Lancaster Street, Belfast, reflects the high-quality design by NIHE architects and consultants.

preferred. The houses were stepped and staggered to add variety to the design which was further emphasised by the use of contrasting brickwork and render which gives individuality to each dwelling. Semi-mature trees and generous landscaping all add to the sense of place.

B, Housing Design Awards, *Building Homes*, 27/9/95, p. 29.

Divis Estate redevelopment, Milford Street/Cullingworth Road
1998, NIHE Design Services

The 795 Divis flats were built between 1966 and 1972 by the Northern Ireland Housing Trust. Its urgent need was to redevelop Belfast's slums by replacing the dense warren of streets known as the Pound Loney. The complex of 12 medium-rise blocks and the 20-storey Divis Tower became the largest single development of flats in Northern Ireland. However, the drab concrete appearance never appealed to its residents and by the early 1980s parts were being demolished. In 1986, the result of an Investment Appraisal indicated a clear preference for replacing the medium-rise blocks with around 260 new dwellings and the phased decanting of the residents from the old to the new housing. The tower would remain to be refurbished and occupied by single people and couples.

363

Figure 6.7 Carrick Hill (photo by NIHE).

There was a high degree of resident participation – questionnaires, consultation with individuals and groups, and door-to-door surveys were carried out. Several strategy layouts were then produced. The outcome was a clear desire for a mixture of one-to three-storey dwellings grouped along traditional open ended streets with some residents asking for courts. Both layout preferences were adopted and the street pattern now echoes the road pattern of the old Pound Loney with a main street, Milford Street, running through the heart of the area with smaller link streets running off towards Cullingtree Road. T-junctions were used as a traffic calming measure. The residents also preferred traditional Belfast red brick housing combined with a measure of individuality. The housing is now complete and very popular. St Peter's Cathedral, previously overshadowed by the deck-access blocks, has again become the focal point (Fig. 6.8).

Perspective, 11–12/93, pp. 19–21.

Laganview Apartments, Bridge End
1993. The Boyd Partnership

A visit to Belfast's new concert hall offers the best viewing point for the first waterfront housing to be developed by the Laganside Urban Development Corporation. The brief for the developer-led competition called for tall buildings for the riverside which resulted in four-storey development with penthouse apartments and strong chimneys to give the scheme verticality when viewed across the river (Fig. 6.9). By orientating the facade south-west towards the curving River Lagan and installing full-length windows in every apartment, the architects gave every occupant a view of the river. They also provided every apartment with a private balcony off the living room. At the entrance to the site, close to a NIHE development at

CHAPTER SIX • NORTHERN IRELAND

Figure 6.8 The cathedral is once more the dominant element in the new Divis Estate.

Rotterdam Court, are townhouses, built along the street frontage, that link the public sector housing to the apartment block.

Perspective, 9/10/93, pp. 56–58.

Tudor Road renewal, Crumlin Road/ Shankhill Road
2003 onwards, NIHE Design Services

The Tudor Road renewal area lies between Crumlin Road and Shankhill Road in North Belfast. It was one of the areas most affected by the past political difficulties. Built in the early twentieth century its housing was small with only two bedrooms. The renewal project included 790 new houses and 30 shops. The residents were heavily involved in the design and, at first they did not want demolition of their homes. However, they soon preferred to live in new housing provided it was the kind they wanted. When taken to see town houses, apartments and other high-density housing being built in regeneration areas in London, they expressed an instant dislike. Most people wanted three-bedroom, two-storey houses with gardens. This they said would offer flexibility for occupation by elderly people as well as families with children. It would therefore be more sustainable. They even wanted semi-detached housing but the NIHE would only permit this form for private housing (Fig. 6.10).

The roads in the area form a three-tier hierarchy whereby the two main arterial roads, Crumlin and Shankland link with Agnes Street and Tennent Street to form an overall boundary grid. The local roads within that boundary form a smaller permeable grid. Movement within this smaller grid is discouraged by designing the roads to 20 mph maximum by the use of junctions, bends and occasional vertical speed restrictions to existing streets.

Figure 6.9 Riverside private apartments inspired by the Laganside Urban Development Corporation.

Figure 6.10 Tudor Road private housing development.

The houses either front on to these roads or on to shared surface courts that provide a safe environment for children. These are through streets designed in a "Z" or "L" shape to create two or more short spaces that appear closed off at one end as if they were culs-de-sac. Entrances at each end were given gateway treatment (Fig. 6.11).

The housing is mixed tenure but mostly social rented. Small groups of private and housing association development are integrated as part of the neighbourhood. Incentives in the form of purchase at construction cost price have had a remarkable affect as many of the better off people in the community jumped at the chance to buy into the community.

Co. Down

The following NIHE schemes in Co. Down indicate how the Executive looked at housing problems in the smaller towns and rural areas in the 1980s and 1990s. They demonstrate a commitment to preserving the Province's distinctive architectural heritage through using housing designs that are in sympathy with the character of the old villages and historic country towns.

Shore Street/Union Street, Donaghadee
1981. McAdam Design. Local Transport

Donaghadee is a small coastal town at the mouth of the Belfast Lough and the new scheme involved the redevelopment of part of its water frontage (Fig. 6.12) along Shore Street and Union Street which had contained cottages dating back to the eighteenth century when the town was the main sea trading link with Scotland. Unfortunately the cottages were too far dilapidated to be refurbished.

Figure 6.11 Tudor Road "L" and "Z" shaped through mews courtyards.

Figure 6.12 Shore Street/ Union Street, Donghadee (photo by NIHE).

Instead the layout and the dwelling design follows their form and retains an old established pedestrian route (Schoolhouse Brae) across the site, which links the new housing with the town shopping area. The slope of the site meant that housing at the rear of the site could be at a higher level than the bungalows fronting Shore Street, which gives them extensive views over the rooftops to the Copeland Islands and Donaghadee Harbour. The 29 dwellings for rent include a mixture of houses, flats and bungalows and are standard housing executive designs. The external treatment of the buildings and the landscaping embody local materials and features to keep the scheme in character with its surroundings; wall finishes are white painted roughcast with contrasting projecting plasterwork features, corner quoins, window and door surrounds and plinths.

New Bridge Street redevelopment, Downpatrick
1986. NIHE Design Services

This small redevelopment scheme containing 17 houses and 5 bungalows for rent lies on the main road from Belfast into the Downpatrick. There is a huge roundabout in front of the site but the housing design is

Figure 6.13 New Bridge Street, Downpatrick.
(Photo by NIHE, from house, home and design, *Architectural Publications Ltd., 1988*, p. 19.)

sufficiently strong to ensure a prominence at this important entrance point to the town. The straightforward strip frontage site gave little scope for layout design except building a single terrace with car parking at the rear, but within this constraint, the architects found a balance of one-, two-, and three-storey dwellings that is visually attractive and reflects the character of Downpatrick.

The visual quality of the terrace was heightened by stepping the rooflines to a climax at the highest point in the centre which was emphasised by placing of strong colour on a single dwelling (Fig. 6.13). Here the footpath is also elevated to separate pedestrians from the busy road below. The landscape treatment at the front is extremely good, using heavy blocks of local stone and large areas of pebbles set in front of the windows and in the areas of attractive planting.

B, Housing Design Awards 1989 Publication, pp. 62–63.

Redevelopment of 34–55 Irish Street, Downpatrick
1992. NIHE Design Services

The town of Downpatrick has a strong eighteenth and nineteenth century townscape structure. The architecture is a mixture of imposing civic buildings, townhouses, and small-scale commercial and residential buildings all of which offer great variety and sense of enclosure. The centre of the town was declared a conservation area in 1985.

The redevelopment at Irish Street followed an options appraisal that considered, but rejected, the possibility of refurbishing the existing buildings. The planning requirements for the new development strictly called for the new development to maintain the building line and be designed to a scale and with materials that reflected the original buildings (Fig. 6.1). This was achieved through building a continuous terrace of two-storey houses and three-storey flats with a single maisonette over an archway in the mid-point of the terrace through which access is gained to car parking at the rear. The bright colours of the rendering are particularly effective. The natural Welsh roofing slates and granite kerbs and setts were salvaged from the previous buildings on the site and reused.

Perspective, 5/94, pp. 15–17.

Abbreviations

A&BN	*Architect and Building News*
AD	*Architectural Design*
AJ	*The Architects Journal*
AR	*The Architectural Review*
AT	*Architecture Today*
B	*Building*
BB	*Brick Bulletin*
BD	*Building Design*
BISF	British Iron and Steel Federation
BRE	Building Research Establishment
CHAR	Campaign for Homeless and Rootless recently renamed Natural Homeless Alliance)
CIOH	Chartered Institute of Housing
CLG	Communities and Local Government
DC	Development Corporation
DETR	Department of the Environment and Transport
DOE	Department of the Environment
DoT	Department of Transport
DfT	Department for Transport
DTLR	Department of Transport, Local Government and the Regions
EH	English Heritage
ELHA	East London Housing Association
ERDF	European Research and Development Fund
GEAR	Glasgow Eastern Area Renewal
GLC	Greater London Council
Ha	Hectare
HAT	Housing Action Trust
IBA	Internationale Bauausstellung Berlin
JRF	Joseph Rowntree Foundation
LCC	London County Council
LDCC	London Docklands Development Corporation
MoHLG	Ministry of Housing and Local Government

ABBREVIATIONS

MoH	Ministry of Health
MT	Ministry of Transport
NFHA	National Federation of Housing Associations
NIHE	Northern Ireland Housing Executive
ODPM	Office of the Deputy Prime Minister
P	Planning
PSI	Office of Public Sector Information (formerly HMSO)
PSSHAK	Primary Support and Housing Assembly Kit
RIBA	Royal Institute of British Architects
RSL	Registered Social Landlord
SAP	(Rating) Standard Assessment Rating (BRE)
SDA	Scottish Development Agency
SLASH	Scottish Local Authority Special Housing Group
SSHA	Scottish Special Housing Association
SRB	Single Regeneration Budget
TRADA	Timber Research and Development Association
UDC	Urban Development Corporation
UHRU	Urban Housing Renewal Unit

Travel Abbreviations

DLR	Docklands Light Railway
M	Metro (Tyneside)
R	Rail Station
U	Underground (London and Glasgow)

English Heritage

Reference is made in several places to English Heritage publications all entitled *Something Worth Keeping? Post-War Architecture in Britain*, 1996. The publications were concerned with building types and, unless otherwise stated, the reference EH (followed by the page number) relates to *Housing and Houses*. See also www.english-heritage.org.uk and book by Elain Harwood, *A Guide to Post-war Listed Buildings*, second edition, B.T. Batsford, 2003.

Bibliography

Aldous, A., *Urban Villages*, The Urban Villages Group, London, 1992.

Alexander, C. *The Timeless Way of Building*, Oxford University Press, New York, 1979.

Alexander, C., and Chermayeff, S., *Community and Privacy: Towards a New Architecture of Humanism*, Doubleday, New York, 1963.

Alexander, C. et al, *A Pattern Language: Towns, Buildings, Construction*, Oxford University Press, New York, 1977.

Balchin, P.N., *Housing Policy: An Introduction*, Routledge, Oxford, 1989.

Barton, H., Davis, G., and Guise, R., *Sustainable Settlements – A Guide for Planners, Designers and Developers*, The University of the West of England/The Local Government Management Board, London, 1966.

Beattie, S., *A Revolution in London Housing: LCC Housing Architects and Their Work, 1893–1914*, The Architectural Press, London, 1970.

Begg, T., *50 Special Years; A Study of Scottish Housing*, Henry Melland, London, 1986.

Begg, T., *Housing Policy in Scotland*, John Donald Publishers Ltd, Edinburgh, 1996.

Bentley, I., Alcock, A., Murrain, P., McGlynn, S., and Smith, G., *Responsive Environments, A Manual for Designers*, Butterworth-Heinemann, Architectural Press, Oxford, 1985, reprinted 1993.

Bentley, I., Davis, I., and Oliver, P., *Dunroamin: The Suburban Semi and Its Enemies*, Barrie and Jenkins, London, 1981.

Birkbeck, D., and Scoones, A., *The New House-building Agenda*, Prefabulous Homes, 2005, Constructing Excellence London, 2005.

Boal, F.W., *Shaping a City, Belfast in the Late Twentieth Century*. The Institute of Irish Studies, The Queen's University of Belfast, 1995.

Borer, P., and Harris, C., *Out of the Woods: Ecological Designs for Timber-Frame Housing*, The Centre for Alternative Technology, Powys, Wales, 1997.

Borer, P., and Harris, C., *The Whole House Book: Ecological Building Design and Materials*, The Centre for Alternative Technology, Powys, Wales, 1998.

Broome, J., and Richardson, B., *The Self-Build Book*, Green Earth Books, Totnes, Devon, 1995.

Burnett, J., *A Social History of Housing*, Routledge, London, 1990.

Chapman, D., *Creating Neighbourhoods and Places in the Built Environment*, E&FN Spon, London, 1996.

Charles, Prince of Wales, *A Vision of Britain: A Personal View of Architecture*, Doubleday, London, 1989.

Chartered Institute of Housing/Royal Institute of British Architects, *Homes for the Future*, CIOH/RIBA, Coventry and London, 1981. Also supplements on the following topics:
Housing Design Brief, 1987.
Housing for Elderly People, 1988.
Housing for Disabled People, 1989.
Housing Rehabilitation, 1988.

Chartered Institute of Housing/Royal Institute of British Architects, *Tenant Participation*, The Architectural Press, London, 1988.

Chartered Institute of Housing (edited by B. Derbyshire, W. Hatchett and R. Turkington), *Taking Stock, Social Housing in the Twentieth Century*, CIOH, Coventry, 1996.

Church of England, *Faith in the City, A Call for Action By Church and Nation*, Church House Publishing, London, 1985.

Coleman, A., *Utopia On Trial: Vision and Reality in Planned Housing*, Hilary Shipman, London, 1985.

Colquhoun, I., *Design Out Crime, Creating Safe and Sustainable Communities*, Elsevier/Architectural Press, Oxford, 2004.

BIBLIOGRAPHY

Colquhoun, I., and Fauset, P.G., *Housing Design in Practice*, Longman UK, Harlow, 1991.

Colquhoun, I., and Fauset, P.G., *Housing Design: an International Perspective*, B.T. Batsford, London, 1991.

Colquhoun, I., *Urban Regeneration*, B.T Batsford, London, 1995.

Commission for Architecture and the Built Environment (CABE) London:
- *Housing Audit: assessing the design quality of new housing in the East Midlands, West Midlands, West Midlands and the South West* (2007).
- *Actions for housing growth: creating a legacy of great places* (2007).
- *New things happen: a guide to the future Thames Gateway* (2006).
- *Building for Life newsletter issue 6: accommodating the motorcar* (2006).
- *Delivering great places in which to live: 20 questions you need to answer* (2005).
- *Housing audit: Assessing the design quality of new homes in the North East, North West, and Yorkshire & Humber* (2005).
- *What it's like to live there: the views of residents on the design of new housing* (2005).
- *Building for Life Standard: A Better Place to Live* (2005).
- *Building for Life newsletter issue 5: regeneration and remodeling* (2005).
- *Building for Life newsletter issue 3: housing growth areas and urban planning* (2005).
- *What home buyers want: attitudes and decision making among consumers* (2005).
- *Better neighbourhoods: making higher densities work* (2005).
- (With ODPM and English Partnerships), *Design coding: testing its use in England* (2005).
- *Creating successful neighbourhoods: lessons and actions for housing market renewal* (2005).
- *Quantity or Quality?* (2005).
- *Housing Audit: assessing the design quality of new homes (London and the South East of England)* (2004).
- *Building for Life Newsletter issue 1: sustainability* (2004).
- *The home buyer's guide: what to look and ask for when buying a new home* (2004)
- (With the Department of the Environment, Transport and the Regions and Design for Homes), *The Value of Housing Design and Layout* (2003).

Communities and Local Government, Planning Policy Statements
- PPS1: *Delivering Sustainable Development* (2005).
- PPS3: *Housing* (2006).
- PPS7: *Sustainable Development in Rural Areas* (2004).

Communities and Local Government and the Department of Transport, *Manual for Streets*, Thomas Telford Ltd, London, 2007.

Communities and Local Government; *Eco Towns Prospectus* (2007) CLG, London.

Communities and Local Government: *Homes for the Future: more affordable, more sustainable* (2007) CLG, London.

Conran, T., *The Essential Housebook*, Conran Octopus Limited, London, 1994.

Cooper Marcus, C., and Sarkisson, W., *Housing Design As If People Mattered – Site Design Guidelines for Medium-Density Family Housing*, University of California Press, Berkeley, CA, 1986.

Cooper Marcus, C., *The House As A Mirror of Self Exploring the Deeper Meaning of Home*, Conari Press, Berkeley, CA, 1995.

Cowling, D., *An Essay for Today, the Scottish New Towns, 1947–1997*, Rutland Press, Edinburgh, 1997.

Dean, P., *The Perfect Village*, BBC, TV programme, London, 2006.

Department of Energy, *Measures to Save Energy, Helping the Earth Begins at Home*, Department of Energy, London, 1992.

Department of the Environment, *Estate Action: Handbook of Estate Improvement*, HMSO, London, 1991.

Department of the Environment, Transport and the Regions (DETR), *Places, Streets and Movement, A Companion Guide to Design Bulletin 32: Residential Roads and Footpaths*, DETR, London, 1998.

Department of the Environment, *Quality in Town & Country*, HMSO, London, 1994.

Department of the Environment/Department of Transport., Design Bulletin 32, *Residential Roads and Footpaths*, HMSO, London, 1977. (2nd edn, 1992).

BIBLIOGRAPHY

Department of Transport, Local Government and the Regions (DTLR), By Design, Better places to live: A companion guide to PPG3, Thomas Telford Ltd, London, 2001.

Department of Transport, Local Government and the Regions (DTLR), Rethinking Construction: The Report of the Construction Task Force (Egan Report), DTLR, London, 1998.

Donnison, D., and Middleton, A., *Regenerating the Inner City: Glasgow's Experience*, Routledge & Kegan Paul, London, 1987.

Duncan, S., and Rowe, A., *Self Help Housing: The Housing: The World's Hidden Housing Arm*. Centre for Urban & Regional Research, University of Sussex, Brighton, 1992.

Dunleavy, D., *The Politics of Mass Housing in Britain, 1945–1975: A study of Corporate Power, and Professional Influence in the Welfare State*, Oxford University Press, Oxford, 1981.

Edwards, B., *Towards Sustainable Architecture*, Butterworth Architecture, Oxford, 1996.

English Heritage, *Something Worth Keeping: Post War Architecture in England*; leaflets: *Housing and Houses* and *New Towns and Rural Housing*, all 1996.

Eserin, A., (compiled by) *Welwyn Garden City, Archive Photographs*, Chalford Publishing Company Ltd, Stroud, 1995.

Essex County Planning Officers Association, *A Design Guide for Residential Areas*, Essex County Council, Colchester, 1973. (2nd edn, 1997).

Fletcher, Sir Bannister, A History of Architecture, Twentieth Edition 1996, Architectural Press, Oxford, 1896, (reprinted 1998).

Girardet, H., The GAIA *Atlas of Cities – New Directions for Sustainable Urban Living*, Gaia Books Ltd, London, 1992.

Glendinning, M. and Muthesius, S., *Tower Block*, Yale University Press, New Haven and London, 1993.

Goldsmith, S., *Designing for the Disabled: The New Paradigm*, Architectural Press, Oxford, 1997.

Goodchild, B., *Housing and the Urban Environment*, Blackwell Science Ltd, London, 1998.

Greater London County Council, *Home Sweet Home: Housing design By the London County Council and Greater London Council Architects 1888–1975*, Academy Editions, London, 1976.

Greater London Council, *GLC Preferred Dwelling Plans*, The Architectural Press, London, 1977.

Greater London Council, *An Introduction to Housing Layout*, The Architectural Press, London, 1978.

Hackney, R., *The Good the Bad and the Ugly, Cities in Crisis*, Frederick Muller, London, 1988.

Hall, P., *Cities of Tomorrow: An Intellectual History of Urban Planning and Design in the Twentieth Century*, Basil Blackwell, Oxford, 1988, (reprinted 1993).

Harwood, E., *England, A Guide to Post-War Listed Buildings*, Ellipses, 2000, Second edition, B.T. Batsford, London, 2003.

Home Office, *Safer Cities Progress Report, 1989–1990*, HMSO, London, 1990.

Housing Awards Publications. These have been published in various forms and are available to see at the British Architectural Library, 66 Portland Place, London W1N 4AD. *They are also available on Design for Homes website: www.designforhomes.org/hda*

Housing Development Directorate (DOE), London, Occasional papers.
    2/74, *Mobility Housing*, HMSO, London, 1974, reprinted from AJ, 3/7/74, pp. 43–50.
    2/75, *Wheelchair Housing*, HMSO, London, 1975.

Howard, E., *Garden Cities of Tomorrow*, Attic Books, 1977, Powys, Wales, (First edition 1902) new revised edition 1985, reprinted 1997.

The Institute of Highway Incorporated Engineers, *Home Zone Design Guidelines*, The Institute of Incorporated Engineers, London, 2002.

Jacobs, J., *Death and Life of Great American Cities*, Jonathan Cape, London, 1962.

Jones, E., and Woodward, C., *A Guide to the Architecture of London*, Weidenfeld and Nicolson, London, 1992.

Joseph Rowntree Foundation, *Housing Quality – A Practical Guide for Tenants and Their Representatives*, 1996.

Jung, C., *Memories, Dreams, Reflections*, Fontana Library, London, 1969.

Latham, Sir M. *Constructing the Team, Final Report of the Government. Industry Review of Procurement and Contractual Arrangements in the UK Construction Industry*, HMSO, London, 1994.

London County Council (LCC), *London Housing*, LCC, London, 1937.

Martin, L., and Marsh, L., *Urban Space and Structures*, Cambridge University Press, Cambridge, 1972.

375

Index

The index provides the following lists:
1. Projects in alphabetical order followed by the name of the city, county, borough or district in which they are located.
2. Cities, London Boroughs, counties and towns in alphabetical order with projects and locations.
3. Projects listed within categories of housing type where appropriate.
4. Architects or designers in alphabetical order followed by their projects.
5. *Italic type* indicates the page on which an illustration appears.

Aaron Evans Associates:
    Calne Town Centre Regeneration, 262, 280–281
Abbotsbury Glebe, Dorset, 270–271, *272, 273*
Abbotts Wharf, Tower Hamlets, 143–144, *144*
Abercrombie, Patrick, 5, 9
Abernethy Quay/Ferrara Square, Maritime Village, Swansea, 306
ABK Architects:
    Container City, Trinity Buoy Wharf, 143, *144*
Abode and Cala Domus, Newhall, Harlow, 172–174, *173, 174*
Accordia (phase 1) Brooklands Avenue, Cambridge, 165–167, *166, 167*
Achamore Road/Katewell Avenue, Drumchapel, Glasgow, 334
Adaptable and flexible housing (PSSHAK), 16–17, 56–57, *58*
Addison Act, 1919, 5
Adelaide Road/Eton Road (PSSHAK), 16–17, 56–57, *58*

Adventurers Quay, Cardiff Bay Regeneration, 303, *304*
Affordable Rural Housing Commission (ARHC), 44
Ainsley Gommon Wood:
    Aquarius, Hulme Redevelopment, 216
Aldington, Peter:
    Turn End, Haddenham, 234–235, *236, 237*
Aldington & Craig:
    Lyde End, Bledlow, Buckinghamshire, 235–238, *237, 238*
Aldington, Craig and Collinge Kenwell Court, Woolstone, Milton Keynes, 244
Alexander, C., 254, 255
Alexandra Road, Camden, 19, 60–61, *61*
Alford Hall Monaghan Morris, Architects:
    Caspar, Birmingham, 184, *185*
    Crown Street Buildings, Leeds, 282, 290–291
    Latitude House, Camden, 67–68, *69*
    Raines Court, Hackney 86–87, *87*

Allerton Bywater, Second Millennium Village, nr Castleford, 291, *292*
Alton Estate, Roehampton, Wandsworth, 147–149, *11, 148, 149, cover*
Anchor Brewhouse, Southwark, 125–126, *126*
Angell Town estate regeneration, 107–108, *109, 110*
APG Architects:
    Port Marine, Portishead, Bristol, 266
Aquarius, Hulme, Manchester, 216
Architecton, Bristol:
    WCA Warehouse conversion, 264
Architype:
    Nicholay Road, 95, *98*
    Diggers and Sea-Saw, Brighton, 261, 263, *263*
Arkheion, Architects:
    Box Works, Castlefields, Manchester, 223, *223*
    Old Haymarket, Liverpool, 214, *215*
Armagh, Co.:
    Castle Street redevelopment, Armagh, 361, *362*

379

INDEX

Arup Associates:
  Point Royal, Bracknell, 231, 233
Ashmill Street, Westminster, 156, *157*
ASSIST, (Index of projects under Glasgow), 319–320
Atelier V, 17:
  Park Hill Road, Croydon, 22, *23*
Atlantic Wharf, Cardiff Bay regeneration, 302, *302*
Austin-Smith Lord, Architects, 343
  Port Marine, Portishead, Bristol, 266
Avanti Architects:
  1-3 Willow Road (restoration), 55, *55*
Ayrshire, North:
  Irvine New Town, 347–349, *350*, *351*, *352*

Bailey, Michael, 253–255
Baillie Scott, M. H:
  Hampstead Garden Suburb, 50–51, *51*, *52*
  Waterlow Court, 51
  6-10 Meadway with 22 Hampstead Way, 51
Baines, Frank, 71
Bain Swan Architects:
  Marine Square, Eyemouth, 353, 355, *355*
Balfron Tower, Tower Hamlets, 99
Ballater Gardens, Crown Street, Glasgow, 337
Baltic Wharf, Bristol, 264
Barber, Peter, Architects:
  Donnybrook Quarter, Tower Hamlets, 144–145, *145*
  Tannel Street, Barking, 50, *50*
The Barbican, City of London, 70, *72*, *73*
Barker, Kate, 44

Barking and Dagenham:
  Tanner Street, 50
Ballater Gardens, Crown Street, Glasgow, 337
Baltic Wharf, Bristol, 264
Barlow Henley Architects:
  The Village, Caterham-on-the-Hill, 260
Barnet, Dame Henrietta, 50–51
Barnet London Borough:
  Hampstead Garden Suburb, 50–51, *51*, *52*
Barnett Winskell:
  George Street/Queen Street regeneration, Whitehaven, 208–209, *210*
Barons Place, 42, 129–130, *130*
Barr, Cleeve, 16, 147
Barton Wilmore Partnership, 256
Basildon New Town, 9, *21*, 169
Basingstoke:
  Oakridge Village, 249, *250*
Bauhaus, 6
Baxter, Alan Associates:
  Poundbury, 272, 274, *275*, *276*
Bean Hill, Milton Keynes, 238, *239*
Beaufort Court, Hammersmith and Fulham, 42, 89–91, *90*
Beaux-Arts, 5, 252
Beetham (The) Tower, Deansgate, Manchester, 202, 227
BedZED (Beddington Zero Energy Development), 30, 41, 45, 107, *131*, 131–132, *cover*
Belfast:
  Carrick Hill, Upper Library Street, 362–363, *364*
  Divis estate regeneration, Milford Street, 358, 363–364, *365*

Laganview Apartments, Bridge End, 364–365, *366*
1-3 Lancaster Street and 1-19 Thomas Street, 361–362, *363*
Belfast Housing Renewal Strategy, 359
Bell Rock Square, Dundee, 324, *325*
Benson, Gordon, 19
Berkshire:
  Bracknell New Town, 9, *21*
  Point Royal, Rectory Lane, 231, *233*
  Earley, Reading:
    The Liberty of Earley sheltered housing, 233–234, *235*
Berwickshire:
  Marine Square, Eyemouth, 353, 355, *355*
Beverley:
  Globe Mews, 283, *284*
  St Andrew Street co-operative development, 284–285, *285*
Bevin, Aneurin, 8
Bevin Court, Islington, 94–95, *96*
Bickerdike Alan:
  Brunswick Centre (construction), 56, *57*
Bill Dunster Architects BedZED factory Ltd:
  BedZED, Wallington, Surrey, 131–132, *131*, *cover*
  BowZED, Tomlins Road, 141–143, *142*
  Jubilee Wharf, Bude, Cornwall, 41, *41*
  Water Lane, Brixton (with PRP Architects), 105, 107, *108*
Birmingham:
  Brindley Place, *182*, 183–184
  Caspar 1, 100 Charlotte Street, 184, *185*

380

Castle Vale Housing Action
    Trust, 184–185, *186*
Enveloping, Balsall Heath and
    other locations, 181, 183,
    183
Park Central, Bath Row,
    186–187, *187*
Post-war prefabs, Wake
    Green Road, 181, *183*
Birmingham City Architects
    Department:
    Enveloping of pre-1919
        housing, 181, 183, *183*
Bishop's Walk, Ely, 164–165, *166*
Bishopfield & Charter Cross,
    Harlow, 170–171, *171*
20b Bistern Avenue, Waltham
    Forrest, 145–146, *146*
Blackheath, Span housing
    (listed under Span
    Developments Limited),
    22, *23*, 72–73, 75, *75*
Black Road, Macclesfield,
    Cheshire, 203–204, *204*
Boundary Lane/Bonsall Street,
    Hulme, Manchester, 216
Boundary Street Estate, Tower
    Hamlets, 4, 132, *132*
Bourneville, 3
BowZED zero carbon housing,
    141–143, *142*
Boxley Street housing, West
    Silvertown, London,
    114–115
Box Works, Castlefields,
    Manchester, 223, *223*
Boyd Partnership (The):
    Laganview Apartments,
    364–365, *366*
Bracknell New Town, 9, *21*
Point Royal, 231, *233*
Bradford:
    Saltaire, 3
    Scalebor Park, Burley-in-
        Wharfdale, 285–286, *286*
Bradwell Common, Milton
    Keynes, 239

Branch Hill, Hampstead, 59–60,
    60
Bradville, Milton Keynes, 238,
    239
Bradville Solar House, Milton
    Keynes, 244
Bramhall Blenkharn:
    Moss Street, York, 299, *299*
Brent London Borough:
    Stonebridge Estate
        Regeneration, 51–52, *53*
Brentwood Place, Brentwood,
    21, 172, *172*
Bretgate/Walmgate, York, 21,
    298–299, *299*
Bridge Care, Bath, 279–280, *281*,
    283
Brindley Place urban regen-
    eration, Birmingham, *182*,
    183–184
Bristol:
    Baltic Wharf, 264
    Capricorn Quay, 265–266, *265*
    Colliers Gardens, Fishponds,
        267, *267*
    The Point, Wapping Wharf,
        264–265, *264*
    Port Marine, Portishead, 266,
        266
    St Werburgs, self-build,
        267–268, *268*
    WCA Warehouse conversion,
        264
Brixton riots, 25
Britannia Mills, Castlefields,
    Manchester, 221, *222*
Britannia Village, West Silver-
    town, Newham, 112–115,
    114, *115*
Broadclose Farm, Bude,
    Cornwall, 269, *270*
Broadwall Housing and
    Oxo Tower Wharf,
    Southwark, 105, *106*
Broadwater Farm, Haringey, 25
Broadway Malyan:
    The Edge, Manchester, 227

Greenwich Millennium
    Village, 80
NV Buildings, Salford Quays,
    230, *231*, *232*
Broadwindsor, Dorset, 44, *44*,
    270–272
Brock Carmichael Associates:
    Co-operative housing,
        Liverpool, 210, 212,
        213
    Sunningdale Community
        Project, Wirral,
        207–208, *208*
Brooklands Park and Blackheath
    Park, 75
Brooks, Alison, Architects Ltd:
    Accordia, Cambridge,
    166, *166*
Brow (The), Runcorn, Cheshire,
    204–205, *205*, *206*
Brown, Neave, 19
Brown Smith Baker and
    Partners (Hull):
    North Hull Housing Action
        Trust, 287–288
Bruges Place, Camden, 64, *66*
Brunswick Centre, Camden, 56,
    57
Bryanston Hills, Blandford
    St Mary, Dorset, 271–
    272, *273*
Buckinghamshire:
    Bledlow:
        Lyde End, 235–236, *237*,
        238
    Haddenham:
        Turn End, 234–235, *236*,
        237
    Milton Keynes, 238–246
        Master Plan, (*see also* Index
        of projects under city
        name), 238
Building for Life, 37
Burgess Partnership:
    Abernethy Quay/Ferrara
        Square, Swansea
        Maritime Village, 306

381

Burrell Foley Fischer LLP, Architects:
  Angell Town, Brixton, 107–108
Burrell's Wharf, Tower Hamlets, 139, *140*
Burton Place, Castlefields, Manchester, 223, *224*
Byker Redevelopment, Newcastle-upon-Tyne, 194–195, *196*

Cadbury, George, 3
Cairnshill, Belfast, 360
Calder Peel Partnership:
  South at Didsbury Point, Manchester, 226, *226*
Calls (The), Leeds, 290, *290*
Calne Town Centre Regeneration, Wiltshire, 262, 280–281
Cambridgeshire:
  Accordia (phase 1), Cambridge, 165–167, *166, 167*
  Bishop's Walk, Ely, 164–165, *166*
  Highsett, Cambridge, 162–163, *162, 163*
  Sudbury Court, Whittlesey, 163
  Southbrook Field, Papworth Everard, 164, *165*
  Tuckers Court, Stanground, Peterborough, 163–164, *164*
Cambridge University, 19, *20*, 170
Camden architects Department, 57, 60, 61
  Alexandra Road, 60–61, *61*
  Branch Hill, 59–60, *60*
  Highgate New Town, 19, 57–59, *58, 59*
  Maiden Lane Stage 1, 61–63, *62*
Camden Building Design Services:
  Kings Cross Estate Action, 64, 66–67, *67, 68*

Camden Gardens, 64, *65*
Camden London Borough:
Alexandra Road, 60–61, *61*
Branch Hill, 59–60, *60*
Bruges Place, 64, *66*
Brunswick Centre, 56, *57*
Camden Gardens, 64, *65*
17 Camden Road (Supermarket and housing), 63, *63*
Highgate New Town, Dartmouth Park Hill, 19, 55, 57–59, *58, 59*
Isokon Flats, Lawn Road, 53–54, *54*
Kent House, Ferdinand Road, 54–55, *55*
Kings Cross Estate Action, Cromer Street, 64, 66–67, *67, 68*
Maiden Lane Stage 1, 61–63, *62*
Ossulston Estate, St Pancras, 53, *54*
PSSHAK Flexible and Adaptable Housing, 56–57, *58*
  Adelaide Road/Eton Road, 56–57, *58*
  St Anne's Close, Highgate West Hill, 55–56, *56*
  1-3 Willow Road, 55, *55*
Camlin Lonsdale, Selwyn Street and Coppice Park, Oldham, 228–229, *230*
Capricorn Quay, Bristol, 265–266, *265*
Cardiff:
Cardiff Bay Regeneration, 301–303, *302–305*
  Adventurers Quay, 303, *304*
  Atlantic Wharf, 302, *302*
  Lloyd George Avenue, 302–303, *303*
  Penarth Harbour, 303, *305*
  Sovereign Quay, 303, *305*

Carnarvon Street/St George's Road, Glasgow, 334
Carrick Hill, Belfast, 362–363, *364*
Cartwright Pickard Architects:
  Murray Grove, Hackney, 84, *86*
Cascades, WestFerry Road, 136–137, *137*
Caspar 1, 100 Charlotte Street, Birmingham, 184, *185*
Castle Court, Sheffield, 294, *295*
Castle Lane Extension, Westminster, 158–159, *158, 159*
Castlemilk, Glasgow, 319, *320*, 334–336, *336*
Castle Street redevelopment, Armagh, 361, *362*
Caterham:
  The Village, Guards Avenue, 260, 260–261, *261*
Centrepoint Soho (housing association), 33
CGHP Architects:
  Castle Lane Extension, 158–159, *158, 159*
  Oaklands Court, Uxbridge Road, 38, *39*
Chamberlin Powell and Bon:
  The Barbican, 70, *72, 73*
  Golden Lane and Crescent House, 68–70, *70, 71*
Chapel, Chapel Road, Southampton, 248, 248–249
Chapter House, Coffee Hall, Milton Keynes, 239
CHAR Inquiry into Youth Homelessness 1995, 34
Charles, HRH Prince of Wales, 26, 35
  Poundbury, 272, 274, *275, 276*
  Urban Villages, 274

INDEX

Charter Consultant Architects:
Port Marine, Portishead, Bristol, 266
Chartered Institute of Housing (CIOH), 25, 26
Chatham Maritime:
Fishing Village, St Mary's Island, 258, 258–259
Chelsea:
World's End, Kings Road, 101–102, 103
Chermayeff, Serge, 128, 254
Cherrywood Close, Tower Hamlets HAT, 141, *142*
Cheshire:
Black Road, Macclesfield, 203–204, *204*
Hamilton Close, Parkgate, Wirral, 203, *203*
Runcorn New Town, 20, 204–205, *205, 206*
The Brow, 20, 204–205, *205, 206*
Sunningdale Community Project, Wirral, 207–208, *208*
Warrington and Runcorn, (see also Projects listed under each town name), 205–207, *207*
Chetwood Associates:
Chapel, Chapel Road, Southampton, *248*, 248–249
Chichester Road, Hulme, Manchester, 216
China Wharf, Mill Street, Southwark, 124, *125*
CHISEL, 261
Church of England:
Faith in the City, 25
Churchill Gardens Estate, Westminster, 150–151, *151*
CIAM X, 12
Circle (The), Queen Elizabeth Street, Southwark, 123–124, *125*

Circle 33 Housing Association, 83–84, 97, 140
City Grant, 33
City Challenge, 33, 215–216
City of London:
The Barbican, 70, *72, 73*
Golden Lane and Crescent House, 68–70, *70, 71*
Civic Amenities Act 1967, 21
Clague Architects:
Lacuna, Kings Hill, West Malling, *259*, 259–260
Claredale Street, Cluster Housing, Tower Hamlets, 133–134, *134*
Cluster Housing, 12, 15
Usk Street and Claredale Street, 15, 133–134, *134*
Cockaigne Housing Company, 253
Code for Sustainable Homes, 40–41
Coffee Hall, Milton Keynes, 238, 239
Coin Street Community Builders, 31, 104–105, *106*
Colchester Borough Architects Department:
Dutch Quarter, 171–172, *161*
Coleman, Alice, 26
Colliers Gardens, Fishponds, Bristol, 267, *267*
Collingwood Court, Morpeth, Northumberland, 197–199, *198, 199*
Colquhoun and Miller:
Oldbrook, Milton Keynes, 242
Commercial Street, Bridgend, Perth, 349, 351, *353*
Commission for Architecture and the Built Environment (CABE) 35–36
Communities and Local Government (Government Department), 35, 38
Communities England, 44

Communities Scotland, 321
Community Architecture, 26
Community-based Housing Associations (Scotland), 319–320, *321*, 334, *335*
Community Renewal Partnership, Glasgow, 319
Compass Point, Tower Hamlets, 137, *138*
Comprehensive Estates Initiative (CEI), 83
Connell Ward and Lucas:
Kent House, 54–55, *55*
Conniburrow, Milton Keynes, 238, *239*
Conran Roche:
Gainsford Street Halls of Residence, 125
Container City, Tower Hamlets, 143, *144*
Cook Sydney, 19
Co-operative housing, 30–31, 261
Beverley, St Andrew Street, 284–285, *285*
Coin Street Community Builders, 31, 104–105, *106*
Glasgow, 31, 334
Achamore Street/Katewell Avenue, Drumchapel, 334
Carnarvon Street/St George's Road, Charing Cross, 334
James Nisbett Street, Roystonhill, 334, *335*
Tollcross Road/Sorby Street, 334
West End Park Street/Woodlands Road, *321*, 334
Hatfield, The Ryde, 19, *232*, 253–256, *255, 256*
Liverpool, 210
Eldonian Village, 212, *213*
Newland Court, Hesketh Street, 212, *213*
Weller Street, 212

383

INDEX

Essex:
 Basildon, 169
 Brentwood:
  Brentwood Place, 172, *172*
 Colchester:
  Dutch Quarter, *160*, 171–172
 Harlow:
  Bishopfield and Charter Cross, 170–171, *171*
  The Lawns, Mark Hall North, 168–169, *169*
  Shoeburyness, Outlook, The Garrison, 174–175, *175*
  Silver End, Braintree, 167–168, *168*
  South Woodham Ferrers, 24, 172
Essex Design Guide, 24, 172
Estate Action, 25–26, 110–111
Evans Roger, Associates:
 Masterplan, Newhall, Harlow, 172–174
Evelyn Road, West Silvertown, 114
Eyemouth High School Art Department, 335

Faith in the City (Church of England), 25
Farrell Grimshaw Partnership:
 125 Park Road, Camden, 152–153, *153*
 Farrell, Terry, Partnership Admirals Road, Oakwood, Warrington, 207
Fashion Architecture Taste (FAT):
 New Islington, Manchester, 219–221, *220*
Ferguslie Park, Paisley, 319
Ferrara Quay/Marina Walk, Swansea, *300*, 306
Fenwick Close, Newcastle upon Tyne, 195
Festival of Britain, 10, 151

Fielden Clegg Bradley Architects:
 Accordia, Cambridge, masterplan, 165–167, *167*
 Beaufort Court, Hammersmith and Fulham, 89–91, *90*
 Bridge Care, Bath, 279–280, *281*, *283*
 The Point, Wapping Wharf, Bristol, 264, *264*
Fielden and Mawson:
 Friar's Quay, 177–178, *177*
 Martlesham Village, 180, *181*
 Queen Elizabeth Close, 178, *178*
Findlay Ian, Architects:
 Northmoor, Manchester, 219, *220*
Finland Quay, Greenland Dock, 119–120, *121*, *122*
Fishing Village, St Mary's Island, Chatham Maritime, *258*, 258–259
Fishermead, Milton Keynes, 238, *239*
Fleming, Owen, 132
Flexible and adaptable housing (PSSHAK), Adelaide Road/Eton Road, Camden, 16–17, 56–57, *58*
Floyd Slaski Partnership:
 Kings Cross Estate Action, 64, 66–67, *67*, *68*
Forrest, G. Topham:
 Ossulston Estate, 53, *54*
Forsyth, Alan, 19
Foster Associates, 238
Foxes Dale, Blackheath, 72
Foyer Housing, 34
 Swansea Foyer, 30, 34, 309–311, *310*, *311*
France Furlong, Great Linford, Milton Keynes, 241
Fraser, Ross, 33
French Alec Partnership:

 Capricorn Quay, Bristol, 265, 265–266
Fresnel Square, 19, *20*
Friar's Quay, Norwich, 177, 177–178
Friendship House, Belvedere Place, 128–129, *129*
Fry, E Maxwell:
 Kensall House, Ladbroke Grove, 98–99, *101*
Fulham Island, 91, *92*
Fullers Slade, Milton Keynes, 238, *239*
Futureworld, Milton Keynes, 245, *245*

Gainsford Street Halls of Residence, 125
Gallions Reach Urban Village, Greenwich, 76
Gammond Evans Crichton:
 North Hull Housing Action Trust, 287–288
Garden Cities, 3–4
 Bourneville, 3
 Hampstead Garden Suburb, 3, 50–51, *51*, *52*
 Letchworth, 3, 4, 249–252, *251*, *252*
 Port Sunlight, 3
 Welwyn Garden City, 5, *21*, 252–253, *253*, *254*
Garden City Association, 3, 5
Gardner Stewart Architects:
 Britannia Village, West Silvertown, 112–115, *114*, *115*
 Ingress Park, Greenhithe, Kent, 256–258, *257*
 Park Central, Birmingham, 186–187, *187*
Gateshead:
 Staiths South Bank, 192–193, *192*, *193*
GEAR, Glasgow Eastern Area Renewal, 317, *318*
General Improvement Areas, 22

INDEX

George, David Lloyd, 5
George Street/Queen Street regeneration, Whitehaven, Cumbria, 208–209, *210*
Gibberd, Frederick:
  Harlow New Town, 9, 10, 12, *21*, 168–170
  Lawns (The), Harlow, 10, 12, 168–169
  Mark Hall North, Harlow, 168–170, *170*
  Pullman Court, 103–104
Glasgow:
  Castlemilk estate regeneration, 319, *320*, 334–336, *336*
  Clyde Street, 341, *343*, 346–347
  Community Based Housing Association Development:
    Carnarvon Street/St George's Road, Charing Cross, 334
    Achamore Street/Katewell Avenue, Drumchapel, 334
    James Nisbet Street, Roystonhill, 334
    Tollcross Road/Sorby Street, 334
    West End Park Street/Woodlands Road, *321*, 334
  Crown Street regeneration area, 35, 336–338, *338*, *339*
    Masterplan, 337–338
    Ballater Gardens, 337
    Errol Gardens and Pine Place, 337–338, *339*
    Gorbals East renewal area, 338, *340*
    Moffat Gardens, 338, *340*
  Ingram Square, The Merchant Quarter, 332–333, *333*
  Red Road tower blocks, 12

Glasgow City Council, 315–316, 318–319, 332, 334, 337, 344, 346
Glasgow City Council, Department of Architecture and Related Services, 334
  Castlemilk estate regeneration, 334–336
Gleadless Valley, Sheffield, 9, 294–295, *296*
Globe Mews Beverley, 283, *284*
Gloucestershire:
  Ebrington, nr Chipping Camden, 277, *278*
  Gloucester Road, Sheffield (5 m houses), 16
  Golden Lane and Crescent House, City of London, 68–69, *70*, *71*
Goldfinger, Ernö:
  Balfron Tower, 99
  Trellick Tower, 99–101, *102*
  1-3 Willow Road, 55, *55*
Goodman, Elinor, 44
Gorbals East renewal area, Glasgow, 338, *340*
  economic regeneration, *336*, 337
  social regeneration, *336*, 337
Gorbals Initiative, 337
Gorgie Millennium Project, Edinburgh, 327–329, *328*
Grand Metropolitan plc, 34
Grange Road/Hartington Road, Middlesbrough, 193–194, *194*
Greater London Council (GLC):
  Expanded Towns Policy, 19–20
  GLC Department of Architecture and Civic Design:
    Odham's Walk, 154, *155*
    New Ash Green, 256, *257*

PSSHAK Flexible and Adaptable Housing, 16–17, 56–57, *58*
  Thamesmead, 75–76, *76*
Greater London Plan 1944, 9
Greenland Dock, 119–123, *121–123*
Greenland Passage, 119, *122*
Greenleys, Milton Keynes, 238, *239*
Greenwich London Borough:
  Gallions Reach Urban Village, 76
  Nightingale Heights, Nightingale Vale, 76–77, *77*
  Span Housing, Blackheath, 72–75, *75*
  Millennium Village, 77–80, *78–81*
  Thamesmead, 75–76, *76*
  Well Hall Estate, Ross Way, 71–72, *74*
Greenwood Housing Act 1930, 6
Grimsby Doorstep, 34–35
Grieve, Sir Robert, 319
Grimshaw, Nicholas and Partners:
  17 Camden Road, 63, *63*
Gropius, Walter, 8, 150
Groves-Raines, Nicholas:
  Craigwell Brewery, Edinburgh, 327, *327*
Guinness Trust, 215, 216, 217, 274
Gummer, John, 35
Gun Wharf, Devonport, Plymouth, 277–279, *279*, *280*
Gwalia Housing Society, 308, 309
Gwynedd:
  Holiday housing, Portmadog, 303–304, *306*

Habinteg Housing Association:
  Lifetime Homes standards, 31, *32*, *33*

INDEX

Hackland and Dore:
  Gorgie Millennium Project, Edinburgh, 327–329, *328*
Hackney London Borough:
  Holly Street Estate Regeneration, 83–84, *85, 86*
  Lea View Estate, Jessam Avenue, 81–82, *83*
  Nile Street, 87–88, *88*
  Murray Grove, 84, *86*
  Woodbury Down Estate, 80–81, *82*
Hackney, Rod:
  Black Road, Macclesfield Cheshire, 203–204, *204*
Hall, The, Blackheath, 72–73, *75*
Hallgate, Blackheath, Greenwich, 72
Halliday Meecham Architects Ltd.:
  Baltic Wharf, Bristol, 264
  Ferrara Quay/Marina Walk, Swansea, *300, 306*
  Penarth Haven, Cardiff Bay regeneration, 303, *305*
Halton Brow, Runcorn, 204–205, *205, 206*
Hamdi, Nabeel, 57
Hamilton Close, Parkgate, Wirral, 203, *203*
Hammersmith and Fulham London Borough:
  Old Oak Estate, Wulfstan Street, 88, *89*
  Thames Reach, 80 Rainville Road, 88–89, *90*
Hampshire:
  Basingstoke:
    Oakridge Village, 249, *250*
  Eastleigh:
    John Darling Mall, 246–247, *247*
  Southampton:
    Chapel, Chapel Road, *248*, 248–249
    Wyndham Court, 246

Hampshire County Architects Department:
  John Darling Mall, 246–247, *247*
Hampstead Garden Suburb:
  Corringham Road, 51, *52*
  Erskine Hill, 51
  Temple Fortune Centre, 51
  Waterlow Court, Heath Close, 51
Handsworth Riots, 25
Hanson Walford Marston:
  Webster's Yard, Kendal, 209–210, *211*
Harbraken, Nicholas, 57
Harlow New Town, 9, 10, 12, *21*, 169
  Bishopfield & Charter Cross, 170–171, *171*
  The Lawns, 10, 12, 168–169, *169*
  Mark Hall North, 168–170, *170*
  Abode and Cala Domus, Newhall, 172–174, *173, 174*
Haringey London Borough:
  Broadwater Farm, 25
  High Point 1 and 2, North Hill, 92–94, *93, 95*
  White Hart Lane, Risley Avenue, 91–92, *92*
Harrison Sutton Partnership:
  Waters Edge, Shaldon, Devon, 268–269, *269*
Harriston Village, Cumbria, 208, *209*
Hartley, Great Linford, Milton Keynes, 239
Hatfield New Town, 9, *21*, 253
Hawkins Brown, Architects:
  Outlook, Shoeburyness, 174–175, *175*
  Park Hill Sheffield, 293, *294*
Hazelwood, Great Linford, Milton Keynes, 239, *241*

Hemel Hempstead (New Town), 9, *21*
Hemingway Designs:
  Staiths South Bank, Gateshead, 192–193, *192, 193*
Hertfordshire:
  Letchworth Garden City, 249–252, *251, 252*
  Hatfield New Town, 253
  The Ryde, *232*, 253–256, *255, 256*
  Welwyn Garden City, 252–253, *253, 254*
  (see also Projects listed under town heading)
Hesketh Street Co-operative housing, Liverpool, 212, *213*
Highgate New Town, Camden, 19, 57–59, *58, 59*
High Point 1 and 2, Haringey, 92–94, *93, 95*
Highsett, Cambridge, 22, 162–163, *162, 163*
Hockerton earth sheltered housing, 189–190, *189*
Hodgkinson, Patrick:
  Brunswick Centre (design), 56, *57*
Holmwalk, Blackheath, 75
Holly Street Estate Regeneration, Hackney, 83–84, *85*, 86
Holmes Partnership:
  Ballater Gardens, 337
Homes for Change, Hulme, Manchester, 216–217, *218*
Homes for the Future, 25
Homes for Today and Tomorrow, 15
Homeworld, Milton Keynes, 244
Homezone:
  Northmoor, Manchester, 219, *220*

388

INDEX

Honddu Place/Beacons View Road, Swansea, 308–309, *309*
Horselydown Square, Southwark, 123, *124*
Hospital conversion into housing: Royal Free Square, Liverpool Road, 97, 99, *100*
Housing Act 1949, 8–9
Housing Act 1964, 21
Housing Act 1969, 22
Housing Act 1988, 25
Housing Action Areas, 22
Housing Action Trust (HAT), 27
   Castle Vale, Birmingham, 184–186, *186*
   Liverpool, 210–214
   North Hull, 287–288, *288*
   Stonebridge, Brent, 51–52, *53*
   Tower Hamlets, 29, 139–140, *142*
   Waltham Forest, 27
Housing Associations, 20–22, 29–30, 42, 360
   Housing Co-operatives *see* Co-operative Housing
Housing Corporation, 21, 152, 249, 267, 281
Housing Cost Yardstick, 15, 289
Housing Development Directorate (HDD), 16
Housing Manual 1920, 5
Housing Manual 1944, 7, 8
Housing Manual 1949, 8
Housing and Town Planning Act 1919, 5, 71
Howard, Ebenezer, 3, 5, 10, 249, 252
Howells Glen, Architects:
   Burton Place, Castlefields, Manchester, 223, *224*
Hull City Council Technical Services Department:
   Gipsyville, 287

North Hull Housing Action Trust, 287–288, *288*
Victoria Dock, 286–287, *287*
Hulme Redevelopment, Manchester, 215–219, *217, 218*
Hunt Thompson Associates:
   Castle Vale HAT masterplan, 184–186
   Kings Cross Estate Action, 64, 66–67, *67, 68*
   Lea View House, 81–82, *83*
   Millennium Village, Greenwich, 77–79
   Nightingale Heights, 76–77, *77*
   Northwood Tower refurbishment, 138
   Oakridge Village, Basingstoke, 249, *250*
   Winterton House, 137–138, *139*
Hurd Rollands Partnership:
   North Hull Housing Action Trust, 287–288
Hurley Roberts Associates (co Architects with Richard Rogers Partnership):
   Montevetro, Wandsworth, 149–150
Hyde Park, Sheffield, 291, *293*, 294, *295*
Hypostyle Architects:
   Cumberland Street, Crown Street, 338

Ideal Home exhibition adaptable/flexible house, 16–17, *17*
Ingram Square, Glasgow, 332–333, *333*
Ingress Park, Greenhithe, Dartford, 256–258, *257*
Innes Wilkin Ainsley Gommon, 210

Irish Street (34-55) Downpatrick, Co. Down, *356*, 370
Irvine New Town, 21, 28, 347–349, *350, 351*
   Abbeygate, Kilwinnin, 348, *352*
   Braehead, 348
   Bourtree Hill, 348
   Bryce Knox Court sheltered housing, 349, *352*
   Harbourside/Cochrane Street Redevelopment, 348, *350*
   Hawthorn Place, Nethermains, Kilwinning, 349, *351*
Irvine Development Corporation Architects, 347 (all schemes listed under Irvine New Town)
Islington, London Borough:
   Bevin Court, Holford Street, 94–95, *96*
   Nicholay Road, 95, 97, *98*
   Spa Green Estate, Rosebury Avenue, 94, *96*
   Priory Green Estate, Collier Street, 94–95
   Royal Free Square, Liverpool Road, 97, *99, 100*
Isokon Flats, Lawn Road, 53–54
Italian Centre, Glasgow, 333, *333*

Jacobs, Jane, 39
Jestico + Whiles:
   Abbotts Wharf, Stainsby Road, 143–144, *144*
   Bruges Place, 64, *66*
   Burrell's Wharf, 139, *140*
   Camden Gardens, 64, *65*
   Tanner Street, 50, *50*
Johnston, Jim, 320
Joint Venture Companies, 26
Judd, Rolphe:
   Tabard Square, Southwark, 130–131, *cover*

INDEX

Karl-Marx-Hof, Vienna, 6
Keeling House, Claredale Street, 134, *134*
The Keep, Blackheath, 73
Kensall House, Ladbroke Grove, 98–99, *101*
Kensington and Chelsea, London Borough:
  Kensall House, Ladbroke Grove, 98–99, *101*
  St Mark's Road/St Quintin Avenue, 102–103, *103*
  Trellick Tower, Golborne Road, 99–101, *102*
  World's End, 101–102, *103*
Kent:
  Lacuna, West Malling, 259–260, *259*
  New Ash Green, 256, *257*
Kent house, Ferdinand Street, 54–55, *55*
Kidder Smith, G.E., 12
Killingworth, Newcastle-upon-Tyne, 195
Kingham Knight Associates:
  Minster Court, 212–213, *214*
Kingohusene, Helsingor, 170
Kings Cross Estate Action, Cromer Street, Camden, 64, 66–67, *67*, 68
Kingston upon Hull:
  North Hull Housing Action Trust, Greenwood Avenue, 287–288, *288*
  Victoria Dock, 286–287, *287*
Kjaer Richter (Aarhus):
  Greenland Passage, 119, *122*
Krier, Leon, 272, 274, *275*, *276*

Lacey, Nicholas and Partners:
  Container City, Trinity Buoy Wharf, 143, *144*
  Crown Reach, Westminster, 156–157, *157*
  Footbridge, New Concordia Wharf, 126
  New Concordia Wharf, 126

Lacie Hickie Caley Architects:
  Gun Wharf, Devonport, Plymouth, 277–279, *279*, *280*
Lacuna, West Malling Kent, *259*, 259–260
Laganview Apartments, Belfast, 364–365, *366*
Lakes (The), 120, 123, *123*
Lambeth London Borough:
  Angell Town, 107–108, *109*
  Broadwall Housing and Oxo Tower Wharf, 105, *106*
  PRPZED, Brixton Water Lane, 105, 107, *108*
  Pullman Court, Streatham Hill, 103–104, *104*
  Lanark Road, 154, 156, *156*
Lancaster Street (1-3) and Thomas Street (1-19), Belfast, 361–362, *363*
Langham House Close, Ham Common, 116, *117*, 118
Lansbury Estate, Tower Hamlets, 132–133, *133*
Lasdun, Sir Denys and Partners:
  Claredale Street and Usk Street Cluster Housing, 15, 133–134, *134*
  St James Place, 152, *152*
Latham, Sir Michael, 30
Latitude House, Camden, 67–68, *69*
La Ville Radieuse, 6
Lawns, (The) Harlow, 10, 12, 168–169, *169*
LCC Department of Architecture:
  Alton Estate, Roehampton, 11, 12, 147, *148*, 149, *149*, cover
  Boundary Street, 4, 132, *132*
  Lansbury Estate, 132–133, *133*
  Old Oak Estate, 88, *89*
  Roehampton Cottage Estate, 146, *147*

Well Hall Estate, 71–72, *74*
White Hart Lane, 4, 91–92, *92*
Woodbury Down Estate, 80–81, *82*
Lea View House, 81–82, *83*
Le Corbusier, 6, 10, 12, 69, 70, 92, 99, 149, 346
Leeds:
  Allerton Bywater, 291, *292*
  Calls (The), 290
  Chapel Allerton, 289, *289*
  Crown Street, 282, 290–291
  Quarry Hill Flats, 6
Leeds City Architects:
  Chapel Allerton, 289, *289*
Leeds City Council, 6, 289, 291
Leicester:
  Living over the Shop, Granby Street, 33–34
Letchworth Garden City, 249–252
  Cheap Cottages exhibition, 250, 252
  English Heritage listed housing, 4
  Urban Cottages Exhibition, 250
Letts Wheeler, Architects:
  Castle Boulevard, Nottingham, 190, *190*
Lever, William, 3
Levitt Bernstein Associates:
  Alexandra Road (refurbishment), 60–61, *61*
  Angell Town regeneration, 107–108
  Brunswick Centre, refurbishment, 56, *57*
  Midsummer Cottages, Milton Keynes, 245, *245*
  Royal Free Square, Liverpool Road, 96, *99*, *100*
Lewisham London Borough:
  Pepys Estate, regeneration of, 110–111, *112*

INDEX

Segal self-build housing, 108–110, *111*
Liberty of Earley Sheltered Housing, Berkshire, *31*, 233–234, *234*
Lifetime Homes, 31, *32*, *33*, 297–298, *298*
Lifschutz Davidson Ltd.: Broadwell Housing and Oxo Tower Wharf, 105
Lillington Gardens, Westminster, 48, 153–154
Liverpool:
    Co-operative housing, 30–31, 210–212, *213*
        Eldonian Village, 212, *213*
        Hesketh Street, 212, *213*
        Weller Street, 212
        Minster Court, Crown Street, 212–214, *214*
        3-12 Old Haymarket, 214, *215*
Living over the Shop, 33–34, 361
    Berwick Street, Soho, Westminster, 33
    Granby Street, Leicester, 33
    Northern Ireland Housing Executive, 34
Llewelyn-Davies, Weeks, Rushbrook Village, 179, 180, *179*, *180*
Llewelyn-Davies, Weeks, Forrestier-Walker and Bor,
    Milton Keynes, master plan, 238
    Washington New Town, master plan, 200
Llewelyn-Davies Planning, Cardiff Bay Master Plan, 301
Llewelyn-Davies Yeang
    Port Marine, Portishead, Bristol, 266
Lloyd George Avenue, Cardiff Bay Regeneration, 302, *303*
Local Housing Companies, 26

Loddon Rural housing, Norfolk, 175–176, *176*
London Docklands, 29, *30*,
Britannia Village, West Silvertown Urban Village, 112–115, *114*, *115*
Greenland Dock, Redriff Road, Southwark, 119–123
    Finland Quay, 119–120, *122*
    Greenland Passage, 119, *122*
    The Lakes, 120, 123, *123*
Isle of Dogs, Tower Hamlets:
    Burrell's Wharf, Westferry Road, 139, *140*
    Cascades, Westferry Road, 136–137, *137*
    Compass Point, Sextant Avenue, 137, *138*
    Dundee Wharf, 139, *141*
Limehouse, Tower Hamlets:
    Roy Square, Narrow Street, 134–135, *135*
Rotherhithe, Southwark:
    Riverside Apartments (Princes Tower), Rotherhithe Street, 127–128, *128*
    Shadwell Basin, Tower Hamlets, 135–136, *136*
South-East of Tower Bridge, Southwark, 123–126
    Anchor Brewhouse, Tower Bridge, 125–126, *126*
    China Wharf, Mill Street, 124, *125*
    Circle (The), Queen Elizabeth Street, 123–124, *125*
    Gainsford Street Halls of Residence, 125
    Horselydown Square, Shad Thames, 123, *124*
    New Concordia Wharf, Mill Street, 126

    Vogan's Mill, Mill Street, 124–125, *125*
    Surrey Quays, Southwark, Wolfe Crescent, 127, *127*
Low energy/eco housing:
    BedZED (Beddington Zero Energy Development), 30, 41, 45, 107, *131*, 131–132, cover
    BowZed zero carbon housing, 41, 141–143, *142*
    Castle Vale, Birmingham, 185
    Hockerton, Earth Sheltered Housing, *189*, 189–190
    Milton Keynes:
        Bradville Solar House, 244
        Energy Park, 244
        Energy World, 244
        Futureworld exhibition, *245*
        Homeworld exhibition, 244
        Midsummer Cottages, 245, *245*
        Round house, 244, *245*
    Swansea:
        Honddu Place/Beacons View Road, 308–309, *309*
        Penplas Urbanbuild, 307–308, *308*, *309*
    Upton, Northampton, 187–189
Lower Shankhill (Weetabix boxes), Belfast, 358
Lubetkin, Bailey and Skinner: Priory Green Estate, 94–95
    Bevin Court, 94–95, *96*
Lubetkin, B., 9
    Peterlee New Town, 9
Lubetkin and Skinner:
    Spa Green, 2, 94, *96*
Lubetkin and Tecton:
    Highpoint I and 2, 6, 92–94, *93*, *95*
Lutyens, Sir Edwin, 51
    Hampstead Garden Suburb, 50–51, *51*
    Erskine Hill, 51

391

INDEX

Lyde End, Bledlow, Buckinghamshire, 235–238, *237*, *238*
Lyons, Eric, 22–24
    Blackheath, 22, 72, 73, *75*
    Parkleys, 115–116, *117*
Lyons, Eric, Cunningham Partnership:
    Mallard Place, 118, *119*
Lyons, Eric and Partners:
    Highsett, 162–163, *163*
    New Ash Green, 256, *257*
    World's End, Kings Road, 101–102, *103*
Lyons Israel Ellis:
    Wyndham Court, 246, *246*

MacCormac Jamieson Prichard:
    Chapter House, Coffee Hall, 239
    Duffryn, Gwent, 19
    France Furlong, Milton Keynes, 241
    Friendship House, Borough Road, 128–129, *129*
    Shadwell Basin, 135–136, *136*
Mackintosh, Charles Rennie, 345, *346*, 348, *350*
Macmillan, Harold, 10, 12, 13
Maiden Lane Stage 61–63, *62*
Mallard Place, Richmond-upon-Thames, 118, *119*
Mallow Street, Hulme, Manchester, 216
Manchester:
    Beetham Tower, Deansgate, 227
    Castlefields:
        Britannia Mill, 221, *222*, 223
        Box Works, 223, *223*
        Burton Place, 223, *224*
        Moho, 223, *224*, 225, 225–6
        Timber Wharf, 223
    Chorlton Park Apartments, Barlow Moor, 220, *222*
    Edge (The), 227
    Hulme Redevelopment, 215–219
        Aquarius, Aquarius Street, 216
        Boundary Road/Bonsall Street, 216
        Chichester Road, *Hulme*, 216
        Homes for Change, 216–217, *218*
        Mallow Street, 216
        Rolls Crescent/Halston Street, 217, *218*, 219
        St Wilfrid's, Mary France Street, 216
    New Islington, 43, 219, *220*, 221
    Number One Deansgate, 227
    Plymouth Grove, Ardwick, 227–228, *228*
    Salford Quays:
        NV Buildings, Huron Quay, 230, *231*
        Waterside at the Lowry, 230
    South at Didsbury Point, 226, *226*
    Stainer Street, Northmoor Road, 219, *220*
Marine Square, Eyemouth, 353, 355, *355*
Maritime Village, Swansea, *300*, 304, 306–307, *307*
Mark Hall North, Harlow, 169–170, *170*
Martin, Leslie and Marsh, Lionel, 19, *20*, *170*
Martlesham Village, Suffolk, 180, *181*
McAdam Design:
    Shore Street/Union Street, Donaghadee, 367, *368*, 369
McDonnell Hughes:
    Co-operative housing, Liverpool, 210, *212*
McLaughlin, Niall and Associates, 114

Evelyn Road, West Silvertown, 114
Merchant City, Glasgow, 332–333, *333*
Merton London Borough:
    Eastfields, Acacia Road, 112
    Pollards Hill, South Lodge Road, Mitcham, 112
    Watermeads, Rawnsley Avenue, 19, 111–112, *113*
Middlesbrough:
    Grange Road/Hartington Road, 193–194, *194*
Midsummer Cottages, Milton Keynes, 245, *245*
Millennium Village, Greenwich, 35, *36*, 77–80, *78–81*
Millennium Village (second), Allerton Bywater, 291, *292*
Mills, Beaumont Leavy Channon:
    Homes for Change, Hulme, 216–217, *218*
Milton Keynes, 238–246
    Bradville Solar House, 244
    Bradwell Common, 239, 244
    Chapter House, Coffee Hall, 239
    Deerfern Close, Great Linford, 244
    Eaglestone, 239
    Early years rental housing projects, 238, *240*
    Energy Park, Shenley Lodge, Knowlhill and Furzton, 244
    Energy World, Farraday Drive, Shenley Lodge, 244
    France Furlong, Great Linford, 241–242
    Futureworld, Crowborough Lane, Kents Hill, *245*
    Hartley, Great Linford, 239
    Hazelwood, Great Linford, 239, 241

INDEX

Homeworld exhibition, Coleshill Place, Bradwell Common, 244
Kenwall Court, Woolstone, 244
Midsummer Cottages, 245, *245*
Neath Hill, 241, *242, 243*
Netherfield, 238, *240*
Oldbrook 242, *243*
Roundhouse, Rutherford Gate, Shenley Lodge, 244, *245*
Skeats Wharf, Pennyland, 244, *244*
Town Plan, 20, 239
Waterside, Peartree Bridge, 238, *241*
Woodley Headland, Peartree Bridge, 244
Minster Court, Liverpool, 212–213, *214*
Mixed Development, 9
Mode 1 Architects:
 Angell Town, Brixton, 107–108, *109*
Modern Methods of Construction, 41–42
Moffat Gardens, Gorbals, Glasgow, 338, *340*
MoHLG adaptable/flexible Ideal Home Exhibition house, 16
MoHLG Research Group, 16
Moho, Castlefields, Manchester, 223, *224*, 225–226, *225*
Monteith phase 1, Tower Hamlets HAT, *29*, 140
Montevetro, Wandsworth, 149–150, *150*
Morgan, Ken Architects (now Carey Morgan Architects, Ltd):
 Abbotsbury Glebe, 270–271, *272, 273*
 Broadwindsor, 44, *44*, 271

Bryanston Hills, Blandford St Mary, 271–272, *273*
Moss Side (Manchester) riots, 24
Moss Street, supported housing, York, 299, *299*
Mozart Estate, Westminster, *28*
Mulberry Housing Cooperative (Coin Street), 105
Munkenbeck & Marshall Urbanism:
 Nile Street, London, 87–88, *88*
Murray Grove, Hackney, 84, *86*

Napper Collerton Partnership:
 New Village, Aspatria, Cumbria, 208, *209*
National Building Agency (NBA), 16
National Trust:
 1-3 Willow Road, 55, *55*
Neath Hill, Milton Keynes, 241, *242, 243*
Neighbourhood Unit, 8, 9
Nelson and Parker:
 Hamilton Close, Parkgate, Wirral, 203, *203*
Netherfield, Milton Keynes, 238, *240*
New Ash Green, Kent, 256, *257*
New Bridge Street redevelopment, Co. Down, *369*, 369–370
Newcastle upon Tyne, *191*, 194–197
 Avondale and Ferndale, Gosforth, 195, *197*
 Byker Redevelopment, *191*, 194–195, *196*
 Fenwick Close, Jesmond, 195
 Killingworth, 195
 Wyncote Court/Jesmond Park Court, Jesmond, 195–197, *198*
New Concordia Wharf, Mill Street, Southwark, 126

New Earswick, York, 296–297, *297, cover*
Lifetime Homes, 297–298
New Gorbals Housing Association, 336–338
Newham, London Borough:
 Britannia Village, West Silvertown 112–115, *114, 115*
New Islington, Manchester, 219, *220*
New Islington and Hackney Housing Association, 97
Newman, Oscar, 27, 39
Newton Aycliffe, 9
New Towns, (housing projects listed under Town names) 9, 19–21, 28
Neylan and Unglass:
 Bishopfield and Charter Cross, Harlow, 170–171, *171*
 Setchell Road, 19, 118–119, *120, 121*
Nicholay Road self-build housing, Islington, *95, 97*, 98
Nicholl Russell Studios:
 Scrimgeours Corner, Perth, 351–352, *354*
Nightingale Heights, Greenwich, 26, 76–77, *77*
NIHE Architects:
 Castle Street redevelopment, Armagh, 361, *362*
 Carrick Hill (phase 2), 362–363, *364*
 Divis estate redevelopment, 363–364, *365*
 Irish Street, Downpatrick, 370, *356*
 Lancaster Street (1-3) and Thomas Street (1-19), 361–362, *363*
 New Bridge Street redevelopment, Downpatrick, 369–370, *369*
 Tudor Road Renewal, Belfast, 365, 367, *367, 368*

393

INDEX

Nile Street, Hackney, 87–88, *88*
Nisbet, James, Street, Glasgow, 334, *335*
Noble, John, 16
Norfolk:
   Ditchingham and Loddon: Rural Housing, 8, *9*, 175–176, *176*
   Norwich:
      Friars Quay, *177*, 177–178
      Queen Elizabeth Close, 178, *178*
Northamptonshire:
   Upton, Northampton, sustainable suburb, 187–189, *188*
North British Housing Association, 215, 217
North British Housing Association Architects:
   Mallow Street, Hulme, 216
   St Wilfred's, Mary France Street, Hulme, 216
Northern Ireland Housing Executive (NIHE), 358, 361
North Hull Housing Action Trust, 287–288, *288*
Northmoor, Manchester, Homezone, 219, *220*
Northumberland:
   Monkseaton:
      Northumberland Village, 199–200, *200*
   Morpeth:
      Collingwood Court, 197, *198*, 199, *199*
Northwood Tower, Walthamstow, 138
Norwich:
   Friar's Quay, *177*, 177–178
   Queen Elizabeth Close, 178, *178*
Nottingham:
   Castle Boulevard, 190, *190*

Nottinghamshire:
   Newark:
      Hockerton Earth Sheltered Housing, *189*, 189–190
Number One Deansgate, Manchester, 227
NV Buildings, Salford Quays, 230, *231*

Oaklands Court, Hammersmith and Fulham, 38, *39*
Oak Meadow, South Molton, nr Barnstable, 269–270, *271*
Oakridge Village, Basingstoke, 249, *250*
Odham's Walk, Covent Garden, 154, *155*
Oldbrook, Milton Keynes, 242, *243*
Oldham:
   Selwyn Street, 228–229, *229*, 230
Old Haymarket, (3-12), Liverpool, 214, *215*
Old Oak Estate, Hammersmith and Fulham, 88, *89*
OMI Architects:
   Boundary Lane/Bonsall Street, Hulme, 216
Ossulston Estate, Camden, 53, *54*

Page and Park:
   Priory Court, Queen Elizabeth Square, 339, *340*
Palm Housing Cooperative (Coin Street), 105
Papworth Village Settlement, Cambridgeshire, 164, *165*
Park Hill, Sheffield, 13, *14*, 43, 291–294, *293*, *294*
Park Hill Road, Croydon, 22, *23*
Park Road, Camden, 152–153, *153*
Parker and Unwin, 5
   Hampstead Garden Suburb, 50, *51*

Corringham Road, 51, *52*
Temple Fortune Centre, Finchley Road, 51
Letchworth Garden City, 249–250, *251*
New Earswick, 296–297, *297*, *cover*
Parker Morris, 100, 150
Parker Morris Report, 15, 16
Parker Morris Standards, 15, 25, 297, 360
Parkleys, Richmond-upon-Thames, 115–116, *116*, *117*
PCKO Architects:
   Cala Domus, Newhall, Harlow, 172–174, *174*
   Fishing Village, St Mary's Island, Chatham Maritime, *258*, 258–259
   Penplas Urbanbuild, Swansea, 307–308, *308*, *309*
   Swansea Foyer, 309–311
Peabody Trust, 3, 41, 42, 84, 86, 87, 114
   Barons Place, 42, 129–130, *130*
   Beaufort Court, 42, 89, *90*, 91
   Boxley Street, 114–115
   Britannia Village, 113–114
   Evelyn Road, 114
   Murray Grove, 42, 84, 86
   Nile Street, 87–88, *88*
   Raines Court, 42, 86–87, *87*
Penarth Haven, Cardiff Bay regeneration, 303, *305*
Penoyre & Prasad LLP:
   Collier Gardens, Fishponds, Bristol, 267, *267*
Penplas Urbanbuild, Woodford Road, Swansea, 307–308, *308*, *309*
People's House, 10
Pepys Estate, Grove Street, Lewisham, 110–111, *112*
Percy Thomas Partnership:
   Ebrington, nr Chipping Camden, 277, *278*

INDEX

Poundbury (co-ordinating architects), 272, 274, *275, 276*
Perimeter Housing, 19
  Duffryn, Gwent, 19
  Eastfields, 112
  Pollards Hill, 112
  Watermeads, 19, 111–112, *113*
Permeable road and footpath layouts, 38–39, 107, 114, 187, 188, 264, 274, *274*, 360
Perth and Kinross:
  Commercial Street, Bridgend, Perth, 349, 351, *353*
  Scrimgeours Corner, Comrie Street and West High Street, Crieff, 351–352, *354*
Peterlee New Town, 9, *21*
Petherick, Ann, 33
Pevsner, Nicholas, 12
Philips/Cutler/Troy:
  Holiday Housing, Portmadog, 303–304, *306*
Phippen, Randall and Parkes (now PRP Architects) 253–255
  Plymouth Grove, Ardwick, Manchester, 227–228, *228*
  The Ryde, Hatfield
Planned Overspill Development, 19–20
Plymouth:
  Gun Wharf, Devonport, 277–279, *279, 280*
  Plymouth Grove, Ardwick, Manchester, 227–228, *228*
  Point Royal, Bracknell, 231, *233*
Pollard Thomas and Edwards:
  Anchor Brewhouse, 125–126, *126*
  Cherrywood Close, 141, *142*

Royal Free Square, Liverpool Road, 97, *99*,
Portmadog, holiday housing, 303–304, *306*
Port Marine, Portishead, Bristol, 266, *266*
Port Sunlight, 3
Poundbury, by Dorchester, Dorset, 272, 274, *275, 276*
Powell and Moya:
  Churchill Gardens Estate, 150–151, *151*
Prefabricated housing, 7–8, 42
Prefabs (post-war), 7
  Wake Green, Birmingham, 181, *183*
Priority Estates Project (PEP), 25
The Priory, Blackheath, Greenwich, 73, *75*
Priory Green Estate, Islington, 94–95
Pritchard, Jack, 54
Private Finance Initiative (PFI), 227, 228
Proctor and Matthews, Architects:
  Abode, Newhall, Harlow, 172–174, *173*
  Barons Place, Southwark, 129–130, *130*
  Stonebridge, estate regeneration, 51–52, *53*
PRP Architects:
  Gallions Reach Urban Village, 76
  Liberty of Earley sheltered housing, *31*, 233–234, *234, 235*
  Plymouth Grove, Ardwick, Manchester, 227–228, *228*
  The Ryde, Hatfield, 19, *232*, 253–256, *255, 256*
PRP Architects and Bill Dunster Architects:

PRPZed Brixton Water Lane, 105, 107, *108*
PRP Architects and Triangle: Chichester Road, Hulme, 216
PSSHAK Flexible and Adaptable Housing, Camden, 56–57, *58*
Pullman Court, Lambeth, 103–104, *104*

Quarry Hill flats, Leeds, 6
Queen Elizabeth Close, Norwich, 178, *178*

Radburn, New Jersey, USA, 16
Radburn layouts, 16, *297*, 298 322
Ranwell Road Estate, Tower Hamlets, 27
Raines Court, Hackney, 86–87, *87*
Research and Development, 16
Red Road tower blocks, Glasgow, 12
Reid, Richard and Associates:
  Adventurers Quay, Cardiff Bay, 303, *304*
  Finland Quay, 119–120, *122*
Reilly, Professor C.H., 5
Ribbon Development, 6
Richards, J.M., 10
Richardson, Martin:
  Bradwell Common, Milton Keynes, 239
  Hartley, Milton Keynes, 239
Richmond-upon-Thames London Borough:
  Langham House Close, Ham Common, 116, *117*, 118
  Mallard Place, Strawberry Vale Twickenham, 118
  Parkleys, Ham Common, 115–116, *116, 117*
Rickinson Philip, Architects:
  Allerton Bywater, Second Millennium Village, 291, *292*

395

INDEX

Right-to-buy, 25, 184
Ritchie, Ian Architects:
   Roy Square, 134–135, *135*
Riverside Apartments (formerly Princes Tower), Southwark, 127–128, *128*
Robin Hood Lane, 13, *13*
Robotham, Matthew & Quinn:
   Southbrook Field, Papworth Everard, 164, *165*
   Sudbury Court, 163
   Tuckers Court, 163–164, *164*
Robson, Brian:
   Fenwick Close, Newcastle-upon-Tyne, 195
Roehampton (Alton Estate), 147–149, *148, 149*
Roehampton (cottage estate), 146, *147*
Rogers, Lord Richard,
   Montevetra, Wandsworth (with co-architects Hurley Robertson Associates), 149–150, *150*
   Thames Reach, 88–89, *90*
   Urban Task Force, 35
Rolls Crescent/Halston Street, Hulme, Manchester, 217, *218*, 219
Ronan Point, 17
Round House, Milton Keynes, 244, *245*
Royal Docks, Newham, 112–115, *114, 115*
Royal Free Square, Liverpool Road, 97, 99, 100
Royal Institute of British Architects (with the Chartered Institute of Housing), 117, 118
   Homes for the Future, 25
   Tenant Participation, 26
Roy Square, Southwark, 134–135, *135*

Rowntree, Joseph, 3, 296
Rowntree, Joseph Foundation, 31, *32*
   CASPAR 1, Birmingham, 184, *185*
   Lifetime Homes, 31, 32
Ruffle, David and Associates:
   Brentwood Place, 172, *172*
   Globe Mews, Beverley, 283–284, *284*
Runcorn New Town:
   The Brow, 204–205, *205, 206*
Rural Housing, 43–44
   Abbotsbury Glebe, 270–271, *272, 273*
   Broadwindsor, 44, *44*, 271
   Bryanston Hills, Blandford St Mary, Dorset, 271–272, *273*
   Ditchingham and Loddon, Norfolk, 8, *8, 9*, 175–176, *176*
   Ebrington, nr Chipping Camden, 277, *278*
   Lyde End, Bledlow, 235–236, *237*, 238, *238*
   Rushbrooke estate cottages, 179–180, *180*
   Scalebor Park, Burley in Wharfedale, 285–286, *286*
   Turn End, Haddenham, 234–235, *236, 237*
   Rushbrooke estate cottages, Suffolk, 179–180, *180*
   Ryde (The), Hatfield, 19, *232*, 253–256, *255, 256,*

St Andrew Street co-operative sheltered housing, Beverley, 284–285, *285*
St Anne's Close, Camden, 55–56, *56*
St Francis Church and Priory Court, Gorbals, Glasgow, 339, *340*

St James Place, Westminster, 152, *152*
St Mark's Road/St Quintin Avenue, Kensington and Chelsea, 102–103, *103*
St Werburgs, self-build, Bristol, 267–268, *268*
St Wilfred's, Mary France Street, Hulme, Manchester, 216, *217*
Salford:
   Salford Quays:
      NV Buildings, Huron Quay, 230, *231*
      Waterside at the Lowry, 230
Sakula, Ash:
   Boxley Street, West Silvertown, 114
Salt, Sir Titus, 3
Saltaire, 3
Scalebor Park, Burley-in-Wharfdale, 285–286, *286*
Scarman, Lord, housing enquiry, 25
Scott, Joanna, 355
Scottish Borders:
   Marine Square, Eyemouth, 353–355, *355*
Scottish Development Agency (SDA), 318, 332
Scottish Homes, 321, 337, 344
Scottish Special Housing Association (SSHA), 315, 317
Scrimgeours Corner, Crieff, Perthshire, 351–353, *354*
Seafar, Cumbernauld, 322, *323, 324*
Secured by Design, 39, 249
Segal, Walter:
   St Anne's Close, 55–56, *56*
Segal, Walter, Jon Broome and Brian Richardson:
   Lewisham Self-build housing, 108–110, *111*
Seidlung Halen (Switzerland), 62

INDEX

Seimensstadt, Berlin, 8, 150
Self-build Housing, 31
   Diggers, Brighton, 31, 261, 263, *263*
   Hockerton earth-sheltered housing, Newark, *189*, 189–190
   Nicholay Road, 95, 97, *98*
   Segal Housing, Lewisham, 108–110, *111*
   St Werburgs, Bristol, 267–268, *268*
Selwyn Street, Oldham, 228–229, *229, 230*
Setchell Road, 19, 118–119, *120, 121*
Shadwell Basin, 135–136, *136*
Shaw Sprunt, AFH:
   Kings Cross Estate Action, 64, 66–67, *67, 68*
   Monteith Phase 1, *29*, 141
   Stonebridge, estate regeneration, 51–52, *53*
ShedKM, Architects:
   Moho, Castlefields, Manchester, 223, *224*, 225–226, *225*
Sheffield, 13–15
   Castle Court, St John's Road, 294, *295*
   Gleadless Valley Blackstock Road, 294–295, *296*
   Gloucester Road, 16
   Hyde Park, St John's Road, 294–295, *295,*
   Park Hill, Duke Street, 13, 14, *14*, 291–293, *293, 294*
Sheffield City Architects Department:
   Gleadless Valley, 294–295, *296*
   Hyde Park, 294–295, *295*
   Park Hill, 13, 14, *14*, 291–293, *293, 294*
Shelter, 34
Shephard, Epstein Hunter:
   The Lakes, 120, 123, *123*

Stonebridge, masterplan, 51–52
Shoeburyness, Outlook, The Garrison, 174–175, *175*
Shore Street/Union Street, Co Down, 367, *368*, 369
Shropshire:
   Telford New Town, 20, *21*, 200
Sidell Gibson Partnership:
   Earls Manor Court, 281, 283, *284*
   Walpole Court, 274, *276*, 277, *277*
Silver End, Critall workers housing, nr Braintree, 167–168, *168*
Silvertown Urban Village, Newham, 112–115, *114, 115*
Simister Monaghan:
   Moffat Gardens, Gorbals, 338,
Simpson, Ian, Architects:
   Beetham (The) Tower, Deansgate, *202*, 227
   Number One Deansgate, Manchester, 227
Single Regeneration Budget (SRB), 26, 110
Skeats Wharf, Pennyland, Milton Keynes, 244, *244*
Skinner and Lubetkin:
   Spa Green Estate, 94, *96*
Skinner Bailey and Lubetkin:
   Bevin Court, 94–95, *96*
   Priory Green Estate, 94–95
SLASH, Scottish Local Authorities Special Housing, 317
SMC Parr Architects:
   Bell Rock Square, Dundee, 324, *325*
   Commercial Street, Perth, 349, 351, *353*
Smith Scott Mullan and Associates:
   Wester Hailes, 324, 326, *326*

Smithson, Peter and Allison, 12–13, *13*
Society for Improving the Conditions of the Labouring Classes, 20–21
Soho Housing Association, 33
Soissons, Louis de:
   Knightsfield, 253
   Welwyn Garden City, 252–253, *253*
Somerset:
   Bridge Care, Bath, 279–280, *281, 283*
Souter, A.S., 88
Southampton:
   Chapel, Chapel Road, *248* 248–249
   Wyndham Court, 246, *246*
South at Didsbury Point, Manchester, 226
South London Family Housing Association, 261
Southwark London Borough:
   6, Barons Place, Webber Street, 129–130, *130*
   Coleman, Alice, study, 26
   Friendship House, 3 Belvedere Road, 128–129, *129*
   London Docklands (see also Projects listed under this heading), 29
   Setchell Road, 19, 118–119, *120, 121*
   Tabard Square, Tabard Street, 130–131, *cover*
South Woodham Ferrers, Essex, 24, 172
Sovereign Quay, Cardiff Bay Regeneration, 303, *305*
Space standards, 15, 45
Spa Green Estate, Islington, 94, *96*

INDEX

Span Developments Ltd., 22, 162
  Blackheath, 22, *23*
    Brooklands Park and Blackheath Park, 75–76
    Corner Green, 73
    Foxes Dale, 72
    The Hall, 72, *75*
    Hallgate, 72
    Holmwalk, 75
    The Priory, 73, *75*
    Southrow, 73, *75*
  Highsett, Cambridge, 22, 162, *162*, 163, *163*
  Mallard Place, Richmond-upon-Thames, 118, *119*
  New Ash Green, Kent, 256, *257*
  Parkleys, Ham Common, 115–116, *116*, *117*
Spence, Sir Basil, 314, *314*, 316, 337
Springfield, Milton Keynes, 238, *239*
Squire, Michael Associates:
  Vogans Mill, 124–125, *125*
Stephenson Bell:
  Chorlton Park Apartments, Manchester, 221, *222*
Stirling, Sir James and James Gowan:
  Langham House Close, 116, *117*, 118
Stockholm City Council, Sweden, 31
Stonebridge Housing Action Trust, 27, 51–52, *53*
Strathclyde Regional Council, 318, 334
Strathclyde University, 320, 333
Student Housing, 333, 337
  Gainsford Street Halls of Residence, 125
Sudbury Court, Whittlesey, Cambridgeshire, 163
Suffolk:
  Martlesham Village, 180, *181*

Rushbrooke, Estate Cottages, 179–180, *179*, *180*
Sunderland/Washington New Town, 200
  Fatfield Village, Malvern Road, 200, *201*
  Lambton Village, Fallow field Way, 200, *201*
  West and East Bridge Streets, Mount Pleasant, 201
Sunningdale Community Project, Wirral, Cheshire, 207–208, *208*
Supported Housing:
  Moss Street, York, 299, *299*
Surrey:
  The Village, Caterham-on-the-Hill, 260, 260–261, *261*
Sussex:
  Brighton:
    Diggers and Sea Saw self-build housing, 261, 263, *263*
  Sussex University, 31
Sustainability, 35, 38
Sutton, London Borough:
  BedZED, (Beddington Zero Energy Development), 30, 41, 45, 107, *131*, 131–132, cover
Swansea:
  Foyer Housing, 34, 309, *310*, 311, *311*
  Honddu Place/Beacons View Road, 308–309, *309*
  Maritime Village, *300*, 304, *307*
    Abernethy Quay/ Ferrara Square, 306
    Ferrara Quay/Marina Walk, *300*, 306–307
  Penplas Urbanbuild, Woodford Road, 307–308, *308*, 309

Tabard Square, London, 130–131, cover
TADW Architects:
  Malton Street, Oldham, 229
  4-8 Market Place and 107 Mealhouse Brow, Stockport, 229
  Selwyn Street housing and Coppice Park, Oldham, 228–229, *229*, *230*
Tanner Street, Barking and Dagenham, 50, *50*
Tayler and Green, 8–9
  Rural housing, Ditchingham and Loddon, Norfolk, *9*, 175–176, *176*
Team 10 (CIAM X), 12
Telford New Town, Shropshire, 20, 21, 200
Tenant Participation (RIBA), 26
Tenants' Choice Programme 1987, 27
Terence O'Rourke:
  Stonebridge, Estate Regeneration, 51–52
Thamesmead, Greenwich, 75–76, *76*
Thames Reach, Hammersmith and Fulham, 88–89, *90*
Thatcher, Margaret, 26
The Edge, Manchester, 227
The Point, Wapping Wharf, Bristol, 264, *264*
Thomas, Peter, 355
Thompson, John, 62
Thompson John and Partners:
  Angell Town, estate regeneration, 107–108
  The Village, Caterham on the Hill, 260, 260–261, *261*
Thorne, Anne, Architects Partnership:
  Boatemah Walk, Angell Town, Brixton, 107–108, *110*

398

INDEX

Tibbalds Monro (Gardner Stewart Architects/Tibbalds Planning and Urban Design):
  Kings Cross Estate Action, 64, 66–67, *68*
Timber Wharf, Castlefields, Manchester, 223
Tindale, Patricia, 16
Tinkers Bridge, Milton Keynes, 238, 239
Tollcross Road/Sorby Street, Glasgow, 334
Totterdown Fields, Wandsworth, 4
Tower block refurbishment:
  Nightingale Heights, 26, 76–77, *77*
  Northwood Tower, 138
  Sunningdale Community Project, 207–208, *208*
  Winterton House, 26, 137–138, *139*
  Tower Hamlets Housing Action Trust, 27, 139–140
  Cherrywood Close, 141, *142*
  Monteith Phase 1, *29*, 141
Tower Hamlets London Borough:
  Abbotts Wharf, 143–144, *144*
  Balfron Tower, St. Leonard's Road, 99
  Boundary Street Estate, 132, *132*
  BowZED zero carbon housing:
  Tomlins Grove, 141–143, *142*
  Burrell's Wharf, Westferry Road, 139, *140*
  Cascades, Westferry Road, 136–137, *137*
  Cherrywood Close, Tower Hamlets HAT, 141, *142*
  Claredale Street Cluster Housing, 133–134, *134*
  Compass Point, Sextant Avenue, 137, *138*
  Container City, Trinity Buoy Wharf, 143, *144*
  Donnybrook Quarter, Parnell Street, 144–145, *145*
  Dundee Wharf, Three Colt Street, 139, *141*
  Lansbury Estate, East India Dock Road, 132–133, *133*
  Monteith Phase 1, Parnell Road, Tower Hamlets HAT, *29*, 141
  Ranwell Road Estate, 27
  Roy Square, Narrow Street, 134–135, *135*
  Shadwell Basin, 135–136, *136*
  Tower Hamlets Housing Action Trust, 27, 139–140
  Usk Street Cluster Housing, 133–134
  Winterton House, Watney Market, 137–138, *139*
Town Development Act 1952, 20
Townsend, G.P. (Span Developments Ltd.), 22
Toxteth (Liverpool) riots, 25
Trellick Tower, Kensington and Chelsea, 99–101, *102*
Troughton McAslan and Tim Brennen:
  Riverside Apartments (formerly Princes Tower), 127–128, *128*
Tuckers Court, Stanground, Cambridgeshire, 163–164, *164*
Tuckley, David and Associates:
  Deerfern Close, Milton Keynes, 244
Tudor Walters Report, 5, *146*
Turn End, Haddenham, Buckinghamshire, 234–235, *236*

Ujima Housing Association, 77
Unité d'Habitation, 10, 12, 69, 99, 346, *349*
Unity Flats, Belfast, 362
Unwin, Raymond, 5, 71, 88
Upton, sustainable suburb, Northampton, 39, 187–189, *188*
Urban Development Corporations, 28
Urban Housing Renewal Unit (UHRU), 25
Urban Space Management Container City: 143, *144*
Urban Splash:
  Castlefields, Manchester, 214, 221
    Box Works, 223, *223*
    Britannia Mills, 221, *222*, 223,
    Burton Place, 223, *224*
    Moho, 223, *224*, 225, *225*, 226
    Timber Wharf, 223
  Chorlton Park Apartments, Manchester, 221, *222*
  New Islington, Manchester, 219, *220*, 221
  3-12 Old Haymarket, Liverpool, 214, *215*
  Park Hill, Sheffield, 293, *294*
  Rotunda, Birmingham, 43
  Royal William Yard, Plymouth, 43
Urban Villages, 35, 76, 112, *115*, 226, *226*, 227, 274
Urban Villages Forum, 35
Usk Street Cluster Housing, Tower Hamlets, 133–134

Vale, Robert and Brenda:
  Hockerton Earth Sheltered Housing, 189–190, *189*

399

INDEX

Village The, Caterham-on-the-Hill, 260, 260–261, 261, *261*
Vogans Mill, Mill Street, Southwark, 124–125, *125*

Waller and Partners, Architects: Scalebor Park, Burley in Wharfdale, Yorkshire, 285–286, *286*
Walpole Court, Puddletown, Dorset, 274, 276, 277, *277*
Waltham Forest London Borough:
  20b Bistern Avenue, 145–146, *146*
Walthamstow London Borough:
  Northwood Tower refurbishment, Wood Street, 138
Wandsworth London Borough:
  Alton Estate, Roehampton, 11, 147, *148*, 149, *149, cover*
  Montevetro, Battersea Church Road, 149–150, *150*
  Roehampton Cottage Estate, Dover House Road, 146, *147*
  Totterdown Fields, Tooting, 4
Waring and Netts Partnership:
  Avondale and Ferndale, 195, *197*
  Wyncote Court/Jesmond Park Court, 195, 197, *198*
Warrington and Runcorn Development Corporation Architects Department:
  Admirals Road/Curlew Grove, 206
  Gorse Covert Road/Stanmore Close and Darnaway Close, 206

Old Hall, 206
Old Hall Road/Nansen Close, 206
Warrington and Runcorn New Town, 20, *21*, 205, *207*
  Admirals Road, Oakwood, 207
  Admirals Road/Curlew Grove, Birchwood, 206
  Gorse Covert Road/Stanmore Close and Darnaway Close, 206
  Old Hall/Cromwell Avenue 206
  Old Hall Road/Nansen Close, 206
  Redshank Lane, Oakwood, 207
  Fatfield Village, 200, 201
  Lambton Village, 200, 201
  West and East Bridge Streets, Mount Pleasant, 201
Washington New Town, 200–201
  Ayton Village, 200, 201
  East Bridge Street, Mount Pleasant, 201
  Fatfield Village, 200, 201
  Lambton Village, 200, 201
  Waters Edge, Shaldon, Devon, 268–269, *269*
  Watermeads, 111–112, *113*
  Waterside Peartree Bridge, Milton Keynes, 238, *239*, 241
Wates, Neil, 22
Watson, Eric, 200
Webster's Yard, Kendall, Cumbria, 209–210, 211
WCA, Warehouse conversion, Bristol, 264
Well Hall Estate, Greenwich, 71–72, 74

Weller Street Co-operative housing, Liverpool, 212
Wells Coates:
  Isokon Flats, Camden, 53–54, *54*
Welwyn Garden City, 5, 252–253, *253, 254*
  Handside Close, Knightsfield, 253
  Parkway, 253
Wester Hailes, Edinburgh, 319, 324, 326, *326*
Westminster London Borough:
  Ashmill Street, 156, *157*
  9 Berwick Street (living over the shop), 33
  Castle Lane Extension, *158*, 158–159, *159*
  Churchhill Gardens Estate, Grosvenor Road, 150–151, *151*
  Crown Reach, Grosvenor Road, 156–157, *157*
  171-201 Lanark Road, 154–156, *156*
  Lillington Gardens, *48*, 153, 154
  Odham's Walk, 154, *155*
  125 Park Road, 152–153, *153*
  St James Place, 152, *152*
  West Silvertown Urban Village, London, 112–114, *114, 115*
  Wheatley Housing Act 1924, 5
  White Hart Lane, Haringey, 91–92, *92*
  Whitehaven: regeneration of George Street and Queen Street, 208–209, *210*
  Wickham and Associates:
    20b Bistern Avenue, 145–146, *146*
    Horselydown Square, 123, *124*

400

Wilkinson Hindle Hallsall Lloyd Partnership:
    Co-operative housing, Liverpool, 210, 212, *213*
    North Hull Housing Action Trust, 287–288
1-3 Willow Road, Camden, 55, *55*
Wilson, Sir Hugh:
    Cumbernauld Master Plan, 322, *323*
Wiltshire:
    Calne Centre Regeneration, *262*, 280–281
    Earls Manor Court, Winterbourne Earls, 281, 283, *284*
Winterton House, tower block refurbishment, 137–138, *139*
Wolfe Crescent, Southwark, 127, *127*

Woodley Headland, Peartree Bridge, Milton Keynes, 244
Wormersley, Lewis, 13
Wyncote Court/Jesmond Park Court, Newcastle-upon-Tyne, 195, 197, *198*

York:
    Bretgate/Walmgate, 298–299, *299*
    Moss Street, 299, *299*
    New Earswick, 296–297, *297*, *cover*
    Lifetime Homes, 297–298
Yorke, F.R.S., 6
Yorkshire:
    Allerton Bywater, Castleford, 291, *292*
    Beverley:
        Globe Mews, 283–284, *284*
        St Andrew Street, 284–285, *285*

    Bradford:
        Scalebar Park, Burley-in-Wharfdale, 285–286, *286*
        Kingston upon Hull, 286–288, *287*, *288*
        Leeds, 288–291, *289*, *290*
        Sheffield, 291–295, *293–296*
        York, 296–299
York University Design Unit:
    Bretgate/Walgate, York, 298–299, *299*
    St Andrew Street, Beverley, 284–285, *285*
Young Builders' Trust, 34
Young people's housing:
    Youthbuild, 34–35
    Grimsby Doorstep, 35
    Swansea Foyer, 30, 34, 309–311, *310*
Young Raymond, 319